THE ARCHITECTURE OF LIFE AND DEATH IN BORNEO

THE ARCHITECTURE OF LIFE AND DEATH IN BORNEO

ROBERT L. WINZELER

 UNIVERSITY OF HAWAI'I PRESS / HONOLULU

Library of Congress Cataloging-in-Publication Data
Winzeler, Robert L.
   The architecture of life and death in Borneo / Robert L. Winzeler.
      p. cm.
   Includes bibliographical references and index.
   ISBN 0-8248-2632-9 (hardcover : alk. paper)
      1. Architecture—Borneo. 2. Vernacular architecture—Borneo.
3. Ethnic architecture—Borneo. I. Title.
NA1526.6.B67W56 2004
720´.9598´3—dc22

                                                          2003019694

FRONTISPIECE: "A Dyak Village," an engraved illustration
of a Land Dayak longhouse in an account of Dayak
architecture first published around 1870.

CONTENTS

ACKNOWLEDGMENTS

The field research in Sarawak and elsewhere in Borneo on which this book is partly based was supported in 1985–1986 by a grant from the National Science Foundation (BNS-8507574) and by a Southeast Asian Studies Research Fellowship from the Fulbright Program. Further work was aided in 1994 by a Small Grant for Southeast Asian Studies from the Luce Foundation and in 1996 by an International Activities Grant from the University of Nevada, Reno. The fieldwork in 1998–1999 and the writing begun in 1999 were made possible by a Sabbatical Leave Award, also from the University of Nevada, Reno. I thank all of these benefactors with deep gratitude.

I am also grateful to the federal government of Malaysia and the state government of Sarawak for giving me research visas on several occasions between 1985 and 1998 and to the government of Indonesia for doing so in 1996. My research in Sarawak was sponsored first by the

Sarawak Museum, to which I am also indebted for much assistance over the years—in particular, regarding this book, by giving me access to its superb photo archives. Research in Sarawak in 1998–1999 was officially sponsored by the State Planning Unit of the Chief Minister's Department of Sarawak; during this time I was attached to the Majlis Adat Istiadat, to which I am also very grateful for a great deal of help, both then and during previous stays in Sarawak. For help with the identification of trees and wood samples I am very grateful to the field staff of the Sarawak Forest Department in Kuching.

It is not possible to adequately thank all of the friends, colleagues, assistants, and others who have contributed so much to the making of this book. Some of my dependence on the work and contributions of others can be seen in the references and endnotes and in the list of credits for photos and illustrations, although this hardly covers everyone. I must, however, thank the following specific individuals for friendship, hospitality, information, and other help: Leo Janek, Peter Minos, Patau Rubis, Mathew Ngau Jau, Candy Biron, Nicholas Bawan, Peter Kedit, Lim Yu Seng, Jayl Langub, Johnny Kon, and Robert S. Ridu. For loaning me photos (always more than could be included), I thank Bernard Sellato, George Appell, Jennifer Alexander, Aloysius Lawai Lau, Jayl Langub, and (in his former capacity as photographer and curator of the photo archives of the Sarawak Museum) Lim Yu Seng. In addition, I am happy to acknowledge my appreciation for the drawings done by Tim Pyles and Barbara Erickson (again, more than could be included) and the work of word processing and copyediting done by Glenda Powell. The University of Hawai'i Press has been a pleasure to deal with throughout the whole process of getting the book published. I wish to thank, in particular, Pamela Kelley for her early interest in the project and her continued support and Bojana Ristich for her meticulous final copyediting. For reading and commenting on the manuscript, I am deeply indebted to the two anonymous readers retained by the Press and to Judy Winzeler.

INTRODUCTION

OVER THE LAST SEVERAL DECADES the indigenous architecture of Southeast Asia has drawn a degree of interest not present in Borneo at least since the latter half of the nineteenth century, when the great longhouses, mausoleums, and other built forms of the interior attracted the attention of many outsiders.[1] Much of the renewed interest in these architectural forms has been focused on the rapidly vanishing or now extinct traditional versions known mainly from photos and illustrations of earlier periods or from a small number of surviving examples or re-creations. The present-day traveler who visits Borneo and sets out to see the marvelous buildings pictured, described, and analyzed in the recent literature is liable to think that he or she has ended up in the wrong place if careful use is not made of up-to-date guidebooks. Much of the architecture of Borneo and other areas of the humid tropics of Southeast Asia was never intended to last, and, built as it was of wood and other organic materials, lasted it has not. This is especially so in areas where governments or others with power or influence over interior peoples have been hostile to traditional architectural practices. The abandonment or transformation of traditional built forms is also, however, a consequence of modern, national, and global processes and influences —technological, economic, cultural, and political. Logging and other processes of deforestation have also strongly affected building practices. And eventually there is also a loss of local knowledge so that those who may wish to perpetuate or revive architectural traditions are not able to do so.

While this book is about the architecture of Borneo, it is not intended to cover the built environment of all of the populations that are or should be regarded as "indigenous." All that can be reasonably said in the way of identifying the indigenous or native groups of Borneo is that they can be differentiated from the Chinese, Indian, Javanese, Balinese, Madurese, Bugis, southern Filipino, and others (not to mention Europeans, who have been only transients) who readily identify themselves as such and who have arrived in the last two hundred years or so. The peoples on whom I focus in the present volume are those of the vast interior who, with a few exceptions, were more or less autonomous before the beginning of colonial rule.

These peoples of the interior have long identified themselves as ethnically separate from the Malays or Melayu and other Malay-speaking (but dialectically diverse) Muslims of the coastal and lower river areas. In contrast, however, to the recently arrived ethnic populations, the Malay peoples of Borneo are also indigenous in that most of them derive from local populations rather than ones from elsewhere. There are also important continuities between the indigenous Malays and the interior peoples, including architectural ones. All of the peoples of Borneo traditionally place their houses and most

other buildings on piles; make extensive use of bamboo, palm thatch, wood, bark, and other organic building materials; and work with similar tools. At the same time, the coastal Muslim Malays belong to a civilization that is spread far beyond Borneo, around the Malayan Peninsula and the great islands of western Indonesia—a civilization that grew and flourished in relation to Indic and then Islamic influence and to trade and political control. While varying from one part of Borneo to another, the village houses (which are always single-family dwellings rather than longhouses), the palaces, mosques, and other built forms that comprise Malay architecture belong more to this larger tradition. When I first arrived in Sarawak, I was struck by the presence of the same sorts of beautiful old Malay houses with which I was already familiar from my previous stays in Kelantan in the northeastern part of peninsular Malaysia. The architecture of the interior peoples of Borneo, in contrast, while having common Austronesian roots with that of the inland or upland peoples of Sumatra, Sulawesi, and other areas, has clearly developed in its own ways, probably over a long period of time—although certainly not entirely without external influence or external material goods. In the present volume I consider Malay architecture mainly in relationship to its influence on that of the non-Muslim groups of the interior and in relation to processes of ethnic differentiation.

Things would be easier if I could simply say that this book is about the architecture or built environment of the "Dayaks," who are relatively well known in both ethnological and popular terms and equated by many with the interior or tribal peoples of Borneo. This would have also relieved the need for many iterations of "indigenous," "native," or, more properly, "indigenous-interior" or "native-non-Malay" and the like or the also frequently used alternative, which is to list the specific groups—Bidayuh, Benua', Iban, Kayan, Kenyah, Kajang, Melanau, Maloh, Ngaju, Rungus, Taman, and others—to which I intend some generalization or other to apply. The term "Dayak" (in local languages *daya*, *daya'*, or *dayuh*) either originated with or was widely disseminated by Malays and then by colonial authorities. While perhaps originally used pejoratively by the Malays to refer to the wild tribal peoples of the interior, the term is perfectly acceptable in much of present-day Borneo and is officially and otherwise used by many groups themselves, as in such autonyms as Bidayuh and Lundayeh. The problem is that not all interior groups refer to themselves or are known by this term. Thanks apparently to the Dutch colonial regime, it is now applied to all the non-Malay indigenous peoples of Kalimantan or present-day Indonesian Borneo, as opposed to both the native Malay and the Chinese, Javanese, Bugis, Madurese, and other immigrant peoples. This is not the case in Malaysian Borneo or in the small nation of Brunei. In Sarawak, while the term "Dayak" is sometimes used in nationalistic contexts in which the various groups of the interior are seeking ways to refer to themselves collectively, it more properly refers only to the Bidayuh and the Iban (the Land and Sea Dayaks respectively of the colonial tradition). In Sabah or Brunei, a Dayak would most commonly be assumed to be a migrant Iban from Sarawak.

Fortunately the term "architecture" does not involve the sort of problems that "indigenous" or "Dayak" do. It means simply the built environment, built forms, or building traditions and practices, depending on the context. While formally trained architects and architectural historians may see a need to distinguish the sort of buildings and building practices found in the interior of Borneo from those in Western countries, I do not. Broad-minded and comparatively oriented experts on architecture sometimes speak of "architecture without architects" and note that the local building traditions of places like Borneo account for all but an infinitesimally small amount of all human architectural effort throughout history.[2] Such building traditions are generally referred to in architectural circles by the special term of "vernacular" (as in Cambridge University Press' admirable *Encyclopedia of the Vernacular Architecture of the World*, which includes various entries for Borneo).[3] In this regard, perhaps, it is formal "architecture with architects" for which a special term should be used, not the more common variety. Nor would it be appropriate to refer to interior Borneo building traditions as "folk architecture." This phrase is appropriately used in regard to Europe, India, or China, for example, in order to distinguish the buildings of local villagers from the monuments, palaces, civic buildings, cathedrals, and temples that form the urban or "great-tradition" architecture of these places. In Borneo a distinction between folk and great-tradition architecture might be made in the case of the Malays but not in that of the Dayaks or other interior peoples, for whom no such distinction exists.

OUTSIDE VIEWS OF BORNEAN ARCHITECTURE: COLONIAL AND POSTCOLONIAL

Whatever it should be called, until recently the architecture of the peoples of Borneo has been treated mainly in works devoted primarily to other matters. By the middle of the nineteenth century (and continuing well into the twentieth) descriptions of longhouses, mortuary structures, and other built forms had become common themes in the writings of explorers, scientific travelers, missionaries, colonial heroes, and administrators.[4] River scenes showing longhouses—sometimes fortified—and other dwellings are especially common. Men's houses, bridges, mausoleums, and other structures are also shown.

Toward the end of the nineteenth century, ethnological accounts began to appear. These were works that focused on peoples, customs, and lifeways rather than the travels and adventures of the writer. The ethnological studies—including Henry Ling Roth's *The Natives of*

FIG. 0.1 (facing top). Mid-nineteenth-century engraving of a Dayak village on the Barito River in southern Borneo.

FIG. 0.2 (facing bottom). Engraved illustration (originally in color) from C. A. L. M. Schwaner's *Borneo* (published in 1853–1854) of Dayak longhouses surrounded by a high stockade (southern Borneo).

FIG. 0.3 (above). Originally colored engraving of a Murut bridge from Spenser St. John's *Life in the Forests of the Far East*, published in 1862.

FIG. 0.4. "A Dyak Village," an engraved illustration of a Land Dayak longhouse in an account of Dayak architecture first published around 1870.

Sarawak and British North Borneo, Alfred Haddon's *Head-Hunters: Black, White and Brown,* and Charles Hose and William McDougall's *The Pagan Tribes of Borneo*—were often explicitly comparative and sometimes synthesized information from different published sources.[5] Houses in Hose and McDougall are discussed under material conditions, along with clothing, tools, pottery, and the like, and house building is treated as a handicraft, along with boat building, weaving, iron forging, and other manufacturing processes.[6] Collecting went along with ethnology, and while entire buildings were not collected, carved posts, finials, and doors could be and were, in addition to statuary, mortuary posts, mausoleums, and an array of other objects. The Sarawak Museum, a vast repository of the material culture and ethnology of the peoples of Borneo, was founded at this time.

Both the early accounts and the later ethnological literature are often illustrated, first with drawings and later with photographs. In contrast to the early photographs, the older drawings are often very good. Those in A.W. Nieuwenhuis' account of the Apo Kayan area in East Kalimantan include technical drawings of a Kayan longhouse that remain unsurpassed. As photography improved, the use of drawings declined.

After World War II the study of Bornean societies came to be dominated increasingly by social anthropologists, whose agenda, as established especially by Edmund Leach in Sarawak, was very different from that of earlier ethnologists.[7] The interest shifted toward matters of social structure, development and change, and ritual and belief. In terms of living arrangements, it was the village and household rather than the physical house that

FIG. 0.5. Print from Frederick Boyle's *Adventures among the Dyaks of Borneo* (published in 1865) showing a feast in progress on the open veranda of the Iban longhouse of Gasing, on the Batang Lupar.

mattered. While social anthropologists needed to say something about the material structure of the dwellings of the group in question, this was done as a prelude to the central discussion of family organization, kinship, marriage customs, community integration, political leadership, social stratification, and to some extent religious ideas and ritual practices. Material culture, whether of buildings, tools and weapons, or heirloom property, was mainly of interest in relation to social organization, not in and of itself, as it had been to earlier observers, who themselves were, conversely, seldom in a position to understand symbolic culture and social organization very well but could often competently enough describe a Dayak house, basket, sword, or tattoo design.

There were, however, some differences among the early social anthropologists. William Geddes, in his no-

table description of the Bidayuh men's house in the upper Sadong area, wanted to convey the feeling of its height—both its roof in relation to the floor and its floor in relation to the ground—and he was able to do so in a very graphic way.[8] But he did not know how high men's houses were in either respect, for he had never obtained measurements of any kind (he explained) and could only guess. This acknowledgment was not offered as an admission of something that he should have done. All that really mattered about how high a men's house was (unless perhaps it happened to fall down when people were in it) was how high it *seemed* to be—which was very high, especially if it was built on a hillside.

What Geddes did and did not do regarding men's houses was also true of his treatment of longhouses. While these were discussed frequently in his scholarly

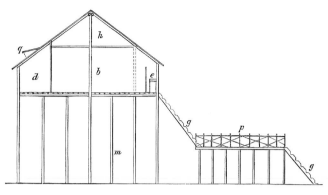

Fig. 72. Section of a house of the Ot-Danom Dyaks on
the Samba River.

b. Large public hall.	*d*. Private apartments.	*e*. Hearths.	*g*. Ladders.
h. Attics.	*m*. Posts.	*p*. Bridge.	*q*. Skylight.

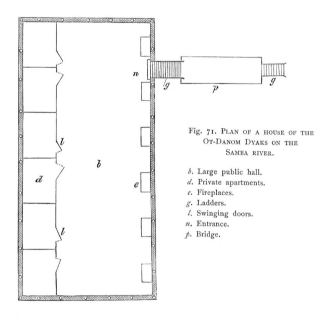

Fig. 71. Plan of a house of the
Ot-Danom Dyaks on the
Samba river.

b. Large public hall.
d. Private apartments.
e. Fireplaces.
g. Ladders.
l. Swinging doors.
n. Entrance.
p. Bridge.

FIG. 0.6. G. A. F. Molengraaff's (1902) diagrams of the Ot Danum longhouse at Roemah Toembang Mentikeh on the Samba River: section (above) and plan (below). The Ot Danum longhouse as shown in these drawings differs from those typical of northern Borneo in having the fireplaces on the front wall of the gallery area (rather than in the interior apartment) and in having an upper and lower entrance ladder and platform.

monograph and form the topic of an entire chapter of his more popular *Nine Dayak Nights*,[9] Geddes' descriptions of longhouses contain less information on their physical features than do his accounts of men's houses. The height, width, and length of longhouses or the numbers of apartments comprising them were left unreported, as were also the methods of construction or materials. Entrance ladders, an unceasing matter of interest and trepidation for European visitors to longhouses, were an exception. Geddes discusses these at some length, partly as a matter of humor for the natives (who welcomed visitors with rice wine as they approached the longhouse and who at the time of his fieldwork had an amusing song about a ladder that breaks beneath the weight of an honored guest), but mainly to make a sociological point. This point was that entrance ladders were the only publicly owned part of a Land Dayak longhouse and therefore once built were hardly maintained, a reflection of the generally low level of civic cooperation in the village.

Derek Freeman, another of the first group of social anthropologists in Sarawak, took architecture more seriously in ways other than purely sociological. His classic *Report on the Iban* includes a description of the Iban longhouse as a physical structure.[10] This description, which includes valuable information on several matters (including the size and number of apartments in longhouses in the Baleh River area), appears in the opening pages of a long chapter on the *bilik* (apartment-household) family and itself focuses on the social uses of longhouse space. Freeman also noted that entrance ladders were the only publicly owned parts of Iban longhouses and that, as such, were not looked after with much diligence once they had been carved from a log, set up, and ritually consecrated.

In bringing issues of social organization of longhouses to the fore, the early social anthropologists were especially concerned with correcting what they regarded as mistaken impressions, with the result that much of

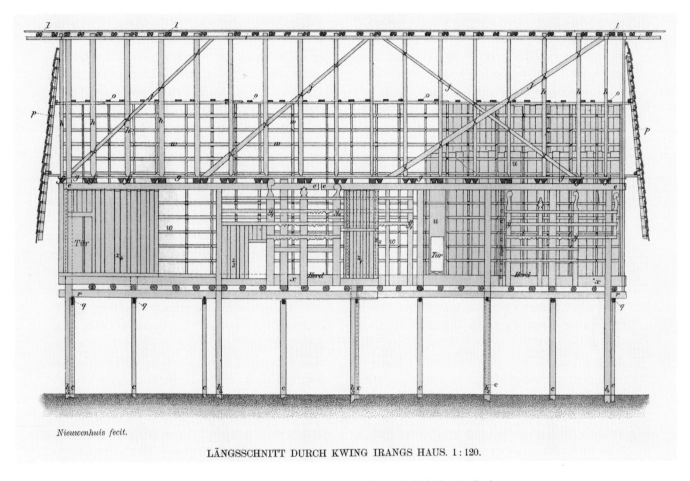

Nieuwenhuis fecit.

LÄNGSSCHNITT DURCH KWING IRANGS HAUS. 1:120.

FIG. 0.7. A.W. Nieuwenhuis' (1907) detailed scale drawings (originally in color) include this longitudinal cutaway of the house of the Kayan chief Kwing Irang, circa 1900, upper Mahakam River, East Kalimantan.

what they stressed was negative—that is, they tended to emphasize what longhouses were not. Perhaps in part reflecting the 1950s cold war reaction to the spread of communism, the main impression to be corrected was the notion that the longhouse was a communal organization—that is, one that acted collectively and subordinated the property rights and other interests of individuals and families to those of the larger group. Geddes

went the furthest and described Land Dayak (Bidayuh) longhouse society as verging on anarchy. Freeman emphasized the cohesion of the Iban longhouse community in some respects but argued that it was based on important but limited ritual concerns. George Appell, a student of Freeman, found a rather similar pattern among the Rungus of Sabah.[11] Stephen Morris, who had studied the coastal Melanau as another researcher in

Leach's early group, encountered a different form of social organization, one involving authority and hierarchy, but since his initial focus was on the economics of sago production, this did not become evident until later.[12]

As subsequent social anthropological studies were carried out among a wider range of longhouse societies, including ones more like the Melanau, a different set of sociological issues emerged. While the earlier studies were concerned with matters of autonomy and integration, the later ones were especially concerned with hierarchy. The Melanau, Kayan, Kenyah, Kajang, and Maloh were variously described in these studies as being strongly, if not always rigidly, stratified into hereditary sectors of nobles or aristocrats, commoners, and slaves. Some, perhaps most, anthropologists have concluded that these groups and others are basically very different kinds of societies than the Iban, Bidayuh, and Rungus. Others have argued that such differences have been overemphasized—that, on the one hand, no longhouse-dwelling peoples are entirely egalitarian and, on the other, hierarchy varies among the formally stratified groups. Jérôme Rousseau, in particular, challenged Freeman's characterization of the Iban as classless, and Freeman responded sharply that they were and delineated in detail the fundamental differences between the egalitarian Iban and the hierarchical Kayan.[13] While the issue of hierarchy has not been mainly about architecture, it does concern it, for the Melanau, Kayan, Kenyah, Maloh, and other hierarchically organized groups customarily tend to build different sorts of longhouses than do the Iban, Bidayuh, and Rungus—or so it has often been claimed. The expression of hierarchy in longhouse design and in other architectural forms is a significant issue with which I will deal in several chapters.

While social anthropologists in Borneo have generally approached domestic architecture from the perspective of social structure, those focusing on the built forms of other islands in the region (especially of eastern Indonesia) have been more concerned with meaning, symbol, and cosmology. In these studies, which began in the 1960s, the house has been taken to be a map or template of the culture. The impetus has been, in part, the influence of Lévi-Strauss, as well as of the work of earlier Dutch structural ethnologists in the region on indigenous cosmologies and exchange practices. The issues and perspectives have been drawn together and discussed especially in Roxana Waterson's wide-ranging *The Living House*, the most comprehensive treatment of the indigenous nonmonumental architecture of Southeast Asia yet produced.[14]

In Southeast Asia, as elsewhere, symbolic approaches to architecture have tended to focus on the metaphorical characteristics of buildings—on how the houses in particular have been used to represent central cultural ideas or are thought to have the attributes of other things, including living creatures.[15] The pioneering work on architectural symbolism in Borneo was done in the early twentieth century by the missionary-ethnologist Hans Schärer (known mainly through the translation of Rodney Needham) on the rituals and beliefs of the Ngaju of the far south of the island.[16] Schärer described Ngaju architecture and other traditions (most famously mortuary practices and beliefs) in terms of several pervasive structural distinctions—male and female, upperworld and underworld, upriver and downriver, hornbill and water serpent. Although scholars have mainly followed up on Schärer's work on Ngaju mortuary ritual ideas and practices, the general cosmic distinctions he identified are important regarding architecture throughout the interior of Borneo. Of course, the linking of the house and the local landscape with the cosmos works both ways. That is, Bornean notions of divinities and the afterlife are also a refraction of the visible, lived-in world—the gods have human characteristics and may appear in the guise of animals (especially birds), and heaven has rivers, forests, rice fields, and longhouses. And Bornean peoples tend to think symbolically of houses and villages in other ways as well, as having some of the same characteristics of human bodies—that is, in humoral terms of hot and cold.

Beyond its connections to social structure and to symbolism, cosmology, and artistry, Bornean architecture has drawn interest in relation to ecological issues and environmental studies. Early descriptions of building practices tended to make only minimal observations about such matters. In the past it was commonly assumed that the availability of building material was unlimited. It was sometimes noted that where possible, house posts, beams, floorboards, and shingles were reused when constructing a new building. Beyond this, getting materials was seen as a matter of going into the forest and cutting down trees and turning them into whatever was needed. Even in the past, however, large villages built in new areas required large amounts of timber.

Perhaps in part in relation to the emergence of environmental studies, more recent scholars have looked more closely at such matters. Several anthropologists have linked the abandonment or absence of longhouses to the disappearance of ironwood trees.[17] Other recent research on building practices and forest resources, including Timothy Jessup's studies in the Apo Kayan plateau of east central Borneo in present-day East Kalimantan, show that interior builders are flexible and make use of a considerable variety of tree species while using their favorites for various purposes.[18] In many areas, however, access to forests of the sort on which builders formerly relied is now a thing of the past, with the result that houses are being built mainly with purchased materials, including bricks or concrete blocks, as well as the more widely used corrugated metal sheets. This was one of the topics on which I worked during my last period of fieldwork in 1998–1999 in Sarawak. Here the Bidayuh, as well as some of the Iban, have been strongly affected by the reduction of the availability of

lumber from forests due to rural agricultural development projects and commercial logging, as well as by the expansion of traditional swidden practices and population growth.

My Own Interests and Biases

My entry into the study of Bornean architecture was by the back door, as it were. Beyond some personal involvement with woodworking and carpentry, my interests in architecture were initially with its relationship to ethnicity, nationalism, and the politics of culture. I was aware that the practice of living in multifamily longhouses has long had important implications for ethnic boundaries along two lines. The first is that in the deep interior areas, where nomadic hunter-gatherers (commonly known as Penan in Sarawak and Punan in Kalimantan) have comprised up to 25 percent of the population, longhouses traditionally form a boundary marker with the more numerous, settled swidden cultivators—that is, the nomads customarily live in small, separate family shelters while the cultivators have longhouses.[19] Over the last several decades or so this pattern has broken down, but in a way that continues to illustrate the association of longhouses with sedentariness and cultivation. That is, at least in Sarawak (and apparently also in some cases in earlier periods in Kalimantan),[20] as nomads have settled into more permanent villages and begun to practice farming, with the encouragement and help of either the longhouse dwellers (with whom they have been affiliated through trade in forest products) or the government, they have commonly moved into longhouses, where many of them are today.

The second ethnic boundary involving longhouses is that between the swidden cultivators of the interior and the Malays, Chinese, and other downriver groups. Except perhaps for the Chinese, whose blocks of shop houses are built in a connected row like longhouses (and appear to have been a model for some of the innovations in long-

FIG. 0.8. Map of Borneo showing national and regional boundaries and places mentioned in the book.

Map labels:
Mainland Southeast Asia · Philippines · Malay Peninsula · Borneo · Sumatra · Sulawesi · Java
Kudat Peninsula · Kota Kinabalu · SABAH · Bandar Sri Bagawan · BRUNEI · SARAWAK · Tutuh · Baram · Tinjar · MALAYSIAN BORNEO · Tatau · Belaga · Apo Kayan · Kayan · Oya · Rajang · Balui · Skrang · Batang Lupar · Ai · Baleh · Lundu · Kuching · Pada-wan · Sambas · Bau · Sadong · Mendalam · Putissibau · EAST KALIMANTAN · Pontianak · Kapuas · Mahakam · Barong Tongkok · Samarinda · INDONESIAN BORNEO · Barito · WEST KALIMANTAN · Kahayan · Palangka Raya · Banjarmasin · CENTRAL KALIMANTAN · SOUTH KALIMANTAN
0 — 500 kms

house form in the Belaga area of Sarawak), these peoples live in single-family dwellings. In an early (1839) account of a Sebuyau Iban settlement on the Lundu River in present-day western Sarawak, James Brooke noted that the village consisted of a single large longhouse, in which all of the Dayaks were living, along with a few scattered single houses of Malay traders.[21] In the past this ethnic interface occurred mainly along the coasts and inland along a few of the larger rivers of Borneo. These were the locations of the sultanates and other Malay and Chinese trading towns that became the focal points of colonial administration and that today are the main centers of government, commerce, education, and development. As noted above, the Malay and other coastal Muslim populations of these regions are probably mainly of local origin, formed as the interior peoples moved toward the coast and altered their identity. This usually involved a shift in religious affiliation (to Islam), in language (to

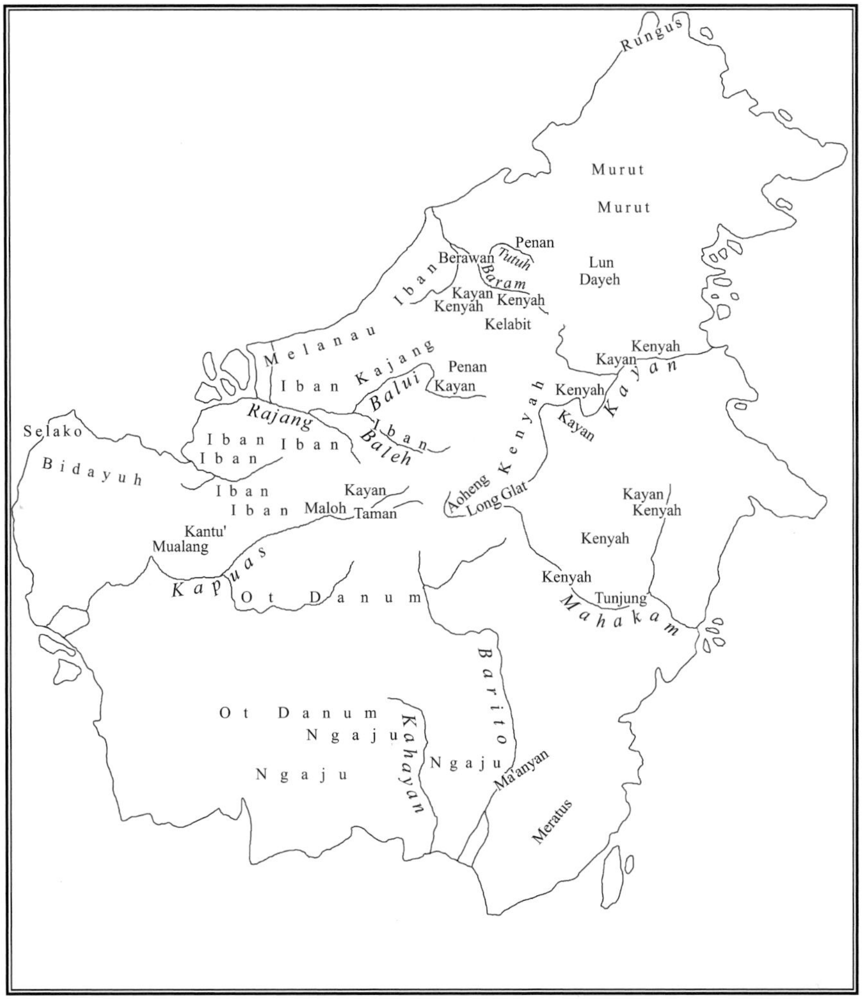

FIG. 0.9. Map showing locations of groups mentioned in the book.

the local dialect of Malay), and in architecture (to single-family houses), all of which are taken to be part and parcel of a Malay way of life.

In the more recent period, architecture and ethnicity have become more complicated, with some interior groups in Sarawak and most of those in Kalimantan having abandoned longhouses while retaining a Dayak or other local ethnic identity. In Sarawak many members of interior, longhouse-dwelling groups have moved to

coastal or downriver urban areas while maintaining family apartments in longhouses in the interior, to which they return for festivals and other visits. The association of longhouses with upriver backwardness notwithstanding, maintaining a residence in one is something of which urban dwellers are proud, and it is an advantage to indigenous political leaders.

Unlike many anthropologists in recent decades, I did not start out doing research in Borneo by living at length among a particular group and focusing on issues of social organization. My initial inquiries in Sarawak were an extension of earlier studies in Kelantan in northeastern peninsular Malaysia on *latah*, a famous culture-bound syndrome. I had wanted to find out about the occurrence of *latah* among some of the main ethnic groups of Sarawak and did surveys among the Selako Bidayuh and Sebuyau Iban in Lundu, the Melanau of Dalat on the Oya River, and the Saribas Iban and Malays of Betong on the Layar River. I also made more limited inquiries in various other areas, especially among the Iban on the middle Rajang and Baleh Rivers. The six months that I initially spent traveling and living in these places were very fruitful in terms of my original purposes, and I continued to return over the next several years to some of the same places and to new areas. More important from the perspective of the present inquiry, my experiences focused my attention on houses and the different patterns of architectural change that had occurred throughout central and western Sarawak. With the exception of the Malays, the various groups of this region had previously lived in longhouses, but by 1985 only some of them continued to do so. All of the Sebuyau Iban of Lundu and the Melanau of the Oya River had abandoned longhouses for Malay-style single dwellings. Most of the Selako and many of the other Bidayuh had also by then moved out of longhouses, while most of the Saribas Iban and nearly all of the other Iban outside of town areas were still living in them and continue to do so at present.

Equally important, the longhouses I saw varied greatly. Aside from the ethnic differences of the sort noted in the literature and discussed below in this book, they varied in terms of change; some were very similar to those discussed and illustrated in nineteenth-century accounts, while others were very modern, two-story, built-on-the-ground brick-and-mortar affairs. The Bidayuh, who had widely abandoned longhouses, had kept those they still had in a fairly traditional form. The Iban, in contrast, who had mainly retained longhouses, tended to favor modern types. While still often living in older, traditional longhouses, the Iban, when replacing older longhouses, were commonly building modernized new ones. While this pattern may seem odd, it was one I subsequently found to be common throughout Sarawak— the Kenyah, Kajang, and Kayan groups had also, to a considerable extent, stayed in longhouses but generally were building very modern versions.

Once I had finished my research on *latah*, I decided to continue to work on projects in Sarawak, to concentrate on the Bidayuh and on matters of ethnicity and change. I was attracted to the Bidayuh for several reasons. They were mainly known from the early social anthropological accounts of Geddes, who had chosen—somewhat contrary to the instructions of Leach to find a village undergoing substantial modern change—a remote and rather traditional community in the deep interior of Bidayuh country. It was also apparent that in ethnological terms there were notable differences among the various Bidayuh groups, specifically between those of the Sadong area in the east and those of the Bau and Lundu areas to the west.

Although Bidayuh longhouses were often not much to begin with (compared to those of some of the other groups) and were gone from many areas, Bidayuh architecture was notable in several respects. The first was that Bidayuh villages had previously been located on ridge tops and steep mountainsides, and a few are still in these locations. Part of the change that the Bidayuh had undergone was to relocate to lower and more open settings, usually at the base of the mountain on which they had formerly lived. While this mountain orientation was formerly common among interior tribal groups of other areas of Southeast Asia, many of the other longhouse dwellers in Sarawak and throughout Borneo generally had primarily been riverside peoples. The architectural changes and continuities involved in the shift also seemed interesting.

The second feature of Bidayuh architecture was the men's houses, which had frequently been referred to in the older literature and which had more recently been engagingly described by Geddes. Although some groups on the other side of the island in East Kalimantan also have men's houses, they are unique to the Bidayuh in Sarawak and to the Bidayuh and related groups in West Kalimantan. By the late 1980s the older men's houses were gone from most Bidayuh villages in Sarawak, and of those that remained none that I learned of were being used as sleeping quarters for unmarried men. In a few villages, however, the adherents of the old or *adat* (traditional) religion were still actively caring for the skulls kept in the remaining men's houses and were once in a while holding major festivals for them. More important from the perspective of my interests in ethnicity and the politics of culture, men's houses were being revived as ethnic cultural symbols at the urging of modern, mostly Christian, Bidayuh intellectuals and nationalists, as well as more traditional adherents of the old religion. Some older men's houses were being refurbished, and many new ones were being built to serve new purposes; the results of these efforts can be readily seen in and around Kuching. Over the years I wrote several papers on these developments.[22]

Between 1994 and 1997 I made several trips to West Kalimantan and East Kalimantan, then again in 1998 to West Kalimantan. These trips enabled me to make comparisons between Sarawak and several regions of Indonesian Borneo, including the upper Sambas area and the upper Kapuas and Mendalam Rivers in the interior of West Kalimantan and the middle Mahakam region in East Kalimantan. These forays, along with the accounts of various colleagues, tended to confirm what had oc-

curred to me earlier regarding architectural change in Sarawak.[23] In Indonesian Borneo few or no longhouses exist in many areas. Those that do tend to be of an older, more traditional style in terms of both design and materials than do those in the areas of Sarawak where longhouses remain the most common form of dwelling. Indeed the contrast was striking. The persistence of more traditional styles of longhouses in Kalimantan is due in some instances to the Indonesian government's attempts to counter the effects of its earlier efforts to have longhouses abandoned and destroyed as backward and otherwise undesirable living arrangements and to preserve the few remaining older ones as museum pieces and tourist attractions. But it could also be seen in the areas where new longhouses were being built or older ones rebuilt in the traditional style, as in some of the Taman villages above Putissibau on the Kapuas and Mendalam Rivers of the interior of West Kalimantan.

There were other interesting developments to be seen. In both Kalimantan and Sarawak various modern political and cultural uses have been made of interior architecture. In Kalimantan, provincial governments and some Christian churches have recently incorporated Dayak built forms and artistry into their architecture. In the case of government efforts, the purpose has been to use local art and architecture to help foster provincial identities. This has included the use of local motifs in modern government buildings, monuments, and other structures, as well as the erection of rather freely interpreted model longhouses in some provincial capitals. In the case of Catholic churches, indigenous carving and painting are now sometimes added to church buildings, a reversal of earlier efforts at extinguishing interior cultural forms in association with conversion. In Sarawak, while Christian religious architecture shows fewer efforts to incorporate native forms than in some regions of Kalimantan, spectacular examples can be found. In addition, perhaps partly in response to the popularity of long-house tourism, internationally oriented hotels, resorts, and other tourist operations in Sarawak have incorporated interior architectural designs to a greater extent than in Kalimantan.

This book, then, is about the longhouses and other architectural forms of the interior peoples of Borneo, especially those of Sarawak (Malaysian Borneo) and the northern region of Kalimantan (Indonesian Borneo), with occasional reference to other areas, including Sabah (also Malaysian Borneo) and the southern part of Kalimantan. My aim has been to both document traditional architecture and note and analyze patterns of change and recent developments. These two concerns are reflected in the general organization of the book, the first in part 1, the second mainly in part 2. In chapter 1 I offer an overview of interior Bornean architecture and building practices, in chapter 2 I deal with longhouses, and in chapter 3 I offer a description and analysis of architectural symbolism. In dealing with change and present-day developments, I turn first in chapter 4 to the Bidayuh in particular and then in chapter 5 to broader changes involving longhouses. Chapter 6 is concerned with the present uses and (uncertain) future of indigenous Bornean architecture.

PART ONE TRADITIONAL FORMS

CHAPTER ONE THE BUILT ENVIRONMENT
OF THE INTERIOR: AN OVERVIEW

THE TRADITIONAL ARCHITECTURE of the interior peoples of Borneo includes longhouses and other multifamily dwellings, single-family houses, granaries, storage sheds, farmhouses, bridges and walkways, river docks, and platforms. Among some groups there is also a widespread and often elaborate mortuary architecture of burial posts and mausoleums, as well as of statuary, ceremonial poles and various other ritual structures, and (in some areas) men's houses.

THE LOCATION OF VILLAGES

With the partial exception of mortuary architecture, the main location of buildings and other structures in Bor-

neo is the clustered village; the dispersed and ribbon settlement patterns found in some rural areas today appear to be mainly a recent development. In the past most villages throughout Sarawak and much of the rest of Borneo were placed in two sorts of locations: on mountainsides, ridges, or hilltops or along navigable rivers. Most peoples were therefore either hill or mountain inhabitants or riverside dwellers, although it needs to be kept in mind that much of the interior is rugged upland country, and therefore many of the riverside dwellers were also situated among hills or mountains if not on them.[1] In the northwestern part of the island the hill dwellers include all of the Bidayuh peoples in Sarawak and related groups in West Kalimantan, for whom mountain villages were a defining characteristic. Until several decades ago the Bidayuh were known as Land Dayaks, or sometimes in earlier periods as Hill Dayaks. In addition, in the far north of Sarawak and adjacent areas of East Kalimantan and Sabah some groups, including the Kelabit and Lundayeh, lived in high valleys and on plateaus that lack navigable rivers and streams, although their culture and languages otherwise link them to the other north-central Bornean groups rather than the distant Bidayuh. Their villages, moreover, were not built on steep mountainsides or hilltops, as were those of the Bidayuh, but rather in open areas near the water courses that were used to irrigate their wet rice fields. The Penan, Punan, Ukit, Bukat, and other nomadic hunter-gatherers of the interior are also land or mountain dwellers who typically lived in the headwaters of the rivers of central Borneo and, until recently, have made little use of boats. Their traditional architecture and way of life is also different from that of the Bidayuh, as well as from the various Kenyah or Kayan, with whom the Penan of Sarawak (who speak languages related to Kenyah) are usually allied. In the southern part of Borneo the hill- or mountain-dwelling peoples include the Dayaks of the Meratus Mountains, who

are sometimes referred to as Bukat, a term generally meaning "hill."

The riverine dwellers are much more numerous and diverse. They include the Iban, the largest single ethnic group in Sarawak, most of whom dwelt along the middle and lower stretches of the rivers of central Sarawak, mainly below major rapids in the case of the larger rivers, as well as in the northern part of the middle region of the Kapuas in West Kalimantan. They also include the Kenyah, Kayan, and various Kajang groups, who, along with the Berawan, are sometimes referred to as the central Bornean peoples, as well as the Melanau, who have shifted to the coast but are closely related to the Kajang peoples of the interior. These groups dwelt both below and above the large rapids of many rivers of central and northeastern Sarawak and in contiguous areas of East Kalimantan. The riverside dwellers of the south include the Ngaju, Ot Danum, Ma'anyan, Benua', and others.[2]

The geographical distinction between the mountain-dwelling and riverine peoples is not absolute. The hill-dwelling peoples are dependent on water for bathing, cooking, and drinking and therefore locate villages beside or near springs or streams that can be relied on throughout the year. But in the case of the Bidayuh at least, aside from the fact that such streams are usually not navigable, longhouses and other dwellings are not placed with any particular orientation to nearby water courses and are often built facing away from them (as can be seen, for example, in the village of Anah Rais in Padawan)—the opposite of the practice of the riverine groups. Similarly, the riverine groups also sometimes built their villages on hilltops or mountainsides at some distance from the river for reasons of security against attack by enemy groups.[3] Although for a different reason, the Iban also occasionally built their longhouses on the upper, unnavigable reaches of streams, leaving their boats at a friendly village farther down. All such groups, however, remained linked to rivers and never developed the sort of mountain-oriented architecture characteristic of the Bidayuh. Unlike the Bidayuh or Kelabit, they traveled by rivers and defined directions mainly in terms of upstream and downstream.

IRON AGE ARCHITECTURE: WOOD, STONE, AND METAL

While the architecture of interior groups varies substantially among regions and specific groups, it has a number of common features that may be noted at this point. To begin with, Bornean built forms are almost exclusively organic in nature—that is, based on wood and other plant materials obtained from the forest or other local sources.[4] An important exception is the use made of stone in mortuary architecture in some areas, sometimes in association with wood, but also in the form of dolmens and other burial receptacles and memorials. The use of stone in the creation of large burial structures among the Kelabit and other groups replicates its much wider use for nonarchitectural ritual objects, either in natural form or in that of small, carved figures. (The creation of stone mortuary receptacles, memorials, and other large objects is part of a much wider Southeast Asian megalithic complex that in Borneo is concentrated in the northeastern quarter of the island.)

In constructing houses, mortuary structures, and other buildings, the peoples of Borneo have been able to make use of some of the richest and most diverse forests in the world. Unlike temperate forests, which tend to comprise concentrated stands of a small number of species of trees in given ecological zones, those of the humid tropics have an enormous variety of trees. Unlike the Native American builders of the Northwest Coast of North America, who relied almost entirely on a single tree—the red cedar (*Thuja plicata*)—in constructing their

FIG. 1.1. Dolmen, Kelabit highlands, Sarawak.

great houses and ceremonial posts,[5] Bornean builders (some of whose architecture is reminiscent of that of the Northwest Coast in terms of artistry, size, and boldness) have had a great variety of trees among which to choose. These include numerous broadleaf trees that yield some of the hardest and most enduring lumber found anywhere, lumber that is straight-grained and knot-free for great lengths.

The importance and variety of broadleaf trees, palms, rattans, and bamboos for building and other purposes is reflected in the large numbers of each that are recognized and distinguished by local peoples. A recent ethnobotanical study of the Iban in Sri Aman Division in Sarawak found that villagers identified more than 675 plant species, including 200 types of trees, 50 of which produced useful timber, bark, or other building materials.[6] In the rural Bau area, Bidayuh villagers have more limited access to old growth forest, which has a much greater variety of species than younger or secondary forest, because of extensive cutting for swidden cultivation and logging concessions. Here, as a result of surveys of several dozen houses under construction, I found about 30 different kinds of timber in use, although the names of a great many more trees are known.

For building purposes various woods are relatively valued for their resistence to insect borers and decay, their absence of noxious or toxic properties, and their strength and working properties in relation to the specific purpose for which they are to be used and to the difficulty in finding and transporting them. Builders are generally most concerned about the properties of lumber that will be partially sunk in the ground (as with foundation posts) or exposed to the rain; somewhat less concerned with those of interior framing timber, which needs to be strong for some uses but can be less durable; and least particular regarding interior uses that do not require either much strength or durability.

Many of the most desirable woods—to both local builders and loggers—belong to one vast single family, the dipterocarps. Especially in the lowland areas such trees predominate to the extent that they provide the name for one of the most common botanical zones on the island—mixed dipterocarp forest. The *Shorea*, one large group of species within the dipterocarps, has been estimated to comprise 67 percent of the stock of timber trees in Borneo.[7] These include the many different *selangan batu*, *meranti*, *chengal*, and *enkabang* varieties. (All such terms are Malay unless otherwise noted.) These trees tend to be large, produce hard wood, and have long trunks.

Villagers in Borneo know and value the characteristics of many kinds of wood, but not all available trees are readily cut. Some are regarded as the home of spirits and therefore potentially dangerous, although the strangling fig or *ara* (*Ficus benjamina*), which is the most common of all the haunted trees, has little or no value as building material. There are also other kinds of trees that are used for other purposes and therefore not readily cut,

even though they may provide valuable lumber. These include the various fruit trees, especially the durian (*Durio* spp.) and the bee trees (like the durian, often individually owned), especially the magnificent *tapang* (*Koompassia excelsa*), the tallest of all Bornean trees.

If there is a single tree in Borneo that begins to approximate the importance of the red cedar for native builders in the Northwest Coast of North America, it is not a dipterocarp but a laurel. In most areas of Borneo where it occurs (mainly lowland and swamp forest) Bornean ironwood (*Eusideroxylon zwageri*, most commonly *belian*, but also known in other local vernacular terms) is valued above all other woods. It has a dry weight of more than a thousand kilograms per cubic meter (or more than a ton per cubic yard) and sinks like a rock in water, with strengths comparable to its weight and legendary endurance to insects and decay when exposed to the weather or placed in the ground. It is considered by far the most desirable for house foundation piles, carved grave posts, mausoleums, and other uses for which both strength and longevity are wanted.

Bornean forests also provide other types of building materials. Bamboos (*buluh*)—specially *Gigantocloa* spp., the large varieties that grow abundantly around villages, along rivers, and in fallow swidden fields—are among the most important of all building materials. Because large bamboo is so readily available and so easy to carry and to work, it is extensively used in many ways. As framing material, it is commonly used in more temporary structures, although the Bidayuh build permanent as well as temporary bridges with bamboo, replacing the individual lengths when they deteriorate. In more permanent dwellings bamboo is split in halves or quarters and used as flooring, especially for exterior drying platforms and for the walkways in longhouse galleries. Bamboo that has been split and flattened into wide sheets is used as wall covering and sometimes as flooring.

Palm trees, while often grown primarily for other

FIG. 1.2. Bamboo sheets to be used as siding for a small Bidayuh house, Gumbang Village, Bau District, western Sarawak, 1997.

purposes—the coconut (*Cocos nucifera*), sago (*Metroxylon sagu*), and sugar palm (*Arenga pinatta*) for food and drink, the areca palm (*Areca* spp.) for betel nut—also yield very valuable building materials. These include *attap daun* or leaf thatch, the most durable of which comes from the sago palm but which is also made from the leaves of coconut, *nibung*, nipa, and fan palms. In addition, very strong and durable cordage is made from the black fiber (*ijuk*) of the sugar palm, while the split outer shell of palm trunk, especially from the *nibung* palm (*Oncosperma* spp.) is also used in construction, especially for some parts of floors and drying platforms. Then there are the various climbing palms or rattans (*Calamus* spp., *Daemon-orops* spp., *Plectomia* spp.) that are collected in the forest and yield edible tips, but their principal use is as a construction material, usually in split form for tying and lashing, as well as for many other purposes, including basketry and mat making.

Tools, Traditional and Modern

The ability or inclination of Bornean peoples to obtain and work with the very hard woods from large trees that they prefer for some building purposes is linked to the use of iron tools. While the prehistory of Bornean architecture is largely unknown, it seems fair to assume that it was different before the use, and probably the manufacture, of iron implements. Iron work appears to have a long history in the interior, as well as in the coastal regions of Borneo.[8] Although information on the spread of iron smelting and forging in the past is scanty, these practices seem to have been in place among all the settled groups by the nineteenth century and had probably been present among most of the longhouse dwellers for hundreds of years before this time. Iron is traded from the coast, but in the past it was produced from nodules of ore collected in rivers and smelted using a double cylinder bellows. It is then forged into swords, knives, adzes, and other tools throughout the interior. The spread of iron forging has continued. In Sarawak the Penan of the Baram (and perhaps other areas) who have settled into longhouses have learned from the Kenyah to make iron tools and now supply these to others.

Trees are traditionally cut down and buildings constructed using a limited variety of locally made iron hand tools, most of which involve a forged blade or head lashed with rattan to a wooden handle. Axes and adzes are the most important customary building tools. The most common version is widely known in Sarawak as a *beliung*. It can be used as either an axe or an adze, the difference being the way that the head is bound to the handle. That is, as an axe the iron head is attached so that the axis of the blade is parallel to the length of the handle, while as an adze the same head is attached with the blade axis at a right angle. In some instances the rattan binding is done in such a way that the position of the head can be easily changed so that the tool can be used alternatively as an axe or an adze. However, other kinds of adze heads are also made that can only be used in one way, including one with a wide blade with a wing or flange on each side that is today used mainly for hollowing boat hulls but in the past was also used for making planks. In either case, the haft always has two parts: a slender, springy upper shaft and a thicker lower handle. The iron head (which, if not made in a local forge, is ob-

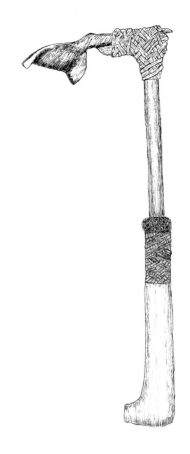

tained by trade or purchased from a Chinese blacksmith in town) is lashed with split rattan to the T-shaped upper shaft made from the intersection of a tree branch and a larger limb of very strong wood such as *belian*. The upper shaft in turn is fitted into a socket in the lower handle and kept in place with *geta perca* resin and by lashing with finely split rattan. The lower handle is often made of a softer wood than the upper and usually embellished with carving on the lower end. Some groups, including the Kayan, also mounted adze blades to straight handles to form chisels.

Locally made adzes are still used, though to a more limited extent than in the past. However, the customary axe has been largely or entirely replaced by imported

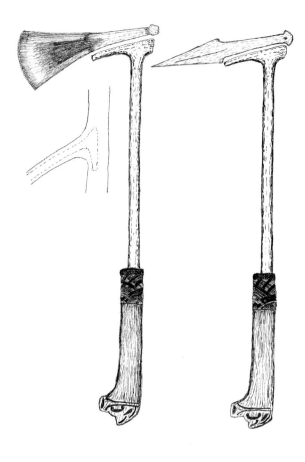

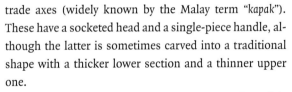

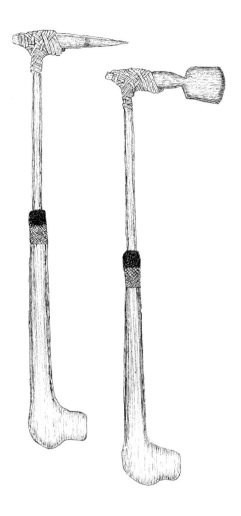

trade axes (widely known by the Malay term "*kapak*"). These have a socketed head and a single-piece handle, although the latter is sometimes carved into a traditional shape with a thicker lower section and a thinner upper one.

In addition to the use of axes and adzes, much work is done with all-purpose heavy chopping or bush knives (commonly known as *parang* in Malay or *duku'* in Iban), which have different shapes and sizes, as well as lighter-weight, long-bladed knives, all of which vary in style from one group to another. Fine carving is done with smaller knives and chisels. Axes, adzes, and larger knives are used for cutting, shaping, and (supplemented in some cases with chisels) most architectural carving. Smaller,

FIG. 1.3 (facing). Flanged adz.

FIG. 1.4 (above left). Forged adz-axe head mounted as an adz (right) and as an axe (left).

FIG. 1.5 (above right). Adz-axe, approximately 73 centimeters long.

PIG. 1.6 (right). Iban *duku'* (chopping knife).

PIG. 1.7 (below). "Dyaks Using the Biliong, or Axe-Adz," engraving in Henry Ling Roth's *The Natives of Sarawak and British North Borneo*, from William T. Hornaday's *Two Years in the Jungle*, 1885.

often long-handled knives are used for preparing split rattan and many other purposes. Although rattan and bamboo are still worked in traditional ways with iron tools, imported hand tools are now extensively used for construction throughout the interior. Chain saws are used both to cut down trees and to produce finished lumber, including flattened or squared beams and thin boards.

PILE FOUNDATIONS AND TIMBER-FRAME CONSTRUCTION

In addition to being built of wood and other organic materials worked with iron tools, nearly all structures are traditionally raised above the ground on posts or, more accurately, piles (that is, posts sunk in the ground). The height to which buildings are raised varies according to the type and location of the building and the group involved. In the past most buildings were built at least two meters above the ground (and often much higher on hillsides or above depressions), while some longhouses, mausoleums, and men's houses were raised eight or ten meters.

The ability to erect large, heavy buildings raised above the ground and, in the case of longhouses, to add to their length by replication requires sophisticated methods of construction. The architecture of the interior in Borneo makes use of several building techniques. One of these involves what may be called pole construction. It is utilized in putting up smaller and lighter buildings, including farm huts, some single-family dwellings, various shelters, drying platforms, and, among the Bidayuh, walkways and traditional bamboo suspension bridges. This method involves tying a framework of sapling posts or bamboo poles together and then adding a floor, walls (if used), and a roof, also by tying. In most instances the upright posts that form the framework for the sides also support the roof and the floor. Structures can be created very rapidly in this way, although this method of building can also be used to erect more complex and time-consuming ones as well.

The construction of longhouses and other larger buildings is accomplished by timber framing. Also often referred to as post-and-beam construction, this method was often used in the past in the United States and elsewhere in building houses and, until more recently, barns. In this form of construction a framework of timbers is erected beginning with a series of upright posts, to which are then attached horizontal joists, longitudinal beams, and cross beams, and eventually rafters, purlins, and braces, all fastened together by mortise and tenon or other appropriate joints or, as in Borneo, combined with lashing. Following the erection of the frame, floors and walls are added. Since the walls do not support the upper framework or the roof (all of which rests on the main framework of posts and beams), they can be made from either boards or light materials such as bark or split bamboo; alternatively, the sides can be left open or partially so. The floor, which is also supported by its own posts as well as the main structural posts, can similarly be made from either heavy boards or light materials, including bamboo strips or sheets.

In contrast to the designs used in carving and painting, the structural architecture of Borneo is one of geometric shapes, rectilinear forms, and sharp corners rather than of curves, although timber framing can be used in the construction of round or octagonal buildings. The framework of rounded buildings, or long buildings with rounded ends, for example, can be made using wooden posts with natural crotches in which beams are set without shaping either part. Such construction needs comparatively little in the way of skill or tools in preparing the framing materials except for making them the right length, and the technique is old in human prehistory. Rectangular framing using heavy timbers, however, generally requires that a mortise or slot be

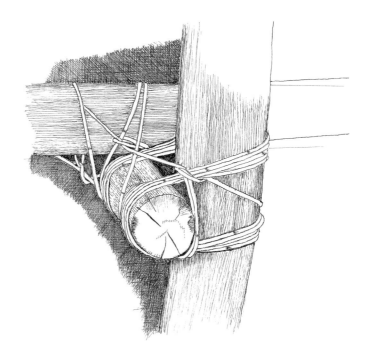

FIG. 1.8. Tied joints.

made in a post or beam and a tenon shaped to fit into it. Both mortises and tenons have to be carefully shaped—that is, usually squared. Rectangular timber-frame joints can also be made using lashing, but except in light construction, this also requires that intersecting parts be squared or at least flattened or notched, although this does not mean that an entire post or beam needs to be shaped (and in fact in the past posts, beams, and other framing parts were often left round or partially round, as some still are). The advantage of rectangular timber framing is that buildings such as longhouses can be massively built and extended horizontally by simply building new segments onto the ends of existing ones. While nearly all buildings are constructed in a rectangular form, there are exceptions. Among the Bidayuh, men's houses are often built in an octagonal or round shape, and some groups round the ends of longhouses.

FIG. 1.9. Mortise and tenon joints.

Roofs and Walls

The use of timber framing in Borneo (as elsewhere) means that walls and roofs are separate, noncontinuous, and partly independent parts of buildings. In smaller structures such as granaries and mausoleums, the walls are attached to the outer posts. In larger buildings the interior and outer walls are attached to various sets of posts that support the roof, but the walls as such do not carry any of the weight. This of course means that walls do not need to be built at all in order to support a roof. Nonetheless, unlike those erected by some Austronesian peoples, the more permanent buildings erected by Bornean peoples are seldom open on all sides. Longhouses are enclosed on the ends and at the back but often partially open at the front. Those that lack open verandas or drying platforms at the front have at least a partial lower wall, while those (such as the longhouses of the Bidayuh) that do have such verandas are sometimes entirely open at the front.

Bornean buildings are, therefore, also similar to those of many other peoples in the region in that roofs rather than exterior walls are emphasized in terms of their height. However, in contrast to the spectacular roof form architecture of some of the peoples of adjacent islands and elsewhere in Austronesia, with elaborate saddle shapes and soaring gables, the roofs of most Bornean buildings have simple, utilitarian shapes. At the same time, roofs are sometimes embellished with carving or statuary, occasionally to a spectacular extent. In southern Borneo roofs often have the characteristic Southeast Asian crossed gable ends, signifying horns, and in the north the Kenyah, Kayan, and some other groups embellish roofs with carved finials. In both regions mortuary structures tend to have the most elaborate of all roofs, with ridge crests, finials, and other embellishments. The use of intersecting roof planes, hipped or dual-pitched roofs, and other departures from simple, two-sided roof shapes that are seen today in some longhouses and other community buildings are recent developments.

BUILT TO LAST OR NOT

The effort and skill that go into the construction of longhouses and other structures in Borneo notwithstanding, these buildings have until recently had a relatively short life. One way to explain this is to say that composed as they are of organic materials, built forms are simply following the normal, inevitably rapid course of deterioration and decay associated with the hot, rainy, and humid equatorial climate of Borneo. To a certain extent this is so. In some instances, buildings are used until they have deteriorated and need to be abandoned or replaced, although here, of course, there are major differences between those constructed mainly from lightweight materials (such as smaller poles, bamboo, bark, and thatch), which deteriorate relatively rapidly, and those made from longer-lasting, larger-diameter hardwoods, especially ironwood.

But it would be an oversimplification to suggest that the limited life of Bornean architecture is simply a consequence of the natural processes of rapid organic decay. Some buildings are not intended to last, for they would have no lasting value. A farm hut built in a swidden field that will be cultivated for a year or so has little use beyond this period unless the next field is to be located nearby. But even in the case of huts built near more permanent fields, such as those for swamp rice, there is an obvious tradeoff between erecting a longer-lasting structure with a heavier hardwood frame and a more temporary one that can be rebuilt quickly and easily from small poles, bamboo, and thatch.

In addition to such utilitarian structures meant to last for a season or two, many traditional ceremonial structures are also built or carved for limited use—often for a single event, after which they are dismantled or left to deteriorate and collapse. Others, such as raised mausoleums, are meant to last and to be used when additional burials of family members or descendants are added. Such mausoleums or ossuaries, built entirely of ironwood, as well as the large, carved burial posts, made also from the trunks of ironwood trees, are probably the oldest wooden structures in the interior of Borneo. The oldest known carved burial post in Sarawak, however, dates only to the late nineteenth century.

While many larger traditional structures are not erected with the evident expectation that they will remain standing for a long period of time, this does not mean that builders are uninterested in the durability of materials. Although builders do not traditionally use preserva-

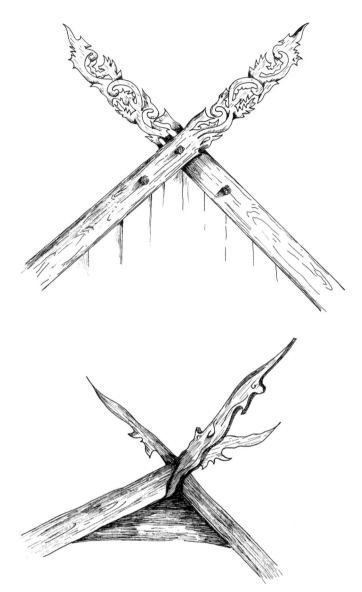

FIG. 1.10 (top). Gable horns, such as those of the Ngaju house shown here, are common architectural features in south Borneo.

FIG. 1.11 (bottom). Ridge beam finial and gable horns on a Modang men's house, East Kalimantan.

tives or protective finishes on buildings, they are very concerned with deterioration through rot and attack by insects. They value woods and other building materials in terms of their resistance and endurance, as well as their strength. They also engage in various practices that are intended to enhance the longevity of building materials. Bamboo and wood used in houses (as well as the hollowed sections of logs used as boat bottoms) are believed to last longer if soaked in water for several weeks or more.[9] In addition, in the past at least attention was paid to various principles concerning the moon and tides that are believed to affect the strength and endurance of wood. The Bidayuh say that trees to be used for lumber should not be cut during periods in which there is a full moon (in general a dangerous time) because the moon at this stage has become soft and crumbly and so has the wood in trees. Similarly, the Bidayuh also say that trees should not be cut during periods of low tide because at this time the remaining water of the sea has been absorbed by the forest; trees at low tide therefore have more water in them and produce weaker, more rapidly deteriorating wood. Present-day Bidayuh may no longer cut trees in accord with such beliefs and recount them with amusement, but they reflect a traditional concern with the endurance of building materials.

THE ARCHITECTURE OF EVERYDAY LIFE

In addition to longhouses, which will be treated in detail in the following chapter, other multifamily dwellings are also built in some areas. The various Ngaju Dayaks and related groups of the far south have for quite some time lived mainly in single-family houses rather than in longhouses. However, they also erect large houses that can accommodate a number of families in separate rooms.[10] In the past, like longhouses, they were intended to provide security against raids and were therefore also raised high above the ground on piles and fortified. They also

reflect a common desire to live together under a single roof in a social group larger than the single-family household, for they continued to be constructed after security against raids was established by the Dutch. Such multifamily dwellings differ from longhouses in that they are constructed and occupied by large extended kin groups comprising several or more nuclear families who are also common owners of land and heirlooms.

Separate individual houses comprising nuclear or smaller extended families (frequently of the stem variety, whereby one married child with children remains in the house) are now common throughout Borneo and predominate in Kalimantan. Among most of the swidden-cultivating peoples of the interior, single-family houses as primary residences are often a recent development that can be attributed to colonial, missionary, or (at least in Kalimantan) postcolonial government efforts to encourage the abandonment of longhouses. In the coastal areas, where single houses are a much older pattern, they are often associated with Malay influence, both among those (such as the Melanau) who have converted extensively to Islam and among groups (such as the Sebuyau Iban of the Kuching and Lundu areas of western Sarawak) who have become Christian instead. In some areas older single houses generally resemble those of the local Malay groups. The design and materials of newer single-family houses, both in coastal areas and in the interior, reflect broader regional or national styles. In some areas of the interior, however, including (but not only) the far south of Borneo and the far north, single houses have been used for a long time.

Farmhouses, Huts, and Forest Shelters
In addition to its main residence, nearly every farming family will build a temporary farmhouse or shelter of some sort close to its current fields. In addition to the small longhouses built by some groups, these include various huts. What sort of farmhouse it is depends on

FIG. 1.12 (above).
Melanau houses,
Oya River,
Sarawak, 1986.

FIG. 1.13 (left).
Bidayuh houses,
Tamong, upper
Seluas area, West
Kalimantan, 1994.

FIG. 1.14. Bidayuh farm hut, Krokong, Sarawak, 1998.

how much time it is occupied during the season, the number of seasons it will likely be utilized, and the uses to which it will be put. Among the Bidayuh farm dwellings range from very small, simply built temporary shelters to fairly large, elaborately built ones that approximate the primary dwellings of some families. The simplest huts (widely referred to in Sarawak by the term "*langkau*") are intended mainly for day use, for shelter in heavy rain, for resting during the hottest part of the day, and for storing tools and supplies. Larger and more elaborate ones are built in or near permanent swamp rice fields and swidden fields that are a long way off. Such houses are sometimes equipped with kitchens and sleeping materials and are used overnight or for longer periods, especially during the harvest. They may also be used for rituals and small feasts. Traditionally farmhouses and field huts are covered with palm leaf thatch. The simpler ones have bamboo frames. They are all raised above the ground, and most have drying platforms on the front.

In many or most areas of the interior the Penan, Punan, Bukat, Ukit, and other nomadic hunter-gathers traditionally build single houses or shelters. Such houses are always raised slightly above the ground and are usually open sided. Some have one-sided or shed roofs, while others have two-sided roofs with a center ridge. They are made of a framework of poles and covered with leaf thatch or sometimes with tree branches and are intended to last as long as a camp is occupied. More recent versions are now sometimes covered with plastic sheet-

FIG. 1.15. Penan forest shelter, Belaga, 1992.

ing that can be reused when the camp is moved. The small number of full-time nomads continue to build such houses as their main dwellings, while the much larger number of those who have settled into either longhouses or single houses in more permanent villages continue to build them while hunting and foraging in the forest.

Granaries and Storage Houses

Among various groups, including the Iban and some of the Bidayuh, rice and heirloom property (especially gongs, other brassware, and ceramic jars) are kept in the longhouse—rice in bark bins in the attic, heirlooms on display in the inner apartment. Other groups—including some Bidayuh, the Kenyah, Kayan, and Kajang—keep rice, and in some cases also heirloom property, in external storehouses. This provides protection against fire, which in Borneo is a threat everywhere, but especially where the village consists of a single longhouse, as opposed to a number of smaller ones. In terms of construction, external granaries and storage sheds for valuables are usually built in the same general way and from the same materials as dwellings. Groups that incorporate painting and carving into their longhouse architecture sometimes also do so with storage houses.

Bridges, Trails, and Walkways

Among many Dayak groups the construction of bridges and walkways is a very minor part of architectural practice. The many peoples who live along larger rivers use

FIG. 1.16 (above). Bidayuh granaries that open from the top (see the one at the far left), built along the front of the veranda, Sadong area, 1988.

FIG. 1.17 (right). Bidayuh granaries, upper Sadong area, Sarawak, 1989.

boats for transportation and as a means for getting from one bank to the other. Many of the rivers in the mountainous country of the interior, however, are narrow enough to be spanned by bridges, and travel is often mainly by foot. Among the mountain-dwelling Bidayuh, the construction of trails and walkways to and within villages is also an important part of traditional architecture. Some traditional bridges are still in use in the interior of Padawan. Like elevated walkways, these are made from bamboo tied with sugar palm fiber or creeper. Where possible, the basic technique is to erect a series of pairs of crossed bamboo posts and then lay and tie long, longitudinal sections of bamboo across the intersections of these. Smaller lengths of bamboo are tied parallel to and above these to form a handrail on each side. As long as the bases of the crossed posts reach the ground, they support the structure—as with a walkway above a muddy or swampy area. Where this is not possible, as with wider bridges over rivers, the middle section is suspended, either from the posts on either side that do reach the ground or by poles tied to trees. Several of the bamboo bridges across the upper Sarawak River in Padawan are suspension bridges that span more than fifty meters. Once it is in place, such a bridge or walkway can last as long as it is maintained. The individual pieces of bamboo do not endure long but can be replaced as they need to be without rebuilding the entire structure. Giant bamboo is usually readily available along rivers and around villages.

THE ARCHITECTURE OF PUBLIC LIFE: VILLAGE HALLS AND MEN'S HOUSES

Village communal buildings used for meetings, various ritual activities, the keeping and display of heirlooms, and sometimes hospitality are found throughout the Austronesian areas of Southeast Asia and beyond. Often known as *balai* (or various cognate terms), such buildings occur also in Borneo, but here (with a few exceptions)

FIG. 1.18 (top). Engraving of a Land Dayak bridge in Alfred Wallace's *The Malay Archipelago*, first published in 1869.

FIG. 1.19 (bottom). Bidayuh bamboo suspension bridge, upper Sarawak River, Padawan, Sarawak, 1992.

FIG. 1.20. Bidayuh men's house, Sadong area, Sarawak, circa 1950.

their presence is generally related inversely to long-houses—presumably because the uses to which *balai* are put are ones that are usually provided for in the gallery area of the longhouse. In the far south of Borneo, for example, where longhouses are generally lacking, such *balai* are common. Alfred Hudson describes those in the Ma'anyan villages of Padju Empat on the Telang and Pa-tai Rivers (tributaries of the great Barito) in Central Kalimantan as follows:

> With the exception of Kararat, which has only two houses, each village has one or more specialized structures that are not used as habitation. Telang, Siong, Murutuwu and Balawa each have a ceremonial hall known as the *balai*. The *balai* is occasionally used for the discussion of village disputes, but its primary function is connected with the *ijambe* cremation cere-mony. The *balai* is square or rectangular in shape, with a heavy wooden floor raised five or six feet above the ground on piles. Most *balai* have shingled roofs, but the one in Balawa has been covered with sheet tin as a mark of modernity. Various temporary porches and walkways are constructed on three sides of the permanent structure when a cremation ceremony is performed.[11]

Balai also occur among the peoples of the Meratus Mountains in South Kalimantan. In this region, how-ever, such buildings appear to be something of a blurred architectural genre—noninhabited public halls in some instances and multifamily houses in others. According to Carl Lumholtz, who traveled in the Meratus Moun-tains as a part of his sojourns in central Borneo early in this century, "The Kampong [village] exists only in name not in fact, the people living in the hills in scattered groups of two or three houses."[12] Of the village of Ang-kipi, which consisted of a "few shanties of one room each," he goes on to say that "The most prominent fea-ture of the place was a house of worship, the so-called *balai*, a square bamboo structure, the roomy interior of

FIG. 1.21.
Bidayuh men's house, Bunuk, Sarawak, 1990.

which had in the center a rectangular dancing-floor of bamboo sticks. A floor similarly constructed but raised some twenty-five centimeters higher, covered about all of the remaining space, and serves as temporary habitations for the people, many small stalls having been erected for the purpose."[13] Upon his arrival at the village of Tumingki, however, he found a similar *balai*, which he describes as a "large structure in which the people had taken a permanent abode, having no houses and possessing *ladangs* [swidden fields] nearby. Many fires were burning inside, round which families had gathered cooking rice."[14]

The use of the *balai* among the Meratus peoples as a sometime or full-time place of residence helps to explain what would otherwise be an anomalous settlement pattern: the dispersal of houses throughout the forest in relation to swidden fields. While in Borneo nomadic hunter-gatherers are traditionally dispersed into small residence groups in remote areas of forest, swidden cultivators live in concentrated villages and have dispersed swidden or farm houses only (at least until recently) as temporary or seasonal secondary dwellings. Aside from the other attractions of living close together, security in the interior areas traditionally liable to raiding and head-hunting encouraged concentrated rather than dispersed settlements, not only in Borneo, but throughout the swidden-cultivating tribal areas of Southeast Asia in general. If the Meratus peoples, who were not apparently headhunters themselves but (according to Anna Tsing) were vulnerable to others who were,[15] used their *balai* as a multifamily home as well as a meeting or ritual hall— at least before the Dutch put an end to head-hunting and slave raiding in southern Borneo—they are not so different from other groups after all.[16]

More recently *balai* have become common in areas where they were formerly uncommon or lacking. In Kalimantan such *balai* have been promoted or supported by the government as an alternative place for the public meetings and other traditional activities formerly carried out in the longhouses. In some instances among Kenyah, Kayan, and related groups in East Kalimantan, such new *balai* are constructed somewhat like longhouses and covered with carving and painting of the sort previously applied to longhouses. In Sarawak, modern *balai* or *balai adat* have also been built with government assistance and are common, for example, in Bidayuh villages where longhouses have often been abandoned. Unlike some of those in East Kalimantan, however, the new *balai* in Sarawak are usually drab, undecorated, utilitarian structures composed of concrete floors, cinderblock walls, and corrugated zinc roofs. Such *balai* lack much appeal or purpose among groups that retain longhouses.

The main exception to the general absence of separate public meeting and ritual halls among longhouse dwellers are men's houses. These also have a particular association with male initiation, with the display of skulls, and, in the past, with head-hunting and defense.[17] Men's houses occur both in East Kalimantan and in far western Sarawak and adjacent areas of West Kalimantan. In East Kalimantan they occur among the Modang groups, a Kayanic people with an otherwise distinctive form. As will be noted more fully in chapter 4, in northwestern Borneo men's houses occur among the various Bidayuh groups.[18]

THE ARCHITECTURE OF DEATH AND LIFE

Like villages, cemeteries are often located along rivers. This is partly a matter of convenience, partly (in some cases) a matter of display, and partly a matter of cosmology. In regard to the last, it is supposed that a location along the river, especially in a high or otherwise prominent place, will help the spirit of the deceased find the right way to the land of the dead. Cemeteries are typically located downstream from villages—this being the direction of death—although not all mortuary architecture is located in cemeteries. Secondary funerary receptacles are often placed directly in villages close to houses.

Mortuary architecture in the form of tombs or mausoleums, grave posts, ossuaries, and memorials is among the most highly wrought and long lasting of all the built forms in the interior of Borneo. However, the building of above-ground funerary structures differs greatly throughout Borneo, from the absence of much of anything to the massive and extensively carved edifices erected by some groups.

Why do some groups have little or nothing in the way of mortuary architectural forms while others have massive and ornate ones, at least for some persons? A simple but not very full answer to such a question would be to say that it is a matter of cultural variation from one region or group to another. Mortuary architecture in general appears to have reached the fullest development in northern Borneo—that is, in present-day central and northern Sarawak and in adjacent interior areas of East Kalimantan, more specifically among the various Kenyah, Kayan, Kajang, Berawan, Melanau, and other peoples that are sometimes said to form a central Borneo ethnological grouping.[19] Mortuary structures are consistent with more general architectural practices common to these groups, including massive construction and the extensive use of ornate carving and painting involving symbols and designs that concern both cosmology and social rank.

A fuller understanding of the development of mortuary architecture in Borneo must also involve consideration of the extent to which it is related to funeral customs. This is so in the general sense that highly developed mortuary structures are linked to lavish or drawn out ceremonies of death. Of course, this is so to some extent for a practical reason. Since funeral receptacles and monuments are usually not built ahead of time, the creation and erection of highly wrought versions takes time, even if large numbers of persons participate in their construction.

Beyond this, the type of mortuary receptacles and monuments created reflects the nature of the funeral rituals that are performed—specifically those involving one in contrast to two stages, or those without and those with secondary treatment of remains. The Bidayuh and some of the Iban are good examples of minimal ceremonial and architectural treatment of the dead, as are the practices of many nomadic groups.[20] Traditional Bidayuh funeral practices are simple and brief. Here the preferred mode was often cremation (still carried out in a few villages), although burial was also practiced and abandonment is reported. None of these practices were or are associated with much public ceremony. In the case of cremation, the soul of the deceased is released by the fire and ascends with the smoke. And here mortuary architecture is absent or minimal.

Iban practices vary from one area to another and in some instances are more complex than those of the Bidayuh. Although the Iban do not (and in so far as we know did not ever) practice cremation, the mortuary rituals of some Iban are similar to those of the Bidayuh, at least in terms of the minimal degree of elaboration in most areas. In their comparative study of death rituals, Peter Metcalf and Richard Huntington stress the brevity of Iban practices:

> Iban funerals are extremely rapid. The corpse is hurried out of the house soon after death, certainly on the same day. The men carrying the corpse to the graveyard stop at some convenient point along the way and prepare a rough coffin from a log cut from a softwood tree. The corpse is stuffed inside, and the

FIG. 1.22. Taman cemetery by the river near Melapi, upper Kapuas, West Kalimantan.

coffin is tied up with rattan. Arriving at the graveyard, the coffin is buried in a shallow grave. Various grave goods are left and a marker may be set up, and then the funeral party returns rapidly to the longhouse. The corpse is not tampered with again, and the graveyard is full of old bones dug from their shallow graves by wild pigs and other animals.[21]

The development of Iban mortuary architecture is also minimal in such situations. The practices of the Iban in the Saribas area are more complex in terms of both ritual and architecture. The Saribas Iban create small but often elaborately decorated grave houses called *sungkup* in association with *gawai antu*, a festival in which the spirits of the dead are welcomed back to the village for a final visit. The *sungkup* are supposed to represent the longhouses in the other world, into which the spirits of

the dead move in their final transformation. They are first set in the longhouse gallery and then moved permanently to the cemetery and placed over the graves of the individuals for whom they have been created.[22] In addition to the ritual and architectural practices of *gawai antu*, the Iban of the Saribas and some other areas memorialize the remains of certain individuals, especially renowned war leaders, by placing them in above-ground mausoleums on the tops of hills near longhouses, or in some instances even bringing them into longhouses.[23]

Such practices stand between the brief and relatively simple ones of the Iban of many other areas, as well as the Bidayuh, and the drawn-out mortuary customs of some groups. The most highly developed of all involve what is often called "secondary burial" but is more accurately referred to as "secondary treatment" in that in Borneo the secondary stage does not usually involve below-ground burial but rather the placement of bones or ashes in an above-ground or raised mortuary structure. Two-stage mortuary practices occur widely in Borneo, and, as elsewhere, all reserve the greatest ritual and architectural elaboration for the second stage, although there are some differences between northern and southern versions.

In northern Borneo two-stage mortuary practices are (or were) followed by all of the Kajang groups, the related Melanau, and the Berawan, Kelabit, and Lun Dayeh, and in some instances by others.[24] They begin with an initial funeral, in which the body, after lying or sitting in state, is placed and sealed in a coffin often carved in the shape of a boat or in a large, imported glazed jar. Here it is kept in the gallery of the longhouse for up to a year or more or transferred after some time to the cemetery. In either case, after decomposition is more or less complete except for the skeleton, the coffin or jar is opened, and the bones are cleaned and replaced or put in a jar and transferred to a new and grander repository. It is this latter phase, which involves the final release of the soul for its journey to the land of the dead, that is the occasion for great feasting,

FIG. 1.23 (above). Iban *sungkup* or grave hut, Saribas area, Sarawak.

FIG. 1.24 (right). Grave post, upper Bahau River, East Kalimantan.

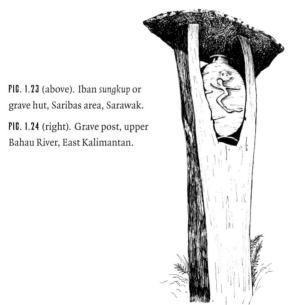

celebration, and sacrifice, including, in the past, human sacrifice. It is also for this stage that the elaborate mortuaries are created and erected.

Drawn-out mortuary rituals in the form of two-stage funeral sequences are linked to architectural practices in that groups that have secondary rituals create some kind of repository for the final remains that differs from the one in which the body was originally interred. Moreover, in some instances the receptacles that contain human remains that have been given secondary treatment are placed directly in villages near houses rather than in separate cemeteries, which are usually located well away (often across the river and downstream) from them. While there may be various reasons for such distinctive placement, they appear to include the common belief that ritual processes of secondary treatment render the remains harmless or transform the spirit of the deceased from being dangerous to being benevolent.[25] And while the mortuary structures created in association with secondary funerary rituals are not necessarily more opulent or monumental than those erected in relation to single-stage mortuary practices, they are usually different.

This is true at least in northern Borneo, where massive and ornate mortuary structures commonly take two forms: the grave post, which is known generally by the Kajang term "klirieng," and the raised and carved mausoleum, which is known generally as salong. Both klirieng and salong are or were (the former do not appear to have been made for many decades) created only for important persons of high rank, for whom they are to be monuments as well as mortuary receptacles, although smaller and simpler versions of both mausoleums and post receptacles are, among some groups, for lower status, more ordinary persons. The more unusual structure is the massive grave post, some version of which was made by the various Kajang groups and by the related Berawan (the lijieng) and Melanau (the jerunai), all of whom engage in two-stage mortuary practices for persons of high

status.[26] The klirieng is made from the trunk of a large belian tree or, occasionally, from two trunks that have been joined together along their length.[27] Such posts may stand ten or more meters above the ground, are covered with carving from top to bottom, and are capped by a large flat stone that covers a slot at the top of the post into which the remains are placed. A wooden boxlike structure may also be built on the top, covered in turn by the massive flat stone. Klirieng are left unpainted, but carved features were originally accentuated with ceramic plates and, in some instances, brass gongs.

Salong are made by various peoples, including the Kenyah, Kayan, and related groups. They are also constructed by the Berawan and the Punan Bah Kajang, who also create grave posts.[28] In all cases salong are made from ironwood, with roofs of planks or shingles, decorated with ornate carved fretwork and finials, and sometimes painted. The most elaborate are also placed up to six meters above the ground on carved posts. They are created for men of rank but also used for the remains of other family members. Many salong in Sarawak have two posts, although the number can vary from a single one to nine and can hold several or more coffins or jars.[29] They are usually placed in prominent locations along the river, sometimes on hilltops. Two reasons are given for this practice. One (as noted above) is that such a location will help the spirit of the deceased to find the right way to the land of the dead. The other and more commonly noted reason is that the tombs are monuments as well as receptacles and therefore are intended to impress and awe those who see them from the river as they pass by, thereby displaying the wealth and importance of both the deceased and those who created the monuments.[30]

In northern Borneo the building of monumental wooden mortuary architecture has declined or disappeared throughout most areas. Carved grave posts for persons of high status have not been made by the Melanau, Kajang, or Berawan groups for several decades

FIG. 1.25. Kajang grave post (klirieng), Punan Bah Village, upper Rajang River, Sarawak.

or more, a consequence of religious conversion and other changes, including the cessation of secondary mortuary practices, which were frowned on or forbidden by the government. Carved wooden mausoleums have continued to be made more recently—a great wooden *salong* was built and erected for the paramount chief of the Balui on a hill across the river from Belaga Town in the late 1960s. Newer, hybrid versions of *salong* constructed from concrete as well as wood continue to be produced in some areas. According to Metcalf and Huntington, the decline of monumental mortuary architecture among the Berawan was preceded by a final fluorescence:

> In the new formula of power, legitimization through the construction of mortuary edifices still had an important role to play. In fact, a certain vying for elegance is noticeable. The tombs grew more lofty, delicate and numerous. The Berawan themselves look back on the period from about 1900 to the arrival of the Japanese in 1941 as a golden age, a time of serenity and cultural fluorescence. They reminisce about the fabulous bridewealth paid by important men and the scale of ritual events. They compare it favorably with the tempestuous times before, when the disruption of headhunters made it hard to accumulate a surplus, and with the modern era. The apogee of tomb construction reached in the 1920s and 1930s bears out their recollections.[31]

The developments that Metcalf and Huntington note can probably be generalized to other central Bornean groups in the north as well. In some instances this apogee of mortuary construction involved the creation of both grave posts and mausoleums by groups that previously seem to have had only one or the other—some Kayan on the Balui erecting *klirieng* as well as their customary *salong*, and the Berawan and Punan Bah Kajang making *salong*-style mausoleums along with, or eventually instead of, *klirieng*. The decline and cessation of head-hunting and warfare brought by colonial rule

FIG. 1.26 (left). Kajang grave post *(klirieng)*, Tatau River, Sarawak, 1990.

FIG. 1.27 (above). Punan Bah (Kajang) *salong*, Tubau, upper Tatau River, Sarawak, 1990.

FIG. 1.28. Sarcophagus of Pastor A. J. Ding Ngo;
made of concrete as a modern Kenyah *salong,*
supported by two dragons, painted in polychrome;
at Padua, Mendalam River, West Kalimantan.

increased intermarriage among Kajang, Kayan, and Kenyah chiefly families and therefore increased contact and acculturative interaction among these groups. The Kayan chiefs of the Balui for whom *klirieng* were erected were of Kajang descent.[32] At the same time, the later adoption of *salong* for Punan Bah aristocrats seems to have been associated with the cessation of secondary mortuary practices after they were forbidden by the Brooke colonial government.[33]

The decline in the construction of *klirieng* and *salong* in northern Borneo has been linked to a more general abandonment of above-ground interment in favor of burial, favored by both Christians and Muslims. In some instances converts have adopted Western-style Christian

markers in cemeteries. In others, however, more distinctly local structures are erected over graves. Such structures often have roofs and resemble houses. They sometimes incorporate wooden carvings that reflect both indigenous and Christian motifs.

There has also been a shift away from the use of wood to concrete as a construction material. Among the Berawan concrete is used to create subterranean or semisubterranean vaults into which wooden coffins are placed. In addition, in the case of those Berawan who have still occasionally practiced secondary mortuary treatment in recent decades, older style raised mausoleums have been constructed by covering a wooden framework with concrete.[34] In other instances concrete has been used to create raised mortuary structures that, while not exactly replicating those traditionally built and carved from wood, are highly distinctive in synthesizing Christian and indigenous designs. This can be seen, for example, in the raised mausoleum created for the remains of Pastor A. J. Ding Ngo that combines dragons and the cross, all constructed of molded concrete.

In the far south of Borneo recent developments among some groups appear to be an exception to the general decline of mortuary architecture in Borneo. Here distinctive mortuary structures continue to be created by some of the various Ngaju, Ot Danum, and Ma'anyan peoples.[35] The practices of these groups differ in ritual and architectural terms from those of the northern groups in several respects. One difference is that final processing of the skeletal remains in some areas often involves cremation, rather than simply cleaning, before they are placed in a final repository. Another difference is that while in the north the secondary mortuary ceremonies are held individually, those in the far south are usually carried out collectively by villages or kin groups, although often initiated by a particular influential family. In addition, the cleaned and ritually treated skeletal remains are placed together in raised wooden

FIG. 1.29. Ot Danum *sandung*, Ketinjau River, south Borneo, 1894.

ossuaries rather than in separate jars. These ossuaries, or *sandung*, are built of ironwood, although in recent decades some have been made of concrete as well. Some *sandung* are elaborately decorated, long-lasting structures that resemble miniature houses but are constructed on a smaller scale than the posts and mausoleums of the north. They are placed in prominent locations in the village—often, as is also done in the north, along the riverbank.[36]

Among the Ngaju the construction of *sandung* has been retained or revived among those who continue to practice secondary mortuary rituals. Not all Ngaju continue to do so. Many have converted to Christianity or Islam, both of which are associated with permanent initial burial. Those who adhere to secondary mortuary practices are adherents of Kaharingan, the version of traditional Ngaju religious practices that is now officially recognized by the Indonesian government as a form of Hinduism, one of the approved "monotheistic" religions of modern Indonesia.

For the adherents of Kaharingan the construction of elaborate *sandung* is not merely a perpetuation of traditional village practices, but also a matter of official doctrine and prestige. Those recently described by Anne Schiller on the Katingan River were required by Kaharingan authorities to be constructed of wood rather than concrete and in a style that derived from another river.[37] And while the erection of grand *sandung*, like the mauso-

FIG. 1.30. Bidayuh altar for rice festival, Bau area, Sarawak, 1989.

leums and grave posts of the north, has always been an expression of the status and influence of those who build them, as well as those for whom they are built, the *sandung* are intended by sponsors and the Kaharingan Council (the official organization of the religion) to be a reflection of the importance and vigor of the movement.

Temporary Ritual Structures

In Borneo as elsewhere in Southeast Asia, temporary ritual structures are also an important architectural form. The notion of temporary is, of course, relative. Most built forms in Borneo, as noted above, have a relatively short life, in part at least because of the effects of the hot, wet equatorial climate on organic matter. There is, however, certainly a range of variation, from forms that are built to last for a few days or less to those that are intended to hold up for a season or two to those that are meant to endure and that may do so for many decades or longer. Ritual structures occur at both ends of this spectrum—that is, they are in some instances the most enduring of built forms and, in others, the most temporary. Mortuary structures, as we have seen, appear to be the longest lasting of all creations made of wood—not to mention the much more rarely occurring ones of stone. At the other extreme are the various altars, shrines, poles, and other ritual paraphernalia that are created for a single ceremony lasting from a few hours to a few days. Not surprisingly, much of the temporary ritual architecture is made quickly and from the least enduring organic materials—that is, bamboo and palm leaf thatch. Such

FIG. 1.31. *Kelaman* statues depicting warrior figures with swords and shields, made for a *save'* ceremony; Sekapan Pi'it village, upper Rajang, central Sarawak, 1991.

materials are usually green at the time they are cut, which seems appropriate for ceremonies that celebrate life, fertility, and renewal.

Not all structures created for a single ceremony are, however, quickly made or from the least permanent of materials. In addition to the bamboo and palm leaf altars, there are also elaborately carved wooden effigies that are also created for single ceremonies and then either taken down or left to stand until they eventually decay and fall down. These elaborately carved (and sometimes also painted) ceremonial structures include the famous *kenyalang* (hornbill) effigies made by the Iban for their *gawai burung* (*burung*: bird, in reference to Lang, the god of war) festivals and the carved *save'* statues sculpted by the Kejaman (Kajang) peoples, also for head-hunting ceremonies. Unlike the grave posts and mausoleums, which are made from ironwood, ceremonial effigies, poles, and statues are usually made from softer, more easily carved woods, but they nonetheless require much more time and effort to create than the bamboo and palm leaf structures. Nor do they disintegrate as rapidly. For this reason the notion of "temporary" architecture should be taken to refer to use rather than physical endurance.

The creation of bamboo and palm leaf ritual structures appears to be very widespread if not ubiquitous. The creation of temporary carved wooden statues, effigies, and poles is more limited but also common. In Sarawak, the Bidayuh make elaborate bamboo and leaf altars and shrines, along with temporary sheds and shelters to house them, and they less often carve temporary ceremonial wooden forms. The Iban create a greater variety of carved wooden forms for limited use, including the fantastic hornbill effigies, which have increased in size and elaborateness over the course of this century.[38] The Kenyah, Kayan, Kajang, and other settled central Bornean groups also create elaborately carved wooden forms, above all for head-hunting ceremonies, as well as the bamboo and leaf varieties.

CHAPTER TWO   THE LONGHOUSE

IN HIS JOURNAL ENTRY of September 1, 1839, James Brooke described a Sea Dayak (Iban) longhouse at a place he called Tunggang on the Lundu River, about two days' travel by boat to the west of Kuching. Brooke had been taken to visit the village after asking his Malay hosts in Kuching to see some of the Dayak towns in the area. The inhabitants were said to be "Sibnowan" Dayaks—that is, Sebuyau Iban who had migrated to the Kuching and Lundu areas from the Sebuyau River (a tributary of the lower Batang Lupar to the northeast of Kuching, in what later became the Second [now Sri Aman] Division of Sarawak) and who became the first allies of Brooke in his subsequent efforts to subdue the Iban of the Saribas and Skrang Rivers. Both the village and the Sebuyau Iban community are still there, although the dwelling and its later incarnations are now long gone, as are all of the longhouses in other Sebuyau communities in far western

Sarawak. While Brooke does not seem to have gotten the name of the place quite right either—it was really Stung-gang—his description is vivid and very interesting in several respects:

> Tunggang stands on the left-hand (going up) close to the margin of the stream and is enclosed by a slight stockade. Within this defense there was *one* enormous house for the whole population. The exterior of the defense between it and the river was occupied by sheds for prahus [boats], and at each extremity were one or two houses belonging to Malay residents.
>
> The common habitation, as rude as it is enormous, measures 539 feet in length, and the front room or *street* [the covered gallery or *ruai*] is the entire length of the building, and 21 feet broad. The back part is divided by mat partitions into the private apartments of various families, and of these there are forty-five separate doors leading from the public apartment [gallery]. The widowers and young unmarried men occupy the public rooms, as only those with wives are entitled to the advantage of a separate room. The floor of the edifice is raised twelve feet from the ground, and the means of ascent is by the trunk of a tree—a most difficult, steep and awkward ladder. In front is a terrace fifty feet broad, running partially along the front of the building, formed, like the floors, of split bamboo. The platform, as well as the front room, besides the regular inhabitants, is the resort of dogs, birds, monkeys and fowls, and presents a glorious scene of confusion and bustle. Here the ordinary occupations of domestic labor are carried out. There were 200 men, women and children counted in the room, and in front, whilst we were there in the middle of the day; and allowing for those who were abroad, or then in their own rooms, the whole community cannot be reckoned at less than 400 hundred souls. The apartment of their chief by name of Sejugah, is situated nearly in the center and is larger than any other. In front of it nice mats were spread out on the occasion of our visit, whilst over our heads dangled about thirty ghastly skulls, according to the custom of these people.[1]

From later evidence, much of Brooke's description appears to be accurate. His assertions about the length of the longhouse, the width of the covered gallery, and the open front platform were probably based on pacing the distance, while the observation that the building was raised twelve feet above the ground was probably an estimate based on the height of two tall men. It would have been easy for him to have counted the separate family apartment sections, even if he was not told the number, once he knew that each had a single door opening onto the gallery. He may have overstated the number of inhabitants at four hundred souls, however, for this would mean that each of the forty-five apartments was occupied by an average of between nine and ten persons. His assumption was that since by someone's count there were two hundred men, women, and children in the gallery during his visit, there were probably another two hundred either away from the longhouse or inside of their apartments, but the assumption seems unwarranted. It seems more likely that just about everyone who lived in the longhouse was probably there and out in the gallery looking at Brooke, especially if his party had been expected, for white men were rare on the northwestern coast of Borneo at that time.

Although there is considerable variation, longhouses of the sort described by Brooke have long been a common form of dwelling in the interior of Borneo. For the people who live in them, the longhouse is at the core of their traditional culture and way of life. At present, for example, in those Bidayuh villages in which some families live in longhouses and others in single-family dwellings, the longhouse people are regarded as the keepers of tradition and *adat* (customary law and ceremonies). In most areas the more important traditional celebrations

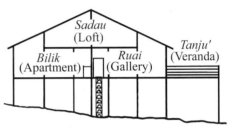

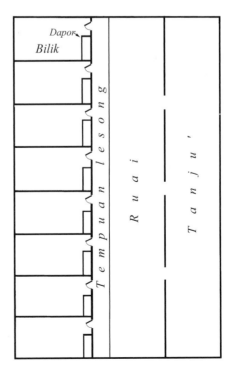

FIG. 2.1 (above). Late nineteenth-century engraving of an Iban
longhouse gallery and exterior veranda. Though with far fewer
people present, these are as James Brooke described them in
his account of the Sebuyau longhouse at Lundu. However,
the carved wooden doors leading to the inner family apartments are shown as being much larger than they should be,
and the rice mortar in use by the two women in the foreground
was probably in actuality located next to the inner wall.

FIG. 2.2 (right). Section and plan of an Iban longhouse.
The *tempuan lesong* is the walkway and area where rice
mortars are stored and used.

and rituals are held in longhouses rather than in separate buildings. One of the important consequences of the now widespread conversion throughout much of the interior of Borneo has been the shift, among Christians, of much ritual and ceremony to an external building, a church, having no particular association with the longhouse. Indeed, conversion has sometimes been noted to be a reason for the breakup of longhouses. At least in Sarawak, the association of the longhouse with traditional culture and ritual activity can hardly be overstated. And yet, as we shall see below, longhouses here have also often changed a great deal.

Longhouses are referred to in a limited number of ways.[2] The Malay/Indonesian phrase "*rumah panjang*," for which "long house" is a literal translation, is reflected in several local terms, including "*ruma' kabang*" (Kelabit and Lundayeh) and "*rumah panyai*" (Mualang). In Sarawak several of the other indigenous terms for longhouse do not take this form but rather imply it. Among some of the various Bidayuh groups and the Iban the terms "*botang*," "*batang*," "*betang*," etc., or trunk, are frequently used, although among the Iban this may also be partly a matter of association of longhouses with rivers, which (in the case of the main stream) are also referred to as "*batang*." Often, however, the longhouse is referred to by one or the other of two general terms. One of these is the widely occurring Austronesian "*rumah*" and its various reflexives (*roman, ruma', umah, uma'*, etc.); the other term is "*levu*" or "*lebu*," as used by the Lahanan and other Kajang and related groups, including the Melanau. Used alone, both such terms usually mean simply "house."

THE LONGHOUSE AS A PHYSICAL STRUCTURE

While the term "longhouse" has been frequently used for multifamily dwellings elsewhere in the world with varying degrees of appropriateness, the term is entirely apt in Borneo. Here longhouses really are long in the sense that the entire structure takes the form of a rectangle that is much longer than it is wide. In some instances, longhouses are very long indeed. In the late 1940s the Uma Pliau Kayan longhouse at Long Laput on the middle Baram River comprised ninety-eight apartments, and the Lepo' Tau Kenyah house at Long Moh on the upper Baram included eighty-nine.[3] According to C. H. Southwell, Long Laput was more than 2,200 feet (about 700 meters) in length, while Tom Harrisson reported that the Kayan longhouse at Long Poh on the upper Kayan River in 1945 was more than half a mile long. Most Bornean longhouses did not and do not reach such lengths. Southwell notes that Kenyah and Kayan longhouses, which along with those of the Kajang peoples are the longest in Sarawak, usually range from 400 to 600 feet in length.[4] Such longhouses must still be among the longest single dwellings ever built by tribal peoples.

The size of a longhouse is usually expressed in terms of its number of household apartments—or doors in official colonial discourse, a door representing each such section. In Sarawak at least, the Bidayuh seem to have built the smallest longhouses in both respects. Some Bidayuh longhouses in the mountain villages consisted of only a few apartments, each only a few meters wide and deep, and with a narrow gallery. Traditional Iban longhouses are typically larger than this, again in terms of both the number of apartment sections and the size of each of these. According to Derek Freeman's information on the Baleh River area circa 1950 (when, it can be assumed, longhouses there were still built in a traditional form), the number of *bilik* (or apartment sections) varied from four to fifty, with the average being fourteen and most longhouses having between ten and twenty.[5] A very large longhouse of fifty apartments might be 800 feet (or 250 meters) in overall length. This is based on an average width of 16 feet for each apartment, which is somewhat greater than that of the apartments in a traditional Bidayuh longhouse. The longhouses of the Kenyah, Kayan, Kajang, and other central Bornean peoples are generally larger than those of the Iban, at least in terms of the dimensions of the sections and sometimes also in terms of the number of sections.

Given relatively level terrain and available materials and the combination of raised post and timber-frame construction, it would be possible to extend a longhouse indefinitely. While the main part is traditionally built at one time, further sections can be added to either end if the terrain allows it. Families living in the longhouse may therefore divide and build new apartments, and families from elsewhere who have relatives living there are usually permitted to join it by adding on to the existing building if there is room. In this sense the longhouse appears to resemble a simple segmentary structure—a coral reef, for example—that can multiply by creating additional more or less identical units.

But while observers have described some longhouses in such terms, it would be an oversimplification in all cases and very wrong in some. Most longhouses vary in size within a limited range, for the addition of new apartments is subject to various social and cultural restraints as well as physical ones. In more hierarchical Bornean societies the physical structure of the longhouse is based on the social structure, with aristocrats, commoners, and, in the past, slaves occupying distinct areas and in some instances having apartments with marked physical differences. In such cases the creation of an additional apartment on either end is an expression of social position. Among the more egalitarian groups the segmental replication of longhouse sections is less problematic but not entirely free of social constraints.

Very small longhouses—or at least very small villages—are not generally favored. In the past warfare and head-hunting encouraged larger longhouses or villages as a matter of protection, and at present governments encourage concentrated villages for various administrative reasons. At the same time, the concentration of peo-ple in larger longhouses or villages means that they must travel farther to farm, as the lands nearby are used up and must lie fallow before being recultivated. This problem is commonly dealt with by building secondary houses, including single dwellings and a few small longhouses nearer to the currently used farmlands.

Longhouse Size and Village Size

The size of a longhouse in terms of the number of family apartments may be related to the size of a village but is not the same thing. Longhouses are sometimes said to be "an entire village under one roof." Some of the villages to be seen in Sarawak today are of this type, as are many of those shown in the older literature in other areas of Borneo. In many places, however, longhouses large enough to contain an entire village cannot be built. Among the Bidayuh, the village and the longhouse are seldom if ever the same. In the case of the Kayan, Kenyah, Kajang, and other groups, single longhouse communities were and are often favored, but actual practices vary with local habits, the possibilities of the terrain, and the size of the villages. In particular, the tendency to live in large villages (which are also common among these groups in Sarawak) often takes precedence over a preference for having the entire village under one roof.

In northwestern Borneo, at least, only among the Iban is the village equivalent to the longhouse. Although there are many exceptions today, most Iban villages take the form of a single longhouse—or, to put it another way, in most cases each longhouse is a separate village with a separate name and identity, even if several such longhouses are located in close proximity. In this case, therefore, the inclination for a village community to be a group of families who live together in one longhouse has generally taken precedence over size. While the Iban also value size in a longhouse, Iban villages are typically much smaller than those of either the Bidayuh or the various Kenyah, Kayan, and Kajang groups.[6] This may be

FIG. 2.3 (top left). Iban longhouse in high water, lower Rajang, 1986.

FIG. 2.4 (top right). Mualang longhouse, Terduk Dampak, Mulau River, middle Kapuas area, West Kalimantan.

FIG. 2.5 (bottom). Rumah Julau, an Iban single-longhouse village, 1987.

partly a matter of factors other than the limits placed on the physical size of longhouses by the terrain of the country in which many Iban live, but it is also a matter of Iban customary practices. Among the groups of central and northwestern Borneo, the Iban are most inclined to have small, independent longhouses. Their willingness to establish pioneering longhouses in new areas, in some cases displacing other groups, is part of the reason for the remarkable expansion of the Iban throughout much of present-day Sarawak and beyond. It was for this reason that the Brooke regime adopted the policy of forbidding longhouses of fewer than ten doors.[7]

The Life of Longhouses

Longhouses often have a short life. To some extent this is a reflection of the natural processes that affect all indigenous wooden structures in Borneo (mentioned above). In addition, longhouses in some areas are liable to be destroyed by floods and everywhere by fires. In the case of those built along rivers, while raising longhouses on piles provides protection against high water, they can be destroyed and swept away in floods by water that rises too high and moves too fast. The problem of fire was not only present in the past, but is also common in the present; longhouse fires in Sarawak continue to be frequently reported in the newspapers. Some villages tell of having longhouses burn several times. Beyond physical deterioration and natural disaster, longhouses are sometimes rebuilt in a different location because of illness in the village, crop failures (or in the past, a death from a headhunting raid), or other misfortunes that are viewed as evidence of spiritual decline.[8]

Some groups appear to rebuild longhouses more frequently than do others in relation to their migration behavior. It has therefore sometimes been assumed that building practices vary with migration habits—that more sedentary groups build massive longhouses that are intended to last a long time while more mobile groups build

FIG. 2.6 (top). Part of the Kenyah Badang village at Long Busang, composed of a series of smaller longhouses; upper Balui River, Belaga, central Sarawak, 1976.

FIG. 2.7 (bottom). Kenyah longhouse at Long Busang, upper Balui River, 1986.

FIG. 2.8 (left). Gallery of Nanga Kerapa longhouse, showing a lighter framework of smaller and more numerous supporting posts and beams that is common to traditional Iban and Bidayuh building practices—in contrast to the more massive ones of the Kajang, Kenyah, Kayan, and Taman, for example.

FIG. 2.9 (facing top). Kenyah longhouse gallery, upper Baram River, 1951. Note the massive columns, cantilevered crossbeams that support the longitudinal roof beam, wide plank flooring, and length of the gallery.

FIG. 2.10 (facing bottom). Solidly built Taman longhouse at Melapi, upper Kapuas River, West Kalimantan, 1994. Note the crossbracing used to strengthen the pile foundation.

flimsier ones because they do not intend to remain in them for very long.[9] "An Iban community," according to Charles Hose and William McDougall, "seldom remains in the same house for more than three or four years; it is, no doubt, partly on this account that their houses are built in a less solid style than those of most other tribes."[10]

Some groups do employ more massive forms of longhouse construction than do others. Massive building practices include the use of larger logs for posts and beams and the use of wide, thick boards for flooring and planks rather than bark or split bamboo for walls. Massive building also involves more reliance on mortise and tenon and slot joinery and less on lashing in fastening structural parts together. Lighter construction, on the

other hand, involves greater use of poles or smaller diameter logs, bamboo and bark rather than planks for walls and floors, and a combination of lashing and mortise and tenon joinery. In Sarawak and adjacent areas of East and West Kalimantan, the various Bidayuh and Ibanic peoples in general traditionally used a lighter form of construction, while the Melanau, Kenyah, Kayan, some of the various Kajang groups, and the Taman and Maloh favored a more massive one.

The relationship between building practices and mobility appears to be well illustrated in some cases but not others. It is apparent in northern Borneo in the contrast between the Maloh, on the one hand, and the Iban and other Ibanic groups, on the other.[11] Previously the Iban often moved into new areas, including the middle Ra-

jang, in search of old-growth forest. Colonial and then postcolonial governments sought to curtail longer migrations, as well as the more localized shift of villages, both by increasing protection and security and mediating disputes among groups and by preventing or inhibiting migration into regions that were deemed inappropriate for settlement. With pacification and the establishment of European rule over various areas, the extent of such movement and displacement slowed but did not cease—indeed it is still occurring. Consistent with their migration practices, the Iban, in the past at least, built smaller and lighter longhouses than did some groups. The pattern among the Taman and Maloh in West Kalimantan is the opposite. At least after the beginning of colonial rule these groups lived in fairly perma-

FIG. 2.11. *Tanju'* or outer veranda of an Iban longhouse on the Mujong River, Kapit, central Sarawak, 1986.

nent villages and often built very large and massively constructed longhouses.[12]

The building practices of other groups, however, do not seem to follow such logic. On the one hand, the Bidayuh tend to live in fairly permanent villages but usually build small, lightly constructed longhouses that are similar to those of the Iban. On the other hand, the various Kenyah and Kayan groups build large, massive longhouses while (formerly at least) moving frequently.[13] Further, massive building practices have often been explained in terms of defense—including the common use of supporting posts that were much thicker than necessary to simply carry the weight of the building but, instead, were intended to be more difficult and time-consuming to cut through in an attack. Social hierarchy, to be considered below, may also help to account for differences in building practices.

Platforms and the Gallery

However large, massively built, and long-lasting they are, and leaving aside for the time being the matter of modern innovations, most longhouses have a number of common physical characteristics. To begin with, longhouses generally have open verandas or external platforms, but their location varies between the front and back of the building among different groups. In Iban and Bidayuh longhouses these are at the front and are an important part of the public space of the longhouse. In the case of the Iban longhouse, while the veranda (*tanju'*) is often fairly flimsy and is often used mainly as a drying platform (for rice, pepper, clothing, etc.), it may also serve as a walkway, and in any case it has important ceremonial uses. Among the Bidayuh, the external front platform is usually wider and more solidly built than the Iban *tanju'*. It is usually also much wider than the adjacent covered gallery and often forms a place where people work,

FIG. 2.12. Iban elders preparing an offering on the *tanju'* for *gawai*, 1986.

visit (especially when it is in the shade), and hold rituals. It is also, in contrast to the practice of most groups, the main roadway or street of the longhouse. In those Bidayuh villages where there are several adjacent longhouses, the front platforms are often continuous or connected by raised walkways.

In contrast to the longhouses of the Iban and Bidayuh, those of the Kenyah, Kayan, Kajang, and many other groups in northern Borneo and elsewhere usually lack such front platforms. In these instances there are usually platforms at the rear. Such rear platforms are used for work and drying but do not form a continuous walkway along the apartments and are not used for ritual activities.

The interior or roofed-over part of a longhouse is divided between what is commonly referred to in the literature as the gallery and the inner apartments of each family group. The gallery is open the entire length of the longhouse. It is separated from the inner apartments by a continuous wall (called the "dog wall" in Iban because it keeps dogs, which are usually allowed in the gallery, out of the inner apartments). In some longhouses this wall is built onto the central row of columns that support the ridge beam of the roof. However, in many other instances, such as that of the Bidayuh longhouse, the wall is placed in front of the roof beam and built onto a secondary set of supporting posts. In such instances the gallery is narrower in depth than the private quarters behind it.

In most longhouses the private apartments are located on only one side of the gallery, but occasionally they are built on both sides. One of the few existing Melanau longhouses that remained in the 1960s took this double form.[14] Except in such instances the gallery forms the front area, the other or outer side of which may be open or partially or entirely closed. In Iban and some

Bidayuh longhouses there is a wall that extends from the floor to the roof and has a series of doorways for entering that open out onto the exterior veranda or platform. In Kenyah, Kayan, Kajang, and many other central Bornean longhouses there is usually a parapet made of only a few horizontally placed planks, rather than a full wall. Such an arrangement allows the occupants to sit on the floor or the low benches or platforms along the front of the gallery to see out over the river. Formerly the open upper area above the parapet was sometimes covered by open lattice work (which can still be seen on some Taman longhouses on the upper Kapuas River in West Kalimantan), which provided protection in case of an attack but still provided an open view of the river below. In many of the longhouses built today by the Bidayuh, this wall has been eliminated altogether. This can be done if either the longhouse has an external front veranda on the same level as the covered gallery or (as in many modern longhouses) the floor of the longhouse is built directly on the ground.

Although the gallery of a modern longhouse often takes the form of an undifferentiated open space, that of a traditional building is less likely to do so. In the case of Iban and some Bidayuh longhouses, different parts of the gallery are associated with variations in the levels in the floor and by different construction materials. The area immediately in front of the continuous, lengthwise main wall forms a walkway from one end of the longhouse to the other. If, as is often the case, the longhouse has entrances at its ends, they will usually open onto this walkway. This is the street part of the longhouse, where anyone is free to walk, although it may also be used for storage and often for pounding rice in mortars. In traditional Iban and Bidayuh longhouses this walkway usually has a floor of bamboo slats or sections of palm trunk, while in Kayan, Kajang, and Kenyah longhouses the entire floor is covered with wide planks. In either case, the gallery also includes a wide section closer to the front that is used for work, socializing with neighbors, entertaining guests, and holding rituals and where mats are spread out for sitting and feasting. In Bidayuh and Iban longhouses the floor here is sometimes slightly raised and made of wider boards. In the past this area was also separated from the walkway by a row of hearths and, in some instances, a row of posts.

The frontmost area of the gallery—that is the one adjacent to the outer wall or parapet and beneath the eaves of the roof—often takes the form of a raised platform, occasionally divided by walls into alcoves (one for each apartment) used for lounging in the daytime and for sleeping at night. The unmarried older boys and younger men of the longhouse, as well as male visitors, traditionally sleep in this section (unless, as in the case of the Bidayuh, they slept in the men's house). In the longhouses of the Kayan, Kenyah, and Kajang groups, in which the outer or front wall extends only part of the way to the roof and is generally made of a few boards with open spaces between, this space often provides a view of the river and the outside area in front of the building. In more modern longhouses the platform has usually been replaced with a narrow bench that is used for sitting, with the front wall often remaining at least partially open to the outside.

The gallery is the more public area of a longhouse, although each section of it has been built and is owned by each family who occupies the private quarters on the other side of the wall. Each family, therefore, stores things, works, or entertains guests in its own part of the gallery. Public gatherings, while usually centered in front of the headman's or chief's apartment, may overflow into adjacent sections. Here in the past (and occasionally still) the collection of skulls owned by the longhouse was hung on display on a rack or a beam, again usually in front of the apartment of the chief or founder. Among some groups the gallery is also the locus of extensive artistic elaboration—that is, of carving and painting.

The gallery is a place of ceremony and ceremonial

display, as well as socializing. Rituals may also be held in other parts of the longhouse among some groups (the open or exterior front veranda among the Iban or, especially, the Bidayuh), in other permanent buildings (the men's house among the Bidayuh) or ones constructed especially for the purpose, or in the private quarters of apartments. But these rituals are usually either fairly specific or parts of larger ceremonials that are located mainly in the gallery. In the case of funerals it is usually here that the body is laid out during mourning. Among the groups who practice secondary burial or who otherwise keep the body of a deceased person in the longhouse for a few days or several weeks or longer, the coffin is kept on display in the gallery before it is conveyed to the cemetery. In terms of historical change, Stephen Morris reports that as the Melanau abandoned their longhouses, much of the traditional ceremonial life that had been concentrated in the longhouse gallery consequently also disappeared.[15] On the other hand, groups that have given up longhouses but wish to continue with ritual festivities that were formerly held in the gallery or there and on the external veranda have the problem of where to hold them. Among the Bidayuh at least this problem has sometimes been solved by building special temporary longhouses for the occasion or building a temporary longhouse-like veranda and gallery onto the front of someone's single house. In one example from present-day Kuching, a wealthy urban Kayan, who had converted to Islam but wished to maintain social and public ceremonial ties with fellow non-Muslim Kayans and other friends, built a special, semidetached, long, rectangular room at his house that resembled a longhouse gallery. In doing this, he was able to maintain his ethnic ties while at the same time keeping his non-Muslim friends, relatives, and acquaintances ritually separate from his fellow Muslims.

Apartments and Lofts

The inner apartment is the more private part of each family section. This is where all or most of the cooking is done and where the family normally eats. It is also the sleeping place for the married couple and their children, with the main exception of older but unmarried sons, who spend the night either in the gallery or, among the Bidayuh in the past, in the men's house.

The inner apartment is entered through a door from the gallery. Although today there are often glazed windows as well, these doors were traditionally the only openings in the inner gallery wall. They are normally kept closed, often with a weight attached to a cord. In the past, the door opening was smaller—usually a meter and half or less in height and a half meter in width—and placed above the floor. Such doorways made the apartment more difficult to penetrate in an attack. The doors themselves were formerly made of thick slabs of hardwood, usually ironwood or in some cases the buttress root of *tapang*, which, because of its dense, interlocking grain, is also very strong and could be barred from the inside. At present, even the most otherwise traditional or older longhouses have larger, standard doors mounted with metal hinges. In any case, each door represents a family-household unit. Today, among the Bidayuh at least, some families in one apartment section have taken over the next one and dismantled all or part of the wall separating the two, but in this case only one door is used.

The interior apartments of the longhouses of most groups have common features that are usually arranged in a similar manner and associated with specific activities. These include the hearth (*dapor* in Iban, *dapur* in Malay and Bidayuh), where the routine daily cooking is done (festive cooking usually requires more room and is often done out of doors) and near where ordinary meals are eaten. Among most groups in northern Borneo the hearth is located just inside the main entrance door from the gallery. It consists of a wooden frame filled with a

FIG. 2.13. Living and sleeping area inside a Bidayuh longhouse apartment, with part of kitchen at the right; Anah Rais, Padawan, western Sarawak, 1996.

thick layer of soil and is usually built directly on the floor. Although there is no chimney, the smoke rises and finds its way out through the roof (which, it is said, helps preserve it from destruction by insects). Firewood is stored immediately above the hearth on a shelf or rack, and cooking utensils and foodstuffs are kept on shelves along the sides. At present, in most longhouses the hearth and kitchen area have been moved from the inner apartment to a separate attached or semi-attached building behind it, although in some Bidayuh villages these have been kept in their original locations.

In nearly all longhouses each family apartment is separated from those on either side by a wall. This wall may extend only part way to the ceiling and does not necessarily afford great privacy. People in one apartment may look through holes or cracks to observe what is going on in the next without being considered rude, and questions and answers or banter may be exchanged back and forth through the wall. In many longhouses there are doors in these walls that may be kept open some of the time. This is commonly the case in Bidayuh and Iban longhouses, at least as long as the adjacent families are closely related or on good terms, for a falling out can lead to the closing up of a doorway. In the Taman longhouses on the upper Kapuas in West Kalimantan these doorways are large and placed at the same point in the wall, so that when they are all open they create a striking corridor throughout the entire line of apartments along which continuous ritual feasts are held.

A longhouse apartment is always constructed in such a way that all or part of the area between the two sloping sides of the roof is turned into a loft, the floor of which is supported by the main upper crossbeams. The loft may extend only over the private quarters of the apartment, in which case the main longitudinal wall extends upward to the roof, with the area above the gallery left open. In other instances the loft is extended part way over the gallery, in which case it is also closed off with a vertical wall. This is the case in Iban longhouses, in which the front wall of the loft is supported by secondary posts that divide the walkway part of the gallery from the outer front area. In Bidayuh longhouses the floor of the loft extends entirely across the gallery so that this has an enclosed, often low, ceiling. In all instances the loft is reached by a notched log ladder that leads up through an opening in the ceiling in the inner part of the apartment; this ladder is either left in place or set up when needed.

The most common use of the loft is for storage. Unlike many other groups, the Iban store rice in the loft, traditionally in large round bins made from the smooth bark of various trees but today commonly in gunny sacks. (This means that if an Iban longhouse burns, the main food supply for whatever part of the year remains before the next harvest, along with the vital seed rice, is destroyed.) The Iban also sometimes use the loft for living space in ways to be noted below.

Other Forms of Longhouses

The traditional longhouses described so far—consisting of a single story, divided into family sections arranged in a single line and divided by lateral walls and opening onto a common gallery—are by far the most general type, but there are or were departures from this pattern. One involves the Modang and Long Gelat of East Kali-

mantan, who build a sort of two-story longhouse by placing the main gallery beneath the private apartments, which are reached by a ladder. Another involves the Murut of Sabah, whose longhouses have rows of private apartments on both sides of a narrow hallway and a large open area at the center. In yet another variation, the Ngaju longhouses had the private apartments at the front and the open gallery in the back, as well as an open lateral gallery in the middle. Finally, the longhouses of the Kelabit of the borderlands of highland northern Sarawak and East Kalimantan and a few other groups lacked the interior walls that divide one apartment and the next. In some instances these departures from the more general pattern have disappeared as the groups involved have either switched to more standard designs or have abandoned longhouses altogether.[16]

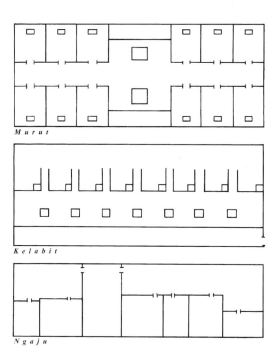

FIG. 2.14. Plans of Murut, Kelabit, and Ngaju longhouses.

LONGHOUSE SOCIAL ORGANIZATION

Space and Gender

Most societies in Borneo provide for some separation of the sleeping arrangements for unmarried men and women. The concerns reflected in these arrangements do not involve sleep per se, for people do not regard sleeping in itself as something that should be done in private, but rather sexual intercourse, which should—although privacy in traditionally built longhouses is limited. The most common traditional arrangement is for married couples and small children to spend the night inside of the apartment and for older boys, bachelors, and visiting men to sleep in the outer or front part of the gallery. The men's houses built by the Bidayuh and some other groups are a logical extension of such an arrangement, in terms of which the separation of unmarried youth and men is carried further. There are, on the other hand, no separate women's houses, although in some instances sexually mature unmarried girls had a separate room in the inner apartment or, among the Iban, some-

times slept in the loft. While the separate sleeping arrangements of unmarried men and women express traditional indigenous Bornean notions of propriety, they were not in the past intended to prevent sexual encounters, for these were accepted as a normal and necessary part of courtship, but, if anything, to facilitate them. They enabled bachelors to come and go as they pleased and for sexually mature women to receive them in their beds if they wished.

Beyond such sleeping arrangements, the organization or use of longhouse space has some relation to gender. The main distinction that has sometimes been stressed regarding male and female areas of activity is that between the gallery, on the one hand, and the inner apartment and loft, on the other. The former is public space and therefore more the realm of men. When guests arrive at an Iban longhouse, the men seat themselves in the outer area of the *ruai*, while the women make their way into the *bilik*. The *ruai* is the particular arena of political discussion, major rituals, feasting, and more casual male drinking and conversation, while the *bilik* is the private arena of intimate visiting, cooking, and female socializing. According to Vinson Sutlive, "The male's place is on the *ruai*, and the man who spends too much time in the *bilik* is liable to be called 'female male' (*laki indu*). The eastward orientation of the house toward the sun reinforces the maleness of the *ruai* which is entered after a climb upon a notched log which, with its decorated head, is recognized as a phallic symbol."[17] Clifford Sather agrees with this general distinction between gallery and apartment but goes on to describe the loft as having especially strong links with female creativity and fertility. Because it is traditionally sometimes the sleeping quarters of sexually mature but unmarried women, it is therefore the place of the sexual encounters that are or were a normal part of Iban courtship. It is or was also used by women for weaving, although this is now done mainly in either the private apartment or the

FIG. 2.15. Gallery of Long Lunuk, a Long Gelat longhouse, with ladders leading up to the apartments.

gallery: "The loft, in particular, is identified with the activities by which women distinguish themselves; namely, weaving and rice agriculture. Women set up their looms, spin thread, dye and weave cloth in the loft, and here the senior women of the family store the *bilik*'s seed rice, including its seeds of its sacred *padi pun*. In addition, the loft was traditionally the sleeping place of women of marriageable age. Here, at night, they received suitors and conducted amours."[18]

"Male" and "female" have important cosmological associations throughout Borneo, but these are not a matter of absolute behavioral practice in the longhouses of the Iban or other groups. No areas of the longhouse are off limits to either men or women, and most are used extensively by both. While women may spend more time in the inner apartment than men, and men more in the gallery than women, both make use of both of the areas. Nor is this a modern development. Earlier (that is, nineteenth-century) illustrations of Iban longhouses show women as well as men in the gallery. This is so, for example, in a sketch in William Hornaday's *Two Years in the Jungle*.[19] It is true that this drawing shows women mainly on their way somewhere or working and men mainly lounging around or conversing. It suggests that women, in contrast to men, use the gallery for specific purposes, especially work, rather than for casually passing the time. In any case, two of the women are shown pounding rice, which, whatever its female associations, is always done in the gallery or, more specifically, the open walkway between the gallery and the inner wall. Iban women also commonly weave cloth and plait baskets and mats in the gallery.

The Apartment Household

In all instances the elementary unit of longhouse society is the family household that occupies a particular apartment. In many or most longhouse-dwelling Bornean societies, terms for the apartment and the household that occupies it are the same. The varying size of the households of a longhouse is partly a matter of family types. At the minimum, households take the form of a married couple and their children. Except perhaps as a result of recent developments, neither single individuals nor married couples alone would have an apartment to themselves. Younger single individuals normally live with their parents and older ones with their children, and newly married couples without children usually live with the parents of the husband or wife. Many or most households therefore consist of extended families. Among the Iban the stem family—one including parents, a married child with his or her own children, and other unmarried children—is typical. Among other groups extended families more often involve several married sons or daughters with children. In some instances two or more married couples with children form separate economic households within a single longhouse apartment, but these are usually temporary arrangements, although they appear to be becoming more common today with the increasing size and complexity of modern longhouse apartments.

Except in the last arrangement, the apartment household is in some sense a corporate group with regard to economic matters, ritual activities, and the political organization of the longhouse. The extent of corporateness varies, however. At the time the Melanau still lived in longhouses, the household, or *sukud*, appears to have been only minimally corporate, according to Stephen Morris, in that it "held no joint property on behalf of all of its members; and though their welfare was in a sense a responsibility, its legal and political rights were the sum total of its members, in so far as they chose to exercise those rights for the benefit of all."[20] Even the physical apartment itself, which formed the most enduring element of the household group, was owned individually, usually by one person, as inherited property, unless it had been built during a marriage, in which case it was marital property.

The Iban apartment household from Derek Freeman's account appears to be the opposite extreme of corporateness. It is "an allodial unit, possessing both land and property in its own right. It is likewise an independent entity economically, cultivating its own *padi*, and a wide variety of other crops. Ritually, each *bikek-family* is a disparate unit with its own magical charms (*pengaroh*), its own particular set of ritual prohibitions or taboos (*pemali*) and its own special kind of sacred *padi* (*padi pun*)."[21] All property, except for personal items (clothing, weapons, and jewelry) is therefore owned jointly by the members of the household. This includes the apartment section of the longhouse itself, heirlooms (most important, gongs and other brassware, large jars and other imported ceramics, and woven ritual cloths), household furnishings, farming implements, and other productive equipment. It also includes land, the rights to which are originally established by clearing old-growth forest.

The other longhouse societies of central and northern Borneo fall somewhere between the Melanau and the Iban in terms of common household property. Among the Maloh and the Bidayuh, land and fruit trees are owned collectively by the cognatic descendants of those who originally cleared or planted them, rather than by a household. Further, at least in areas where farmland is or was abundant, rights are often not a traditional issue. Among the Kayan of the Balui River, farming land is not owned by either households or individuals but is instead allocated each year by agreement among the men of the village. Otherwise, however, the Kayan apartment household, or *amin*, is said to form a corporate group along the same lines as the Iban in that heirlooms and equipment stay with it—except for shares given to those who leave and establish their own families elsewhere.[22]

With the possible exception of those of the Melanau, all of the household apartment groupings of all of these societies are also corporate in terms of the ritual and political life of the longhouse. In the case of the former the apartment makes ritual offerings to common village wide or longhouse ceremonies, and the benefits of these are supposed to be distributed accordingly. In terms of the political organization of longhouses, households rather than individuals are represented at village meetings.

Social Integration, Kinship, and Adat

As we have seen, social anthropological studies tended to stress the primacy of the apartment family over the longhouse community and emphasize the limited and contingent nature of the latter. William Geddes, who went furthest in this respect, described the Bidayuh community he studied in terms of individualism verging on anarchy and went on to expound a view of the longhouse as being not really a *long house* but rather a "series of homes all joined together."[23] The weaknesses in longhouse organization that Geddes described may be in part the result of a long period of pacification and protection under colonial rule—a hundred years by the time of his fieldwork, circa 1950. It is likely that, as elsewhere in the precolonial period, the Bidayuh longhouse was more a device for survival in a dangerous world. It is also likely that the presence of men's houses diminished somewhat the ritual and sociopolitical significance of Bidayuh longhouses.

The longhouse of the Rungus of the Kudat Peninsula in northwest Sabah has also been described as a collection of separate but joined houses rather than an integrated or communal house. According to George Appell, Rungus longhouses come into existence through the "lateral accretion of individual domestic family apartments." No part of the longhouse is "jointly constructed or communally owned." Appell goes on to say that over time Rungus longhouses are constantly changing in membership. Families "join onto a longhouse for a few years, and then move on to others," the average length of occupancy being somewhat less than three years.[24] He

FIG. 2.16. Rungus longhouse, Kudat Peninsula, Sabah, 1960.

does say that the longhouses may have lost importance as a result of the establishment of Pax Britanica, prior to which they were more important as defensive structures.

The Iban case adds the further complication that apparent organizational weakness is not necessarily a liability. Derek Freeman stresses in his discussion of their social structure and history that the Iban have been an extraordinarily successful people who in the nineteenth and twentieth centuries have vigorously expanded into vast new areas, including ones occupied by other groups, as well as ones mainly devoid of other inhabitants. The

patterns of voluntary and reciprocal cooperation, household autonomy, and limited authority that have been characterized as liabilities among the Bidayuh by Geddes are in Freeman's view among the main strengths of the Iban.[25] In addition, the integration of the Iban longhouse is enhanced in that it is, customarily at least, equivalent to the village.

The differences among them notwithstanding, the accounts of the Bidayuh, Rungus, and Iban raise the question of what holds their longhouses together at all, at least since head-hunting and warfare ended, and indeed many Bidayuh and apparently many Rungus families have abandoned longhouses for separate dwellings. Part of the attachment of individual households to the longhouse is based on cognatic kinship. Longhouses are not kin groups as such. Clans and lineages do not exist, descent and kin relationships are reckoned bilaterally, and the rights and obligations of the membership in the longhouse have little or nothing to do with ties of kinship. Many or most families in a longhouse, however, are related in one way or another, in many instances closely. Closely related families often live side by side and have connecting interior doors between their apartments. Among the Iban, households made up of families of brothers are supposed to occupy adjacent apartments.

In addition, longhouses throughout Borneo are by tradition governed by customary law, known as *adat* (the Malay-Indonesian term, which is derived from Arabic), *adet,* or some other local version of this word. Although modified by colonial and postcolonial governments, *adat* continues to operate throughout the interior of Borneo. Under Brooke rule, later colonial rule, and then postcolonial rule in Sarawak, *adat* has been recognized and codified for the various ethnic groups as identified by the government. *Adat* concerns many areas of life and makes the longhouse a moral and jural community. It is intended, among other things, to keep behavior within acceptable bounds, to compensate those who have been wronged by others, and to protect the spiritual state of the longhouse. Compensation and fines are customarily reckoned in terms of ceramic jars, gongs or other brassware, and other valued goods.

Along with offenses against other persons, matrimonial matters, property issues, and ritual restrictions, *adat* includes provisions or rules concerning the obligations of members toward other members of the longhouse community. In the case of the Bidayuh, such provisions are listed in a recent government compendium (*Adat Bidayuh 1994)*, together with fines and restitutions to be paid for the breach of each rule. The provisions define as offenses various actions that threaten the unity of the longhouse. These include breaking a promise to join a longhouse, failing to erect the posts of a section of a longhouse after work has begun or pulling down the posts, disturbing the building site of a longhouse or disturbing an offering that has been made at the site, failing to construct the roof of an apartment section of a longhouse, and constructing a shed at the end of a longhouse that causes an obstruction. Other proscriptions aimed at protecting the integrity of the longhouse include moving out of an apartment section and removing the roof ridge and dismantling a section of a longhouse without the permission of both the neighboring apartment households and the *piayuh* (headman)—and if this is done while the neighbors are observing a ritual restriction, it is an additional offense.

Social Distinctions

As noted above, the longhouse societies of Borneo have often been divided into egalitarian and hierarchical types.[26] The latter are structured in terms of hereditary distinctions in social rank—and in related distinctions in social and economic status and political organization.[27] The nonhierarchical or more egalitarian societies, on the other hand, are those that (while having rich and poor) are without formal hereditary distinctions in social rank and most of the other political and cultural differences that go along with them. The simple dichotomy between hierarchical and egalitarian groups made by earlier observers has by now been widely disputed or questioned. This is so regarding both the importance of hierarchy among most of the groups mentioned and the assertion of its presence among supposedly egalitarian ones or of the existence of mixed or intermediate types.[28] The latter include groups that may have been more hierarchically oriented in the past or ones that have become more so as a result of cultural borrowing. Such criticisms suggest that, in contrast to the thoroughly egalitarian nomadic hunter-gatherers, the swidden-cultivating longhouse dwellers form a complicated continuum in stratification from the very hierarchical to the nonhierarchical. The Kenyah and Kayan have been described in some detail as the most thoroughly hierarchical societies, followed by the Kajang, Melanau, and Maloh, all of which have or had pervasive distinctions among aristocrats, commoners, and slaves.

At the nonhierarchical end of the spectrum, the Bidayuh—who apparently did not keep slaves except occasionally debt slaves[29]—appear to have been the most thoroughly egalitarian group, followed by the Rungus and Iban, who did. Finally, somewhere between the most hierarchical groups and the least are others such as the Berawan, Lundayeh, and Kelabit in northern Borneo and the Ma'anyan, Ngaju, and Ot Danum in the south, among whom hereditary distinctions are present but less important or less rigid or in which acquired wealth as well as ascribed rank is significant (although in some cases among such groups, weaker stratification may simply be a result of extensive social change).[30] Such intermediate or anomalous groups also include those, such as the Saribas Iban, that have borrowed hereditary ranking to a limited extent from neighboring stratified peoples, in the case of the Saribas Iban, from the Malays.[31]

Aside from the intermediate or ambiguous instances, architectural practices and patterns in Borneo have been explained in relationship to social stratification in several ways. One of these concerns the general differences between the building practices of the more egalitarian groups, on the one hand, and those of the more hierarchical ones, on the other. Jan Avé and Victor King note the following:

> The Iban and the various Iban-related peoples like the Desa and Seberuang usually build houses of quite light materials; the support posts are quite slender and the whole dwelling is not raised very high off the

ground; rather more light woods, bamboo, bark and leaves are used in the building of the house itself. In contrast some of the central Bornean groups like the Kayan, Kenyah and Kajang, Maloh and Ot Danum erect very solid houses, using mainly heavy timbers for walls and floors, ironwood shingles for the roof, and massive ironwood support posts which raise the whole house very high off the ground.[32]

These observers do not attribute the differences between massive and modest building practices and longhouse architecture to social stratification per se. Such differences do not, however, appear to have an environmental, ecological, or otherwise simple practical basis. That is, there is no reason to suppose that the Kayan, Kenyah, Kajang, or Maloh creators of lavish or monumental longhouse architecture have had better access to richer forests or larger trees than architecturally modest Iban or Bidayuh builders. As we have seen, the suggestion has also sometimes been made that the architectural differences between the Iban and the Kayan and Kenyah can be attributed to the varying lengths of time that longhouses are occupied.[33] While this may or may not help to explain Iban architectural motives in particular, the tendency to build relatively modest longhouses appears to be characteristic of the more egalitarian groups in general and is therefore probably a matter of social organization as well as migration practices, which in the case of the Kenyah and Kayan of the Apo Kayan were also frequent.[34]

One of the variations in social organization between the more and the less hierarchical groups that may help to account for their different architectural practices concerns cooperation and authority. Among the more egalitarian groups each family household is responsible for building its own apartment, using materials of its own choosing. Families assist one another and work together but on the basis of strict reciprocity. Among the formally hierarchical groups, on the other hand, the construction of the entire longhouse is traditionally carried out as a single communal project under the direction of the chief and with commoners, and formerly slaves, providing material and labor for both their own household apartments and those of the aristocrats.[35] The resulting longhouses, including their size and the quality of their materials, are a reflection especially of the status and influence of the chief and other aristocrats.

Another way in which longhouse architecture relates to social hierarchy involves the depiction of social distinctions. There are few if any indications of wealth or status of the households to be seen in the most public front areas of the longhouses of the Bidayuh or Iban, for example. To look down the gallery of the longhouses of these groups is usually to gaze upon an undifferentiated succession of front walls, doors, and floors; there is sometimes some variation to be seen, but if so, it usually indicates little if anything about the status of the households. The front walls may be made of different materials (bark or planks), as may also the floors, but to the extent that they are present at all, such differences are not very significant. In the past, apartments often had guarding figures carved on doors, but these were not subject to restrictions of rank. The situation is different on the inside of the private apartments. Here furnishings (today including furniture and appliances) and especially heirloom property (including gongs, other brassware, and jars) are on display. Such property does indicate something of the economic standing of the household. There may also be swords or even a brass cannon if someone in the household has been associated with political or military affairs.

Among the more fully hierarchical groups architectural indications of social rank are more likely to be present and emphasized in the public, front areas of the longhouse and in some instances in the overall form of the longhouse itself. There is, to begin with, the location of the apartments. Those of the chief and other aristocratic families will be in the most favorable part of the longhouse. As will be discussed more fully below, the upstream end of the longhouse has higher status than the downstream end.[36] In the case of the Maloh, "*Samagat* [aristocrats] lived at the upriver end of the longhouse with *pabiring* [lower aristocrats/higher commoners] below them, and *banua* [ordinary commoners] and debt-slaves at the downstream end of the house."[37] In most instances, however, despite the general desirability and ritual superiority of the upstream direction, the favored location is the middle of the longhouse. Among the Melanau, according to Stephan Morris, "The political control of the village was in the hands of a small group of aristocratic elders (*a-nyat*) whose families ideally owned the centrally placed apartments of the longhouse, and who were said to be descended from the founders of the village. On each side of this core were apartments owned by freemen (*a-bumi*); and at each end of the house were the apartments of slaves (*a-dipen*)."[38] The last positions were also considered to be the most vulnerable in the case of an attack.[39]

The practice of having the political core of the longhouse in the middle is not, however, limited to the hierarchical groups. The Iban, who in most instances lack the traditional hereditary ranks of the Kenyah, Kayan, Melanau, Taman, Maloh, and others, also emphasize the center. In this case central families are those of the original founder and closely related kin. Further, since longhouses can normally expand only by adding new apartments to either end, the oldest apartments will remain at or near the center, while those of newcomers or of newly founded local families will be on the periphery. The political core therefore remains in the middle, although, while such families may have more wealth and greater influence, they are not designated as aristocrats and their apartments are not otherwise differentiated from those of more recent arrivals on the periphery.

Among the formally stratified societies the position of the apartment is linked with other physical differences that also imply status. The apartments of aristocrats are larger for practical reasons, as well as a matter of rank: "*Samagat* had more spacious long-house apartments or living areas than either *pabiring* or *banua*, partly because aristocrats possessed house-slaves and had to accommodate them. The covered veranda space outside *samagat* apartments was also larger than that of non-aristocrats since it was there that most house meetings and ceremonies were held."[40] The walls and house posts of the *samagat* sections of the longhouse gallery were also decorated with designs that were restricted to their rank.

The embodiment of social rank and political authority in the design of longhouses appears to have reached the highest development in the traditional chiefs' houses of the Kenyah. Some of these longhouses are or were a virtual architectural tableau of hierarchical social structure. They had roofs that were stepped down from the center to the ends in accord with the status of the occupants. Since longhouses are constructed with the roof ridges running longitudinally (that is, without intersecting lateral ridges) and since the galleries of the aristocrats' apartments extend farther outward than do the others, the raising of their roofs to a higher level is perhaps a matter of structural necessity. It is also, however, a matter of status, as Herbert Whittier makes clear:

> The highest section of the roof, usually in the middle of the longhouse marks the *lamin* of the *Paran Uma* who is usually a full *paran*. Immediately adjacent to his *lamin* on both sides are several *lamin* with roofs slightly lower than that of the *Paran Uma* but higher than those of their outside neighbors.... The next descending level of roofs on either side of the house are the *lamin* of the commoners or *panyin*. Small *lamin* on either end of the house may be inhabited by either a new couple who wishes to join the longhouse and who will add in a regular *lamin* when the house is rebuilt or are the *lamin* of *panyin lamin* or war captives and the descendants categorized as slaves. The *lamin*

of the *Paran Bio* [ranking chief of a village comprising several longhouses] has a roof not only higher than the others of his house, but also higher than the highest roofs of the surrounding houses.[41]

The longhouses of the aristocratic groups are also in some instances embellished by painting and carving, and this too is traditionally concentrated in the galleries of the chief and other aristocratic families. As with other architectural features of social standing among the stratified societies, the display of cultural figures in carving or painting was not meant only to indicate or enhance aristocratic status. The figures were also intended variously to offer protection, promote fertility, and depict important mythical themes. However, among the strongly hierarchical groups most of the representational designs—to be discussed in some detail in the next chapter—are emblems of social rank as well.

THE LONGHOUSE AS A RITUAL COMMUNITY

As we have seen, longhouses are subject to customary law, or *adat*. The point to be made here is that *adat* has an all-important ritual dimension. One of the purposes is to protect or repair the spiritual state of the community. In addition to such common activities as invoking spirits, conducting sacrifices and making other offerings, dancing, feasting, and drinking, the inhabitants of a longhouse are collectively responsible for observing taboos or restrictions (widely referred to by the Iban term "*pemali*"). Most major festivals are followed by a prohibition on entering or leaving the longhouse for a fixed period of time, usually several days. Death in particular places strong restrictions on longhouses that adhere to customary practices. Visitors are expected to learn of or inquire about any restrictions that may be in effect before entering a longhouse. The failure of either local inhabitants or outsiders to observe restrictions is a threat to the

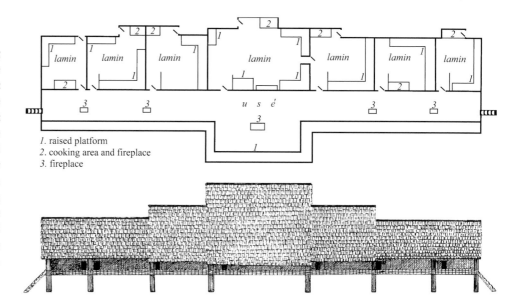

FIG. 2.17. Idealized drawing of a Kenyah chief's longhouse in the Apo Kayan area of East Kalimantan; above: plan (note the cooking areas in the first and next-to-last [from the left] apartments are located on the front wall, the customary location in most longhouses in the northern part of the island); below: front elevation showing the apartment of the chief, flanked by those of other aristocrats and then those of commoners.

1. raised platform
2. cooking area and fireplace
3. fireplace

well-being of the entire longhouse and is therefore a breach of *adat*, for which violators can be fined. The unwillingness of religious converts to participate in ceremonies or to observe restrictions has often been a reason for the split or abandonment of longhouses. In the past, however, ritual was a cohesive force, as it continues to be in many longhouses.

The basic notion underlying *adat* is that of balance, which has both a social and a spiritual dimension. Offenses that harm persons by disturbing the balance among them also distort the spiritual balance of the longhouse. In order to readjust the balance between persons, compensation (in Bidayuh, *takud*) as well as restitution (in Bidayuh, *prosis*) must be paid. In contrast, offenses against *adat*, including those provisions concerning the integrity of the longhouse, are a matter of spiritual or ritual concern. As the introduction to *Adat Bidayuh 1994* puts it,

> The primary function of *adat* is to maintain a harmonious relationship among members of the community and to preserve the physical and spiritual well-being of the *kupuo* [village]. Proper conduct in

accordance with the adat is believed to maintain the community in a state of balance or ritual well-being with the gods and spirits. Any breach of the customs may threaten individual relationships and the spiritual well-being of the community, such as the health and prosperity of the people. Therefore remedial action must be taken immediately by offering ritual propitiation.[42]

The spiritual or ritual balance of Bidayuh, Iban, Maloh (and probably other) longhouse communities is expressed in humoral terms. As Derek Freeman puts it, when the Iban

> speak of the ritual condition of a long-house they liken it to the temper of a human organism. When in sound and normal health, a man's body is said to be chelap, or cool, and when it is afflicted by disease or disorder, angat, or feverish. These same terms are applied to the long-house. Ritually it may be in a "cool" and benign state (*rumah chelap*), or, what is greatly feared, it may become "heated" (*rumah angat*), charged with a kind of evil and contagious essence that threatens all of its inhabitants.[43]

When the spiritual balance of the longhouse has been disrupted, it becomes hot, as a result of which people may become sick and die and crops may fail.[44] The purpose of restitution and sacrifices is therefore to restore the spiritual balance upon which the health and well-being of the community depends and to make it cool once again.

Maintaining the proper spiritual balance of the longhouse and keeping it in a healthy, cool state is also a matter of positive ritual action. The rich and diverse ceremonial life of all Bornean longhouse societies includes many rituals and festivities that involve an entire longhouse. The various agricultural ceremonies culminating in the harvest festival are the most common of all yearly collective traditional ceremonies. These include ones that may take place only once during the entire development of a longhouse. Most or all longhouse dwellers traditionally practice a series of collective architectural rituals involving the selection of a building site for a new house, the clearing of the ground, the erection of the main center post for the entire building, and the initial occupation of the apartments and the use of the hearths. There may also be closing ceremonies—that is, ones that are held when a longhouse is to be dismantled or abandoned. In addition, there are collective rituals held occasionally, including ones aimed at countering an outbreak of illness or crop failure. By tradition in most areas every death in a longhouse places the entire community in spiritual danger and involves rituals in which representatives of all households participate.

The Placement of Villages

The spiritual state of a longhouse is also a matter of its placement, which involves various considerations. Especially before the cessation of head-hunting, these included security, as well as access to farmlands, forest resources, water supplies; convenience; and other such needs—considerations that vary in relation to geograph-ical and political circumstances. Security and prosperity, however, are traditionally regarded as being as much or more a matter of unseen or spiritual circumstances as visible, utilitarian ones.

Notions of alignment appear to be most fully developed (or at least most extensively described) among the riverine groups rather than the mountain dwellers. Among the Bidayuh most villages were previously located on steep mountainsides, ridges, or hilltops that were readily defended and that afforded a view of the surrounding countryside, although not usually on the tops of the higher mountains. In these mountain locations small longhouses or sometimes single dwellings are crowded in as best they can be where there is a stretch of gently sloping or level land, facing in general away from the mountain. The main directions are simply up and down. In such circumstances villages, and houses within villages, are above, below, or beside one another, and to go somewhere is usually to go up or down the hill.

In the case of the riverine dwellers the elevation of villages relative to one another does not have the same significance as with the mountain peoples. As we have seen, however, among some of the stratified river dwellers the height of roofs of longhouses or of specific apartments within longhouses is a matter of social rank. Also among the riverine villages the main orientation is to and with the river itself rather than with the contours of a mountain or hillside. Houses are customarily built facing the river, usually at a point where a side stream enters the main one. Single houses are commonly placed in a row along the bank or along a road that runs along it, while longhouses are usually built with their longitudinal axis parallel to the river. Such an alignment often reflects the best use of the natural setting in that in much of the interior the relatively level stretches of land needed for building longhouses will take the form of terraces that run parallel to the river. Further, building a longhouse so that all or most of it is more or less equidistant to the river means that the convenience for everyone is maximized, an important consideration in that people use the river as the main means of travel, as a source of water, and for bathing. Finally, being able to watch the river and to see who is coming and going is important to people who live along it, and in the past this was a matter of security as well as interest.

Such practical considerations are not, however, the whole story. Writing about the Kenyah and other groups of northeast central Borneo, W. F. Schneeberger makes the following point:

> Although this [parallel alignment] may superficially appear to be dictated by topography, it is a strong belief among all interior tribes that building a longhouse transverse to the river would be inviting disaster. "Malang . . . signifies across athwart, and figuratively unlucky" (Crawfurd 1856:249). *Untung malang* or *nasib malang* means bad luck, adverse destiny. Therefore, a house built transverse to the natural way of things, the flow of the river, would stand *malang* and its inhabitants would experience many reverses.[45]

A second and apparently less common or important consideration is the path of the sun, that it rise in front of the longhouse and set behind it. For some riverine peoples the ideal alignment for houses is one in which they face both the river and to the east. This is the case among the Ngaju according to Hans Shärer and Anne Schiller.[46] Since the Ngaju mainly build single houses, they have considerable flexibility in aligning them to the river as well as to east. Nonetheless, this would be possible only where the course of the river lies on a north-south axis (the main direction of flow of the rivers in the Ngaju region is from north to south), and the houses are built on the west bank. If a house is built facing north or south (so as to face the river at a point where it has an east-west axis), the sun will pass over it from end to end rather than from front to back.

The difficulty of placing a longhouse of several hundred meters or more in length so that it is both facing the river and the rising sun to the east is much greater. For this reason Iban practices are especially interesting. According to Derek Freeman's account of the Baleh River Iban circa 1950 (when existing longhouses appear to have been built in an entirely traditional manner), finding sites for longhouses was often a difficult matter:

> The Baleh and its tributaries drain broken and hilly country, and their involuted courses contain many rapids. These difficulties of terrain mean that suitable sites for long-houses are often hard to find. What is needed is a terrace, some twenty yards wide, sufficiently elevated to escape the threat of floods (some of the rivers rise 30 or 40 feet above their normal levels following exceptionally heavy rains), and sufficiently level to extend the house lengthwise. . . . Another limitation on the length of the house is the ritual prohibition against the long-house spanning a tributary of the stream of the river to which it abuts. The spanning of such a tributary, even if it be no more than a trickle, is believed to bring misfortune to all the people of the house. The ritual danger is that the river spirits, offended by the filth and refuse cast beneath the long-house, might seek retribution. . . . In some areas suitable sites are so rare that houses have to be built on steep spurs, several hundred feet above the river from which the unfortunate women have to fetch, in gourds, all of the water required for domestic purposes.[47]

Elsewhere Freeman stresses yet another factor that further restricts selection of a site for a longhouse: a favorable response from the omen birds, as sought and interpreted by the *tuai burung* (literally bird chief), or augur. He does not mention how often otherwise suitable or ideal sites for longhouses are passed over because of an unfavorable message from the right bird, although he does state, regarding omen taking generally, that if an initial response is unfavorable, a further effort may be made a few days later to secure a favorable one, but if the responses continue to be negative, the proposed course of action must be permanently abandoned.[48]

Freeman stresses the magico-religious dimensions of Iban longhouse architecture (as, indeed, of all things Iban). He does not, however, mention that the Iban of the Baleh River area seek to place their longhouses facing the rising sun, and, with the exception of the ritual prohibition on building across a tributary stream and the seeking of omens, he otherwise treats the selection of a site as an often difficult matter of finding a large enough piece of suitably even ground above the likely high water level. He does provide a schematic diagram of Rumah Nyala, the longhouse on the Sungai Sut (a tributary of the Baleh) that was the main site of his fieldwork. This indicates the position of the longhouse relative to the river and its flow and to the compass and shows that the longhouse (which was built in 1922–1923), while facing the river, is placed with its longitudinal axis diagonal to the path of the sun and at one in which the sun would rise nearer to the end of the longhouse than to its front.[49]

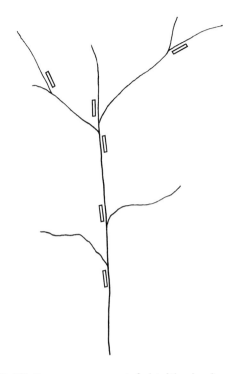

FIG. 2.18. Common arrangement of related Iban longhouses on a main river (*batang*) and side streams (*sungai*).

Upstream and Downstream

Whether they live in longhouses or in single dwellings and however exactly they align them, the fundamental geographical attraction of the riverside inhabitants is to the river, and the most important and widespread notions of direction are those of upstream (*ulu* in Malay and in Iban and many other Bornean languages) and downstream (*illir* in Malay, *illi'* in Iban). Throughout Borneo generally "*ulu*" and "*illir*" appear to have the same basic implications and associations. These include the use of "*ulu*" to mean "upper" (as in *ulu* Baram or *ulu* Balui), interior (as in Orang Ulu, the official Sarawak term for the various Kenyah, Kayan, Penan, Kajang, Kelabit, Lundayeh, and other indigenous peoples of northern Sarawak), or rustic or backward. In geographical terms the general direction of "*ulu*" is the interior, and "*illir*" is the coast.[50]

"Ulu" and "illir" have various cultural and historical implications for indigenous peoples. Enemy raids in the past might well have come from upriver (as when war parties would cross from one river to another by land above and then move downriver to attack). But in Sarawak they often came from downriver, at least when they involved the Iban, who were known as Sea Dayaks because they sometimes attacked from the sea, having first traveled downriver and along the coast. Further, as political control has been established over indigenous groups, either by the traditional Malay sultanates; the Brooke, British, or Dutch colonial regimes; or the postcolonial Indonesian or Malaysian governments, it has been extended from *illir* to *ulu*, usually weakening on the way. Religious conversion and associated Western influences have also generally moved from the coast to the interior, although there appear to be exceptions.[51]

Today, of course, the opportunities and temptations of modern life, whatever their value or their undoubted attraction, are eroding or destroying traditions and emptying upriver villages of young people (or of everyone, in the case of entire villages that relocate), who are moving toward the coast in search of economic opportunities or schools for children. Conversely, forests are being cut by logging companies that move from the coast to the interior, while trees in the form of logs are carried downstream by river or truck. Rivers are, therefore, clearer and fish and game more abundant in their upper reaches than in their lower ones. Human waste, which commonly goes into the river also, of course, passes from upstream to down. The sea is so salty, a native supposedly once explained to a European, because so many people have urinated into the rivers by the time that they flow into it.

In the interior "ulu" and "illir" also have an important ethnic-economic dimension. While valued heirlooms (ceramic jars, brassware, beads) and other trade goods come from the coast, the wealth that is used to procure them comes from the forests of the interior. In Sarawak a common network of exchange involves nomadic Penan (or Ukit) hunter-gatherers, who live in the headwaters or upper reaches of a river; the Kenyah or Kayan or Kajang peoples, who live below them along the navigable stretches of the river; and the Malay or Chinese, who dwell yet further down in trading towns and on the coast. In this system forest products are obtained by the nomads, traded to the longhouse groups, and then by the latter to the downriver or coastal groups.

It is therefore not surprising that "ulu" and "illir" have widespread cosmological significance and are important principles of architectural alignment. Insofar as long-

houses are built more or less parallel to the river, as is usually the case, each will have an upstream and a downstream end. Further, since houses or family apartments are built beside one another, each will normally be either upstream or downstream from each of the others; further still, each single house or apartment in a longhouse so aligned will have an upstream side and a downstream side. In all instances, upstream is cosmologically fortunate and downstream is the opposite. According to Victor King, among the Maloh, a stratified riverine longhouse people who live in the upper Kapuas area of West Kalimantan near the center of Borneo, "Upstream regions were seen . . . as sources of goodness, health and life . . . the home of benevolent spirits . . . linked with the heavens, the Upperworld where ancestor spirits and aristocratic deities such as Sangyang Burong and the hornbill and omen birds dwell." In contrast, cemeteries are located below the village, and downstream leads to the land of the dead, the sea, and the underworld—the domain of serpents and fish.[52]

In the far south of Borneo, the Ngaju people (the term itself means "upriver") do not (or no longer) live in longhouses, but such ideas are also important. Houses are commonly placed facing the river, and if so, the upstream part is more important than the downstream one: "In the upriver part we find the sleeping-rooms of the family, and there are also kept the most valuable possessions; in the downriver part is the kitchen, and this is where young unmarried men and servants (formerly slaves) slept if they do not sleep on the verandah or in a separate hut. . . . The siting of the house thus expresses its divine cosmic character and, together with its whole form, can only be understood through the conception of God, for the house is an architectural expression of this conception of God."[53]

To the north, Iban beliefs and practices regarding "ulu" and "illir" are very similar to those of the Maloh and Ngaju. Burial grounds are ideally located downstream

FIG. 2.19. Raising the sacred main post of a new Aoheng longhouse, Long Bangun Hillir Village, upper Mahakam River, East Kalimantan.

from the village. Corpses are normally buried with the head pointing downstream—the initial direction of the soul on its journey to the other world—and guests enter the longhouse at the auspicious upstream end.[54]

Building Rituals

Among the Kayan, Iban, and undoubtedly most other groups, the building of a longhouse begins with the erection of the principal post of the chief's apartment, usually at or near the center. This is typically the most important of all house building rituals and includes a sacrificial offering of a chicken or pig, the blood put on the post or the animal and other offerings crushed beneath the base of the post as it is raised into place. In the past this was one of the occasions on which a slave might be sacrificed in the same way. After the main post of the entire longhouse, those of the other apartment sections are erected in order, with a sacrificial offering performed by the head of the household involved in each case.

Among the Iban the central origin post (*tiang pemun*) is associated with the *pun rumah*, the human originator of the longhouse. The origin post reaches the peak of the roof and supports the ridge beam. It is located in the middle of the longhouse from front to back, which is the point at which the wall is built that separates the open veranda or front part of the apartment from the private, enclosed, rear part. More specifically, it is located at the upriver end of the founder's apartment. In addition to the sacrificial ceremonies associated with its erection, the *tiang pemun* must be offered blood sacrifices on subsequent occasions—when breaches of *adat* have occurred, for example—in order to cool the longhouse.[55]

The construction of a new longhouse begins with the selection of a site. In addition to the various considerations noted above in choosing a location, this customarily involves the taking of auguries. If these are favorable, offerings are made to the spirits of the area that will be displaced, and the clearing begins. Formerly, at least in the case of the Kayan, taboos on the killing of various animals in the area had to be observed for a year.[56] While building practices have changed substantially, the process customarily involves two phases, the first of which is the more lengthy. It involves the felling of trees; the cutting of posts, beams, and boards; and the preparation of shingles, thatch, and other materials. The second phase involves the erection of the building. Among the Kayan this was done in a short period, sometimes a matter of days. People worked together to build the longhouse as quickly as possible, in part because the period in which the building was being put up was one of potential spiritual peril. Gongs were struck during the entire period of building, and people avoided looking up so as to avoid hearing or seeing bad omens, the danger of which persisted until the building was completed. Many other restrictions were also in effect:

> People who coughed blood were not allowed to participate in house building, as their condition would have polluted the building and the community. Minor rituals fostered prosperity. For instance, a member of the chief's household threw pieces of bitter pumpkin (terak) under the house so that pigs would be healthy and fat. House building could be affected by various unfavorable circumstances: among the Mahakam-Kayan, if a worker fell from the scaffolding, his loin-cloth had to be buried where he fell; work was halted for eight days and a priest carried out a purification. All tools and pieces of clothing had to be buried where they fell. Objects associated with women were not to be brought under the unfinished house. Visitors from other communities were not allowed to go through the house because they might bring with them foreign spirits.[57]

The wood used in building longhouses was also traditionally subject to certain ritual principles and restrictions. While ironwood is highly valued as a building material throughout Borneo, especially for posts and mortuary structures, its use was taboo for a few groups, including the Aoheng and the Mahakam-Kayan of East Kalimantan.[58] Lumber is commonly recycled when longhouses are rebuilt, but there are restrictions on salvaging otherwise usable materials from a building that has burned.[59]

Boards, posts, and beams are traditionally aligned according to ritual principles. Both the Kayan and the Iban, and again undoubtedly many other groups, aligned posts and beams in accord with the top and base of the tree from which they had been cut. In the case of posts, the principle is that the top end should correspond with the top of the tree, while longitudinal beams are aligned with the river, either—as among the Kayan—with the base-of-the-tree end pointing upstream and the tip downstream throughout the entire longhouse or—as among the Iban of the Paku (Saribas) River in central Sarawak—with bases pointing consistently either upstream or down, depending on whether they are in the upstream or downstream half of the longhouse.[60] While placing the heavier, lower end of a post downward might be done for simple practical reasons (the erection of a massive main supporting post would be even more difficult if it were top-heavy as well), the alignment of beams with the flow of the river would appear to be more purely a matter of ritual concern, as would the Iban practice of keeping the tree-top tenon-end of a beam above the butt-end tenon of another where they cross over one another in a mortise. Among the Kayan the alignment of wall boards would appear to follow a different but similar principle, in this case involving life and death. Boards are placed vertically in longhouse walls, in contrast to those used in raised mausoleums, which are placed horizontally. In the past the Kayan also, apparently for ritual reasons, made doors and door frames from a single piece of wood.[61]

CHAPTER THREE THE ARCHITECTURAL SYMBOLISM OF LIFE AND DEATH

INTERIOR BORNEAN PEOPLES make use of carving or painting in the construction of longhouses, mausoleums and mortuary posts, storehouses, and other buildings, although there is a great deal of variation in the extent to which this is done. The building traditions of some groups involve considerable purposeful embellishment, while those of many others include a minimal amount of carving and little or no painting. In northern Borneo the most common forms of architectural carving appear to be the sculpting of guarding figures on the notched-log ladders used to enter longhouses and on the slab doors of longhouse apartments. The tops of entrance ladders are typically carved into anthropomorphic faces or heads

and sometimes into more elaborate figures; occasionally in some areas the sections between the steps are also carved into images so that the ladder resembles a leaning statue. The figures on carved doors commonly consist of dragons or other powerful animal motifs. Iban carved doors, for example, usually have dragons or realistically represented lizards or snakes, often with a single figure on each door, though sometimes with a combination of several. The carved doors of the Kenyah, Kayan, and Kajang peoples generally have more stylized or abstractly rendered figures, often dragons, covering the entire surface. In addition, the frames surrounding the doors made by these groups are also sometimes carved—occasionally instead of the door panel itself—as are the handles, and if so, usually also into dragons. Carved slab doors are no longer made except for sale in shops, al-

though some modern doors in longhouses are painted as a part of larger wall murals.

Architectural carving and painting among some groups goes far beyond carved entrance log ladders and doors. In Sarawak the various Melanau and related Kajang peoples have highly developed traditions of carving involving large ritual poles and mortuary posts and in some places mausoleums. In both Sarawak and Kalimantan the Kenyah, Kayan, and related peoples apply architectural carving and painting to several kinds of buildings, including longhouses and storage buildings, as well as *salong*. In some instances, especially in the Apo Kayan and the middle and upper Mahakam areas of East Kalimantan, sculpture and fretwork are used to create roof finials, and carving is applied to the posts, beams, and rafters of longhouse galleries, as well as to doors,

FIG. 3.1 (facing left). Mualang carved longhouse ladder, West Kalimantan.

FIG. 3.2 (facing right). Ot Danum carved lower house ladder.

FIG. 3.3 (left). Carved longhouse entrance ladder, Eheng Longhouse, East Kalimantan.

FIG. 3.4 (below). Carved lizard figure on an Iban door. In contrast to those of the Kayan, Kenyah, and Kajang peoples, Iban door carvings are relatively simple.

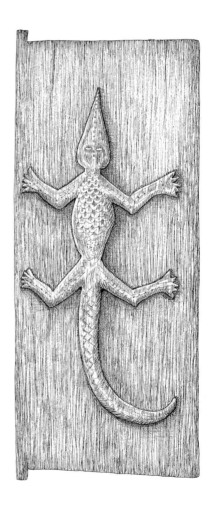

wall panels, and ladder tops.[1] In many areas the most lavish or extensive large-scale carving involves mortuary architecture, a reflection of the emphasis often placed on death rituals throughout Borneo. In Sarawak, as well as in Kalimantan, the Kenyah, Kayan, and others also apply designs to modern community halls and Christian churches.

TOOLS, TECHNIQUES, AND GENDER

The customary tools of architectural carving are basically the same as those used in building in general—that is, axes, adzes, and chisels of various shapes and sizes, with bigger versions used for roughing and larger-scale work and smaller ones for finer detail. Chopping or bush knives are also used as all-purpose chopping, cutting,

FIG. 3.5 (right). Sebop (Kenyah) carved doorframe showing monkeys and a dragon.

FIG. 3.6 (below). Kenyah granary, Datah Bilang, East Kalimantan, 1996.

FIG. 3.7. Kayan men carving main post with adzes, Apo Kayan, East Kalimantan, late nineteenth century.

and planing tools, as are small, long-handled carving knives for the finest details. The traditional axes and adzes most commonly used in architectural carving have forged iron blades that can be mounted either parallel or perpendicular to the axis of the handle (as noted in chapter 1), depending on the type of work to be done. The cutting tools of some groups included these adz-axes; the wider, flanged adz; and various knives that suited their needs. The Iban are meticulous carvers of smaller objects but tend to confine their creation of larger carved forms to the relatively simple motifs on door panels and ladder tops. The Kenyah, Kayan, and Kajang, who engage in much more elaborate large-scale carving, were also highly skilled at iron forging and made and worked with chisels and gouges as well as adzes, axes, and knives. While various adzes are still used for carving and other woodwork and carpentry, indigenous axes have been replaced with imported ones that have handles mounted in a socket. At present in Sarawak, craftsmen make use of modern tools, including chain saws for some of the initial rough work of carving, followed by finer work with axes, adzes, and chisels.

Carving and painting are not traditionally separate realms of activity. Similar images are created by carving or painting or by a combination of the two. That is, a carved figure or repetitive design may be left as bare wood or enhanced with color. In addition, painted images are created on flat surfaces. Lime or other pigments

FIG. 3.8. Punan Bah (Kajang) craftsman carving a ridge beam with an adz, 1998.

are often rubbed onto an otherwise unpainted carved wooden surface in order to enhance the lines of the design.

Carving and painting are related in an even more fundamental way in that both are often done as negative or reverse processes that are common to Bornean artistry in general.[2] The creation of an image or design in wood is basically a process of removing material, with the figure or design consisting of what remains. This is rather obviously the case with much sculpture, but it is also involved in the creation of relatively flat work, including low-relief carving and fretwork (in which parts of a piece are cut through). It is also used to create images in greater depth, either in deeper-relief carving or in work done in the round.

It is also true, however, that the more ornate architectural carving of some groups, including the Kayan and the Kenyan, includes the positive creation of composite work. That is, separate pieces are cut out or carved and then attached to others, traditionally by mortise and tenon joints or (at present) by modern techniques of fastening. The recently created (in late 1998 and early 1999) *salong* at the Sarawak Museum has dragon roof finials created by bolting together separately cut out spiraling tendrils. Such creations may again be either basically flat, as are the above-noted dragon finials, or they may be three-dimensional. The Kenyah in particular create extraordinary three-dimensional composite sculptures in the form of roof finials or as internal attachments to posts, beams, or rafters.

The creation of images on flat surfaces through the use of pigment is also done in reverse when a figure is created by painting around (rather than within) an outline of its shape. Traditional painting in the interior is based on the use of black and white pigments (derived from soot or charcoal and lime respectively), supplemented with small amounts of red (from ocher, usually used for eyes). In some instances images are created directly or positively, as when, for example, a black dragon is painted on a white background. Much more commonly, however, such a figure will be created in the opposite way, by applying black pigment negatively on a white background, so that the figure is what is left in white, as outlined or surrounded by black. The same general result is obtained if a light background is left unpainted and surrounded by black. If designs are sufficiently abstract, formalized, or convoluted, it is not necessarily possible to distinguish the parts that are the figure from those that are the background, but where the images are representational, this is usually clear. In modern Kenyah and Kayan mural painting the same basic reverse technique is followed, but with more colors. That is, the background or negative parts of the design are painted black, while the positive areas are left unpainted or are painted white, red, pink, green, yellow, or blue.

While in terms of symbolism, male and female principles are given equal emphasis, the creation of the important images is the work of men. This may be in part a simple matter of general practice in that building, including the activities of painting and carving, is done by men. According to the art historian Sarah Gill, however, it also involves a basic cultural principle:

> Carving and painting are the exclusive prerogatives of men, and the ornament reserved for these forms of art includes all the figural items of Sarawak iconography. These items—human figures, dragons, hornbill birds, and demonic faces—are those which bear special spiritual or social meaning. The art produced exclusively by women includes only woven textiles, beading, and plaited matwork, and the ornament on these forms is, except for figured Kayan [by which Gill also means Kenyah and Kajang] beadwork and Sea Dayak [Iban] textiles, restricted to non-figural geometric designs of no special significance. Even the exceptions can be fitted into this principle, since the ornament used in Kayan beadwork is always designed by men, and the figured Sea Dayak textiles are never worn by women.[3]

If the scope of these observations were to be extended to all of Borneo, further exceptions—or partial exceptions—would probably need to be noted, but as a general rule they appear to have wide applicability.[4]

ARCHITECTURAL IMAGES AND COSMOLOGY: SOME GENERAL FEATURES

The main motifs used in Bornean architecture are generally the same as those used in other ways—as designs in beadwork, tattoos or carved-on containers, work boards, pack boards, and many other things. Although the styles of each group are unique, the figures, designs, or images that are carved or painted in architectural contexts recur widely. In Gill's words, "Even the complex patterns of Kayan [and Kenyah] ornament are made up of a handful of emblems joined by *kelawit* [hook] tendrils. . . . All style regions select their ornament from a limited vocabulary of forms, the most common of which are human figures, dragons, hornbill birds, and demonic faces."[5] Gill is writing of Sarawak, but the list would not be expanded much if it covered all of Borneo. Even among the same groups, however, most images occur in varying degrees of abstraction or explicitness, although the versions used in architectural carving or painting tend to be more explicitly representational than those used in other ways. This is perhaps partly because carving and painting lend themselves more readily to the creation of singular images than do basketry or weaving, and partly because of social restrictions involving gender and hierarchy. Many of the specific figures occur widely throughout Southeast Asia but are highly developed in distinctive ways in Borneo, a result of a long period of internal development.

The images and designs that are used in architectural (and other) contexts have several purposes, including, of course, aesthetic enhancement and in some instances amusement. Often the images created through carving and painting in architectural contexts are intended to offer protection. Frightening monster or dragon faces with large round eyes and protruding tongues and fangs are carved on doors, ladder tops, war shields, and baby carriers. Guarding statues are erected at entrances to longhouses. Such figures are intended to frighten dangerous spirits and human enemies. They reflect the same general concerns that traditionally motivate efforts to prevent the spirits of the recently dead from returning to disturb the living.

FIG. 3.9. Painted Taman coffin lid (originally red, black, and white) showing a human soul entering the mouth of a dragon; near Melapi, upper Kapuas River, West Kalimantan, 1994.

The promotion of the fertility of crops, animals, and human beings is another general animating force in Bornean architectural imagery. Various figures, including the bamboo shoot and the jar, are associated with fertility, as are (again rather obviously) copulating figures. Male statues often have erect phalluses, though these may be intended to threaten rather than to invoke fertility. While the portrayal of sexual organs and copulation is intended to threaten or frighten, reproduction is a form of power, and fertility is a basic part of well-being. Fertility is closely associated with death and, in the past, especially with sacrifice. A main purpose of headhunting was to enhance fertility as well as general well-being. The protruding tongue is also a common motif in Bornean carving that is related to death and sacrifice.

Among the Benua' and other southern groups the anthropomorphic figures carved on sacrificial posts are often shown with long, protruding tongues, presumably for licking blood. Similarly, a Kenyah door in the Sarawak Museum shows a dragon devouring human heads.[6]

The close association of death and fertility reflects a more general tendency in indigenous symbolism to emphasize opposites, as well as proximity and synthesis. As elsewhere, binary distinctions or oppositions can be readily noted in Bornean symbolism and ritual practice.[7] In the elaborate realm of augury, for example, the meaning of the call of a certain omen bird is not only a matter of what kind of bird it is, but also whether the call comes from the right or the left, or whether the bird is flying from left to right or right to left, or from the front or be-

FIG. 3.10. Dragon face carved on a Punan Bah (Kajang) *klirieng.*

hind. Among the Bidayuh at least there is also a general distinction between day birds (which can provide either good news or warnings) and night birds (which are generally bad news). Similarly, Bornean thought about the ritual condition of persons and places tends to humoral oppositions of hot and cold and of the need to balance the two—although (perhaps because of the association of illness and fever) coolness (sometimes associated with the color white and the upperworld) is the generally desired state for both bodies and villages; spiritual anger, turmoil, crop failure, disease, and death are usually associated with heat.

In the realm of direction and the alignment of longhouses, the common distinction between upstream and downstream has already been noted. Such notions also figure prominently in Bornean conceptions of the journey of death and the geography of the land of the dead. At least among riverine dwellers in the north, the road of death is a long and perilous journey that may begin by boat but typically also involves travel overland to a high mountain range, beyond which lies the land of the dead in the form of the basin of a river, along which departed souls live in longhouses and practice rice cultivation. Such notions vary within as well as between groups, but in general there are upstream and downstream regions to which souls are assigned according to their manner of death.[8] In some versions there is a place set apart near the river mouth for those who died a bad death—that is, those who died by violence, drowning, sacrifice, or suicide, or who were eaten by crocodiles, or who (in the case of women) perished in childbirth; those, on the other hand, who died a good or natural death by disease or old age occupy a place upriver. The Kenyah of Sarawak add to this upstream-downstream dimension a further one of left and right. In the ascent of the main river of the dead (Alo Malou), there are two tributaries; the one on the left (and downstream) is reserved for those who have died unnaturally, while the one on the right (and upstream) is for those who have perished in a natural way.[9]

Although, as we have already also seen, in the daily world of the living, gender appears to be less important than in many other places, cosmology in Borneo also has an important male-female distinction. For some groups and probably in a general way, "male" and "female" as symbolic categories are linked to broad divisions of the cosmos, including an underworld and an upperworld, with the human world of everyday experience in between.[10] The underworld is the female realm of water, reptiles, death, and fertility, while the upperworld is the male realm of the air; of generally benign deities, birds, and mountaintops; and often the final home of departed souls and ancestor spirits.[11] The distinction, which is also between downstream and upstream, was first brought to attention through the study of the Ngaju of southwestern Kalimantan by Hans Shärer.[12]

UNDERWORLD MOTIFS: THE DRAGON, THE JAR, AND OTHER FORMS

The dragon is the preeminent underworld creature and generally the most commonly utilized of all motifs in architectural and other realms of material culture.

> The dragon goddess, being close to mankind, provides protection in daily life—mostly through dragon spirits represented as emanations from her—and sacrifices to her secure agricultural and human fertility. She guards over the dead and ensures their passage from this world to the next. As men must be initiated into the next world she is represented on men's coffins. She is associated with earth, water—particularly primal waters—storms and lightning. She is represented on virtually all artifacts, from kitchen utensils to funeral monuments, and particularly in symbolic or real boats.[13]

Like some other figures (especially anthropomorphic ones), dragons are shown either in their entirety or as heads or faces and in varying degrees of explicitness or abstraction. Explicit dragon characteristics include recognizable—usually reptilian—features, including eyes, tongue, teeth, scales, and tails. In more abstract versions scales disappear; the eye is enlarged; and jaws, legs, and tail become tendrils that end in spirals or connect with other dragons or other creatures. Some dragons have a more serpentine appearance. The *nabau*, or Iban dragon, usually takes this form, with either no legs or very small ones. Other dragons have four legs with claws. Whole dragons are always shown in profile, with one eye visible, an open mouth, a protruding tongue, teeth and often long tusks, and a curved or undulating body. The eye is especially important. It is traditionally usually round, often very large, and the only part of the image done in red rather than black and white.

The dragon is not always identified as such. Among the Kenyah, Kayan, Kajang, and related groups, dragonlike creatures are called "*aso'*" or "*asu'*" or some cognate term that means dog. This term refers to figures with explicit reptilian characteristics, including scales and a serpentine body (as well as to more abstract versions), in addition to ones that might be said to represent other things, including dogs. Some observers have taken this usage literally to mean that the creature portrayed really is a dog and that the dragonlike characteristics developed as a result of the influence of the dragon images on imported ceramic jars. This view gains support from the fact that dogs also have some prominence in Bornean mythology as ferocious guarding animals encountered

FIG. 3.11. Carvings of dragons on the gallery wall of a Long Ulai (Kajang) longhouse, late nineteenth or early twentieth century.

by the soul in its perilous journey to the afterlife. Others, however, regard the *aso'* as nothing other than a version of the widespread dragon that somehow got to be called a dog by mistake.[14] The ethnologist Robert Heine-Geldern takes this view.[15] He makes the diffusionist argument that the Bornean dragon is a Chinese import dating back two millennia, to the late Chou period. As evidence, he notes several stylistic characteristics common to the Bornean dragons and the animals on Chou bronzes. One of these involves an image of the dragon in profile, with its head turned completely backward and upward—a pose impossible for a real animal, he points out—and another involves the rendering of the body in a double curve.

For his part, Bernard Sellato suggests that the dragon got to be called a dog in some cases because it came to be regarded as such a powerful and dangerous creature that another name for it had to be used—something done also by the Kayan with regard to the tiger.[16] If so, then the dragon-as-dog took on a life of its own, with the result that while some Kenyah and Kayan *aso'* have scales, horns, and other usual dragon characteristics, others look more like dogs. Such *aso'* are shown often sitting in a doglike posture, and with upright, pointed ears instead of horns and dog-shaped heads. The *aso'* that are carved or painted on buildings, however, usually have serpentine rather than doglike features.[17]

To complicate matters further, both the Kenyah and Kayan recognize a separate, non-*aso'*, dragonlike water spirit that lives in the river, as do also the Berawan.[18]

Among the Kayan are beliefs that several kinds of snakes can transform themselves into dragonlike creatures, one of which is the *lengunan,* a kind of python that lives under water and can also change itself into a tree trunk that can swim.[19] Among the Kenyah and Kayan such non-*aso'* water spirits do not, however, appear as images in architectural contexts, but among the Berawan the *butiert belungin,* as the dragon is known, "can often be seen snaking along the ridge of a *salong.*"[20]

In addition to such versions of the dragon, natural lizards, snakes, and crocodiles are also common motifs, though less frequently in architectural contexts than in others. All are related to the dragon in cosmological terms as underworld water creatures associated with protection and fertility but are kept separate from it. The Iban, for example, carved snakes (*ular*) and lizards (*menarat*) as well as dragons (*nabau*) on longhouse apartment doors and have separate terms for them all. Further, in architectural contexts at least, snakes and lizards are more or less realistically depicted, as are frogs. As often elsewhere, when represented in two dimensions snakes and lizards are usually shown from the back—that is, more or less symmetrically, the lizard with two flexed legs on each side and two eyes. Whole dragons, on the other hand, are shown asymmetrically—that is, from the side, with only one eye in view.

While imported ceramic jars have long been recognized as likely sources for dragon images in Borneo, their significance goes far beyond this. The jar motif is widely carved as the base figure on sacrifice posts and statues and painted or carved into Tree of Life designs. In some areas the lower parts of posts for longhouses and community halls are also carved as jars.

The importance of the jar as a design motif presents no great mystery. Of the three main forms of imported prestige and heirloom property—brassware, glass beads, and ceramics—glazed earthenware jars of up to three feet or a meter in height are used in the widest

FIG. 3.12 (above). Door handle carved as a dragon.

FIG. 3.13 (facing top). Jars displayed as heirlooms and used for storing rice and for making and storing rice wine in a modern Iban longhouse apartment in Rumah Gensurai, Layar River, Betong area, western Sarawak, 1993.

FIG. 3.14 (facing bottom). Jars used as mortuary receptacles in a Kajang *salong,* Tubau, Bintulu River, central Sarawak, 1997.

range of symbolic and practical ways.[21] Along with gongs and other brassware, jars are often displayed in longhouse apartments as valuables. Imported into the interior for perhaps a thousand years, first from China; then also from Vietnam, Cambodia, and Thailand; and finally from coastal kilns in Borneo itself, jars were and are widely sought, held, and exchanged. In the past they were sometimes used as substitutes for heads or sacrificial victims and, as such, are sometimes broken or "killed" at funerals.[22] Old jars of a particular type or reputation trade for very large sums and were sought in distant lands, including Java and Sumatra, by adventuresome men from the interior. Well-known jars are given honorific titles, and many types are recognized on the basis of color, glaze, shape, size, and image design. Such jars are believed in some instances to have mystical powers and are used for divination—one owned by the sultan of Brunei in the nineteenth century was said to be able to talk and would give warnings of approaching misfortune.[23] Stories are common throughout Borneo of various creatures—including deer, snakes, crocodiles, fish, and humans—miraculously turning into jars and of jars turning into animals and running away.[24] One famous type, the *rusa*, or deer jar, is so called, according to Barbara Harrisson, not because it has a deer design (which is extremely rare) but because such jars were said to have originally come to Borneo as deer. She quotes J. M. Mallinckrodt telling of being shown such a jar while on the Kahayan River in southern Borneo and saying that "it had been speared and the wound was closed with a silver stud. Its history was that it had been discovered during a hunt, while in the guise of a deer. At the moment it was speared, the deer changed into a valuable old jar."[25] Harrisson also recounts a Skapan (a Kajang group) story of the folk hero Galau, who acquired six jars that had come to his longhouse as mysterious human strangers and turned into jars on the veranda following a dream that he had about them.[26]

FIG. 3.15. Kenyah carved and painted post showing an anthropomorph sitting on a jar; community hall at Datah Bilang, middle Mahakan River, East Kalimantan, 1996.

While the idea that jars could be male or female is widespread, jars in general are classic womb and tomb symbols, and their meaning as such is closely associated with their practical importance and ritual use as containers of fertility and fermentation.[27] Jars are used to store rice that has been prepared for cooking and for brewing and storing rice wine, both of which are the essence of fertility. Jars are also one of the most common containers for human remains.[28] In some cases, bodies are placed in the fetal position in large jars that have been broken around the circumference at the widest point and resealed with damar. Among those groups in central and northern Borneo with secondary mortuary practices, human bones are collected and placed in a jar that is then put in a grave post or raised mausoleum. Among the Iban and some other groups jars are sometimes partially buried in the ground above a grave.

THE HORNBILL, OTHER UPPERWORLD MOTIFS, AND THE HUMAN SKULL

Birds in general are associated with the upperworld. This includes especially the various omen birds that are the messengers of the gods. Most important, it includes the rhinoceros hornbill *(Buceros rhinoceros)*, widely known in Sarawak by its Iban name, *kenyalang*, and portrayed in architectural decorations and on ritual objects throughout Borneo.

While the hornbill occurs elsewhere (in Sumatra, for example) as a spiritual motif going back to the bronze age,[29] it appears to have a particular emphasis in Bornean design and mythology. The basis of this importance is perhaps less obvious than that of the dragon, the crocodile, or the jar. It may be in part the distinctive reproductive practices of hornbills, which make nests in holes of trees, the female entering the orifice to lay her eggs, the male then closing the hole with mud and leaving only a slit through which he then feeds the female until the wall is torn down and she emerges with new life. Beyond its mating habits, the rhinoceros hornbill is a very large and impressive bird, with black plumage on its body and white tail feathers marked with black and a red horn above its bill that curves upward. Black, white, and red are the traditional colors used in architectural and other paintings and carvings, and rhinoceros hornbill feathers are worn on hats and cloaks. The casque ivory of the rhinoceros hornbill (as well as of the helmeted hornbill) is carved into male earrings, belt toggles, and pendants, and dried hornbill heads are sometimes incorporated into Iban male ceremonial gear.[30]

FIG. 3.16 (above). Hornbill as a roof finial in the Kenyah village of Datah Bilang, middle Mahakam River, East Kalimantan, 1996.

FIG. 3.17 (left). Hornbills as roof decorations on a small Bidayuh men's house in Batu Dendang Village, Serian, western Sarawak, 1992.

FIG. 3.18. Tigers in a modern Kenyah polychrome mural on granary, Datah Bilang, middle Mahakam River, East Kalimantan.

The supernatural status of the hornbill as a symbol is also somewhat ambiguous. Among the Ngaju and perhaps other southern groups the hornbill is regarded as one form of the chief upperworld deity and the male opposite or counterpart of the female dragon or water serpent, and it is widely depicted as such. In central and northern areas the hornbill is also widely used in architectural and ritual contexts, but here it is rather a representative of a hawk god (specifically the white-headed Brahminy kite, or *Haliaster indus intermedius*). Among the Iban this is Lang Singalang Burung, the god of war, and among the Kenyah, it is Burung Elang or Pelaki, neither of which are often, if ever, carved or painted as a hawk.[31]

But however ambiguous its mythical status, the rhinoceros hornbill has been made into a spectacular and widely used image, especially with the special emphasis given to its upward curving casque in both carved or painted representations. In stylized versions—most spectacularly in the Iban *kenyalang*, or hornbill effigy, used in *gawai burung*—the casque becomes a great spiral. Hornbills, often shown with wings outspread, are also used by other groups as roof figures, except in mausoleums, which usually have dragons instead. If placed on a ritual post or other structure the hornbill is the highest figure and is usually paired with a jar or other underworld figure at the base.[32]

As a male, upperworld image, the hornbill is linked with objects associated with warfare and head-hunting, including swords, spears, and human skulls. Among the Bidayuh, men's houses in general are replete with such associations. The beam from which the skulls hang in the *baruk* (men's house) in Opar Village in Bau has a hornbill head carved at one end, while the *baruk* in Gumbang has several spears and a shield set up near the skulls. Old swords are sometimes also kept near skulls taken in head-hunting. In addition to their collections of skulls and other male heirlooms, men's houses are supposed, for both practical reasons (to keep watch for approaching enemies) and symbolic ones, to rise above the other buildings in a village, and they are often decorated with carved flying hornbills as roof pinnacles or other decorations. Among the Kajang and other groups, skulls are sometimes attached to the tops of ceremonial poles, as they are also on some Ngaju Tree of Life sculptures.

THE TIGER AND THE HUMAN FORM

In addition to the figures that are clearly associated with either the underworld or the upperworld, there are several other important and widespread ones that are not. One of these is the tiger, a mythically powerful creature that is usually represented realistically, at least in present-day architectural contexts. Among the Kenyah, Kayan, and related groups the tiger is often present in mural paintings; it is also used in the mortuary art of some groups. Although tigers do not now exist in Borneo, they have been long known, and teeth and skins have sometimes been imported and used as symbols of rank in hierarchical societies. Tigers are also believed to be ferocious enforcers of *adat* by some groups.

Since they are generally important in the symbolism and mythology of a much broader region of Asia,[33] tigers are probably a part of the ancient cultural heritage of Borneo that became mixed with other symbols that arrived or developed later. It is perhaps therefore for this reason, as Sellato suggests, that tigers are ambiguous in terms of the more general male upperworld and female underworld distinction: "Among the Barito people the tiger . . . is a major god of the male sphere, supposedly an emanation of the upperworld. But it is sometimes described as a fish-like creature, hinting at an underworld affiliation. The Benuac substitute it for the dragon in funeral art, as do some central-northern groups. The Kenyah tiger appears closely associated with the dragon . . . but occasionally replaces hornbill on top of ritual poles."[34] To make matters even more complicated (but by

FIG. 3.19. Ngaju sacrifice post (*sengkaran*) showing a tiger standing on the head of a man, Central Kalimantan.

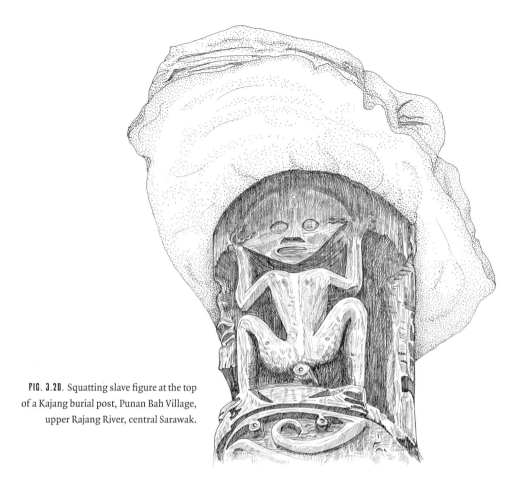

FIG. 3.20. Squatting slave figure at the top of a Kajang burial post, Punan Bah Village, upper Rajang River, central Sarawak.

now perhaps predictably so), the tiger, like the dragon, is sometimes changed into a dog or a bear "for fear of its power."[35]

Anthropomorphic Forms

Some of the anthropomorphic images in common use in Borneo also appear to have ancient origins. The carved heart-shaped faces that appear on *klirieng* are very similar to ones that sometimes appear on the prehistoric Bronze Age (1000 B.C.–A.D. 500) Dong Son bronze drums found in Borneo and elsewhere throughout Southeast Asia.[36] The squatting figure, which is among the most common

of all images in Bornean designs, occurs in many areas outside of Borneo as well and undoubtedly also extends far back in time. It is common in Iban *pua* (ceremonial cotton blanket) weavings and in beadwork done by many central Bornean groups, as well as in architectural contexts. Carved squatting figures are also shown as supporting the stones that are placed on the tops of Kajang *klirieng*, for example.

As with the tiger, the various human or anthropomorphic figures that occur widely in Bornean architectural and other contexts also do not fit simply with an upper-world-underworld dichotomy, though for different reasons. It is rather in part because the human form or humanlike features are used to portray a variety of beings. Anthropomorphic images in some instances represent humans as such, the squatting figure being perhaps the most important and widespread example. Those that are shown supporting the columns of buildings or the stones at the top of grave posts are intended to represent slaves, for in hierarchical societies bearing burdens and squatting in the presence of nobles are appropriate for slaves. But, once again, matters are not so simple, for smiling, squatting anthropomorphic figures also sometimes represent benign, godlike characters among the Kenyah.[37] Such figures, in which the hands, feet, ears, and hair are shown as spirals and tendrils, are referred to in general as "*kalung kalunan.*"

In yet other instances humanlike features are used in images of frightening demons, like the monster (or dragon) faces that are often created by combining two dragon images side by side. These tend to combine distorted human characteristics (such as round, forward-set eyes and occasionally thick lips and square teeth) with animal ones, especially long, curving fangs and long, sometimes serpentlike tongues. Known among the Iban as "*gerasi*" and among the Kayan as "*udo*'," such images are widespread. They involve either the head or the entire body, in either case with large, round eyes and great fangs; if the entire body is shown, the torso, arms, and legs are small in relation to the head. In addition to being painted on war shields, such monster images are painted on house and mausoleum posts.

COMPOSITE IMAGES, THE TREE OF LIFE, AND PLANT FIGURES

In architectural carving and painting, some motifs are created either as single images or in combinations. Dragons, hornbills, and anthropomorphic images are often shown by themselves, in pairs, combined with one another, or with yet other figures. Two dragons, for example, may be placed together in profile in such a way that a frontal demonic face is also created. Similarly, the extremities of a dragon or a humanlike figure may become hornbills. Other figures, including jars, swords, the tiger, and other animals, are usually created in composite images. Carved posts usually have a series of figures carved one above the other, and in some instances side by side as well.

The Tree of Life, which combines upperworld and underworld symbols, is by far the most important and widespread of the composite images. Among the Kayan it is called the "Big Tree" (Kayo' Aya') and, as is common, is associated with the origin and well-being of humans.[38] While as a motif the Tree of Life may be shown only as a tree, it is often depicted as combining several other elements—often the jar, human figure, tigers, swords and spears, and a hornbill. In his account of Ngaju religious imagery, Shärer describes the Tree of Life as the basis of the creation of the world and its human occupants, and he shows the various ways in which it is depicted—sometimes as a tree growing from the body of a slave; sometimes as a house; and sometimes as a post, a spear and banner, or an umbrella.[39] In his comparative summary of the main motifs of Bornean myth and imagery, Sellato attempts to show the widespread occurrence of the image and notes that the general features and meaning of the figure involve the destructive-creative synthesis of underworld and upperworld forces, although, again, such notions are not necessarily explicitly or consciously held.[40] Sometimes it is an actual tree or plant, such as the widely sacred cordyline plant in the Barito area in the far south or the strangling fig (*Ficus* spp.) in many other places. The latter tree, which begins as a vine that grows on and then around another tree, ultimately destroying it, is an especially potent image—a natural symbol and one that expresses the basic Bornean cosmological theme of sacrifice and the creation of life from

FIG. 3.21. Contemporary (1996) Tunjung sacrifice post *(belontang)* showing a demonic figure standing on the head of a woman who is standing on a skull that rests on a jar; Barong Tongkok, middle Mahakam, East Kalimantan.

death. In modern Kenyah and Kayan murals, in which it is a favorite central image, the fig tree is shown with a profusion of outwardly and upwardly spiraling tendrils. The tree is usually shown as growing out of a jar and often has an anthropomorphic figure in the center, sometimes flanked on each side by tigers and, in any case, a hornbill at the top. Other Tree of Life designs, especially those carved as ritual posts, do not have actual trees but combine lowerworld and upperworld figures—a jar or dragon (or often both) at the base, an anthropomorphic figure or face in the middle, and a hornbill or skull at the top. A syncretic Bornean Christian Tree of Life recently created by a Penan group shows a crucifix mounted on a jar and embellished with tendrils, with a hornbill sitting on the top with outspread wings.

Beyond the Tree of Life, floral or foliate designs are commonly used among those groups that live near the coast and have been influenced by Malays—the Iban and the Bidayuh in Sarawak and West Kalimantan and the Ngaju in Central Kalimantan, for example. The tendrils ending in hooks and spirals that occur in rank profusion in the figures and designs of the Kenyah and Kayan may have been partly inspired by the plant forms of garden and forest, but if so, they are not usually identified as such; and while tendrils are used to depict the branches and foliage of the Tree of Life, they are also even more commonly displayed as attributes of the hornbill, dragon, and anthropomorphic motifs. Among these groups tendrils, hooks, and spirals are all often referred to as "*kelawit*," or hooks. Among the Iban, who make shorter and thicker ones, they are called leeches.[41]

CARVING, PAINTING, COSMOLOGY, AND SOCIETY

Aside from their cosmological bases and purposes involving protection, the promotion of fertility, and general well-being, Bornean designs are subject to social restrictions among some groups, specifically the more hierarchically organized ones. Writing of such groups in Sarawak, Gill states that art involving representational designs, "which include some of the most impressive forms in Sarawak, is essentially aristocratic, since it appears to function chiefly to reflect and magnify the prestige and power of the aristocratic class."[42] Such a statement may underestimate other, more distinctly religious motives that also underlie the production and display of the important representations in Bornean art and architecture—motives that are now better understood than in the 1960s, when Gill conducted research and wrote her study. Gill, however, goes on to state that "purely ritual requirements used to account for some of the forms, such as figures of deities, but these have gradually ceased to be made in Sarawak [or elsewhere in Borneo, it might be added] as people turn away from the old gods and inconvenient taboos of their ancient religion."[43]

The images so affected among such groups—the Kenyah, Kayan, and related groups; the Maloh and Taman; and to a lesser extent the Kajang peoples—are more or less the same as those involving gender (although with the difference that in the case of gender it is the creation of images more than their display that is involved). Lower-status persons among these groups are customarily limited to displaying mainly formal, nonrepresentational designs of the sort often produced in the work of women in basketry and matwork and in some weaving and beadwork.

The images involved are generally important throughout Borneo, including the human figure. As we have seen, anthropomorphic figures in architectural painting and carving take several common forms. One of these is the squatting slave or sacrificial victim. Since among the Kenyah and Kayan only aristocrats (*paran*) could own slaves, they also had the exclusive right to display the figure. Another anthropomorph is the benevolent god shown either as a face or head or as a full figure. In either case, among the Kenyah the display is limited to aristo-

FIG. 3.22. A carved and painted Penan Christ done as a Tree of Life, with a jar at the base and a hornbill at the top; Long Urun, Belaga, central Sarawak, 1998.

FIG. 3.23. Dragons and a demon face painted on a square supporting post in a Long Gelat community hall, upper Mahakam River, East Kalimantan.

crats, but with the additional distinction that only high aristocrats could display the body as well as the head, while lower aristocrats could display only the head or face.[44]

The privileged images also include several natural animals, in addition to the dragon or dog-dragon. The two most important animals are the tiger and the rhinoceros hornbill. The display of either among the Kenyah and Kayan is customarily also restricted to aristocrats. Further, this restriction usually extends to the display of physical materials from these animals—that is, feathers and ivory from the rhinoceros hornbill or the skin and teeth of tigers.

The aristocratic domination or monopoly of the important symbolic forms has been explained in various ways. Sellato notes that among the Kenyah, Kayan, Modang, and related groups the aristocrats themselves were often artists: they could devote time to painting and carving since they were freed from the need to work in the fields by the labor of the slaves they owned (the ownership of slaves also being a privilege of rank).[45] It has also been pointed out that among the hierarchical societies it is believed that only the aristocrats had the spiritual strength needed to deal with the supernaturally powerful images, for the aristocrats were supposed to be of divine descent. This meant that the display of a restricted image by someone who was not entitled to do so was not only a social breach, but a ritual one as well and was, therefore, subject to supernatural punishment. Peter Metcalf similarly reports that he was told by the Berawan that the improper display of an image such as the human face on a *salong* meant permanent denial into the land of the dead.[46]

For his part, Victor King has sought to explain artistry and rank among the Maloh (and perhaps among other groups) in terms of a larger scheme of cosmic symbolism, noting that there is some general association between nobility and masculinity, the color white, the up-

FIG. 3.24. A black-on-white dragon mural in a Long Gelat community hall, upper Mahakam River, East Kalimantan.

river direction, and the upperworld and between lower social strata and femininity, the color red, downriver, and the underworld.[47] This works in the case of the hornbill, which is the most important of all the upperworld creatures and which has plumage with white markings on a black background, although the hornbill is less exclusively restricted to the nobility than are other motifs. It does not work so well in the case of the dragon, which, while a female and underworld creature, is among many or most groups the most important of all motifs, especially in architectural contexts. Further, restrictions on the display of motifs are based on rank rather than gender. The most general point is that all of the most important or powerful mythological creatures, whether upperworld, underworld, or anomalous, have been claimed by and are associated with the aristocrats.

As with other aspects of the relationship between social stratification and architecture, therefore, all of this needs some qualification. A simple distinction between societies that are egalitarian and place no restrictions on the display of images (except for ones reflecting achieve-ment or wealth) and those that involve rank by birth and have strict restrictions can be misleading in some instances. The number of societies that are or were fully stratified into rigid classes of nobles, commoners, and slaves is limited, and even in the case of some of these the extent of stratification has been disputed. It is also apparent that notions of hereditary rank and the symbolism and images of privilege that went along with them sometimes had an attraction for other groups and tended to diffuse to them, especially in places where the highly stratified groups had political power or influence. In northern Sarawak this seems to have been the situation with the Kayan and Kenyah in relation to the various Kajang and other horticultural groups of the region. Writing of the Berawan, Metcalf observes that claims of the sort noted above—that an improper display of the human face on a *salong* would bring disaster to the soul of its occupant—were suspect "because the Berawan lack any rigid system of social classes. It seems clear that this usage, along with the face design itself, has been imported from the Kenyah, who do have such class sys-

FIG. 3.25. Modern Kayan polychrome murals covering the veranda walls of Uma Juman longhouse (subsequently destroyed by fire), Balui River, Belaga, central Sarawak, 1986.

tems.... In effect, anyone who is wealthy and powerful enough to build a *salong* is *ipso facto* of sufficient rank to employ the coveted designs.[48] Even the very powerful, independent, and expansive Iban in some areas appear to have borrowed not only Kenyah artistry and designs, but also associated notions of restriction by hereditary rank.[49] Finally, ideas about rank and images have also been widely discarded, leaving many younger members of these societies, who have been raised as Christians, with little awareness of the significance of the older ritual bases of the symbolic motifs or of the spiritual claims of the aristocrats.[50]

MODERN DEVELOPMENTS

Both architectural carving and painting have been affected by the availability of modern tools and materials, as well as by the widespread conversion of local peo-

ples to Christianity and other modernizing influences. While the reproduction of bowls, doors, statues, and other objects for the tourist market (a major cottage industry in East Kalimantan) has proliferated in recent years, architectural carving in general has been on the wane throughout Borneo for many decades. Although grave markers, ritual posts, and statues are still created, the embellishment of buildings with carving is mainly limited to community halls, tourist longhouses (a recent development, discussed in chapter 6), and churches. In particular, the carving of longhouse ladders, posts, doors, and rafters, as well as mortuary posts and mausoleums, except for display at museums and other modern places, has largely ceased.

In contrast to longhouse and mortuary carving, the creation of painted images in architectural contexts has flourished and grown, in some places at least.[51] This may be in part perhaps because of the ready availability of commercial paints and in part because Western cultural influences may provide better models and incentives for architectural painting than for carving. In any case, the main form here is the mural, consisting of figures or scenes painted on large surfaces of buildings. Modern murals—the sort now found in some longhouses (in Sarawak mainly in the Balui River area above Belaga), churches (especially in some areas of Kalimantan), civic buildings, and other urban settings, including private residences—are mainly the work of Kenyah and Kayan painters. Such murals have developed out of the older architectural traditions of these and related groups in Sarawak and East Kalimantan. The Apo Kayan area (from which many of the Kenyah and Kayan peoples of Sarawak derive) is generally acknowledged as the center of architectural painting and carving, and it is evidently here that the more contemporary forms first emerged. From here Kenyah and Kayan artists came to Sarawak to paint murals, especially in civic and religious buildings.

The modern painted murals differ from the more traditional ones in a number of respects. The older murals mainly involve either single dragons, combinations of dragons, or monster faces.[52] They are painted in black and white in the traditional style with tendrils and spirals, mostly on the outer front walls and posts of longhouse apartments, storehouses, or mausoleums of chiefs or other nobles, usually using the reverse technique described above. While the newer murals by Jok Batu and other artists are still created using the older technique of painting in reverse, more of the design is now applied in a direct or positive way. Similarly, while the traditional colors of black and white are still common and in some instances predominate, paintings have generally become truly multicolored, with the addition of blue, yellow, green, pink, and other colors. Such colors are made possible by the use of commercial paints, which are also used to create the traditional black, white, and red colors previously gotten from soot, lime, and iron oxide. While the colors of the old murals are soft and muted and often do not entirely conceal the underlying color of the wood, those created by modern paints are much brighter and more completely hide the underlying surface on which they are applied.

A further development is that the designs have generally become more complex. In contrast to the older, black-and-white murals that typically have a single dragon figure (or several in profile that form a face) with spiraling tendrils, the new ones are often intended to illustrate a traditional story or a modern scene. A modern mural generally consists of a central figure or set of figures (a Tree of Life, several dragons, a human figure) surrounded by others, all surrounded by a lavish thicket of connected tendrils. Dragons continue to be important but less often as single, central figures than as secondary or supporting ones. They also have a less ferocious, more benevolent, or even friendly appearance, with a modern eye complete with lashes. Monster faces have disappeared or become less threatening.

FIG. 3.26 (top). Contemporary Kayan mural showing legendary scenes and individual portraits on the doors to the inner apartments, Uma Daro' longhouse, Balui River, Belaga, central Sarawak, 1997.

FIG. 3.27 (bottom). Wedding celebration participants in front of a mural featuring dragons with flowers for eyes, Uma Daro' longhouse, 1988.

FIG. 3.28. Interior of St. Pius Catholic Church at Kenyah village of Long San on the upper Baram (since torn down and replaced); the work of the late Apo Kayan artist Tusau Padan.

Modern murals also incorporate more realistically rendered figures. In the past both the human form and those of other creatures were treated abstractly. While much of a modern mural (and all of some murals) consists of abstractly rendered human and animal figures done with tendrils, it may also contain realistic versions of these, some from mythology, but engaged in recognizable activities, such as shooting a blowpipe. Portraits of individuals have also been added, in some instances in modern clothing. A woman in a short dress, a man wear-

ing shorts and playing a *sape'* (a stringed musical instrument), and a man in a soldier's uniform are painted on doors as a part of larger murals on the outer walls of longhouse apartments of the Kayan village of Uma Daro'. And while some of the most extensive and lavish longhouse murals have been painted on the apartment walls of nobles, wall paintings are no longer restricted by rank. In several instances murals cover the entire length of the gallery wall. Finally, Christian motifs, as well as traditional mythological ones, are now common—especially, of course, in church murals, but also in longhouse wall paintings.

These various innovations have also been associated with different styles of individual artists and ethnic groups.[53] The Kenyah artists from the Apo Kayan who came to Sarawak to paint murals include the late Tusau Padan, whose work is prominent around Kuching; he created the marvelous interior of the old (now demolished and replaced) St. Pius Catholic Church at Long San in the upper Baram and in turn influenced younger Sarawak artists. In this style, while the human figures and other creatures are realistically depicted in some instances, the most striking characteristic is the intricate elaboration of abstract forms, especially tendrils, spirals, and double spirals, with which all available space is filled up. There is also, in Sarawak at least, a more distinctly Kayan style in which murals include realistically drawn animals (monkeys, lions, tigers, hornbills), as well as mythical beings in anthropomorphic form and portraits. In the Kayan murals painted on the walls of Uma Juman and Uma Daro' longhouses on the Balui River, figures are presented more boldly, and tendrils and spirals are shorter and thicker than the modern Apo Kayan Kenyah style of Tusau Padan.

PART TWO MODERN TRANSFORMATIONS

CHAPTER FOUR THE DEVELOPMENT OF BIDAYUH ARCHITECTURE

BEFORE WE CONSIDER ARCHITECTURAL CHANGE in more general terms in the next chapter, it is worth examining what has occurred among the Bidayuh in some detail. The built forms of the various Bidayuh peoples have by now undergone a great deal of change. In most areas many of the older buildings are gone as a result of shifts away from previous village sites and the adoption of modern building types and materials. The more traditional forms are still evident, however, in a few places, especially in the more rugged and remote regions along the border in the Bau and Padawan districts of Sarawak and in adjacent areas of West Kalimantan.

GENERAL CHARACTERISTICS OF BIDAYUH ARCHITECTURE

While the architectural traditions of the various peoples of the interior each have distinctive features as well as commonalities, those of the Bidayuh tend to depart from the general pattern more than most. To begin with, Bidayuh domestic architecture shows more internal variation than does that of other peoples of northern Borneo. While most groups in northern Borneo have or had a single characteristic traditional main house form, the Bidayuh did not. As described in accounts written in the middle and latter part of the nineteenth century, Bidayuh villages consisted of longhouses in some instances, houses joined in more irregular ways in others, and separate houses in yet others—examples of all of which can still be found.[1] While these differences are partly a matter of regional differences among the several Bidayuh groups, they probably cannot be entirely accounted for in this way. Further, the architecture of the Bidayuh includes a separate men's house, commonly referred to in the literature as a "head house" because it is used to store skulls. While such men's houses have been reported for the Modang and Kenyah in East Kalimantan, they are distinctive to the Bidayuh groups in western Borneo.[2]

The longhouses of the Bidayuh most closely resemble those of the neighboring Iban. In contrast to those of the Kajang, Kayan, Kenyah, and many other groups, the longhouses of both the Iban and the Bidayuh always have an open or outer front veranda, as well as a covered or inner gallery. Both the Iban and the Bidayuh, moreover, tend to build less massive longhouses than do the former groups. Such similarities between the building practices of the Bidayuh and the Iban may be in part a matter of borrowing or influence, but they probably also reflect commonalities in social structure. Both groups lack the hereditary hierarchy of the Kenyah, Kayan, Kajang, and Maloh, all of whom are well known for their large and solidly constructed longhouses. Among these groups hierarchy seems to have been architecturally expressed in massively built and differentiated longhouses, as well as in often elaborate mortuary structures for aristocrats.

The relatively modest nature of Iban and Bidayuh building practices may therefore be linked to the more limited scope of hierarchy and authority in these societies and their reliance on reciprocal forms of cooperation. Although the tendency of the Iban to build less massive longhouses has also been attributed to their habits of frequent migration, this cannot be said of the more sedentary Bidayuh. In any case, the more egalitarian nature of Iban and Bidayuh social orders is also reflected in the absence of the various architectural indicators of hereditary rank sometimes found in the longhouses of the hierarchically organized groups.

While Bidayuh longhouses resemble those of the Iban, there are also differences. Bidayuh longhouses tend to be smaller and to have a much narrower covered gallery than do those of the Iban—not to mention the even wider galleries of the larger longhouses of some other groups. The relatively narrow covered gallery of Bidayuh longhouses—often little more than a walkway without an outer wall—is partly a matter of the relatively narrow overall width of the longhouse. But it is partly also a matter of the allocation of space between the covered gallery and the inner apartment, as determined by the location of the wall. In the Iban longhouse, this wall is directly below the roof ridge and therefore divides each apartment section into two equal parts (the gallery and the inner apartment). In Bidayuh longhouses, the dividing wall is placed well to the front of the roof ridge, thereby allocating more space to the inner apartment than to the gallery.

The narrow gallery of most Bidayuh longhouses is offset by a wide outer veranda (tunju, tanju', tanju, etc., in different dialects), which also runs continuously along the entire front of the building. This wide veranda, which provides entry into the longhouse, is generally well built, usually of split bamboo lath lashed to a solid framework of joists and posts. It serves as the main walkway for the longhouse and sometimes connects two or more adja-

FIG. 4.1. Longhouses at Anah Rais, upper Padawan, western Sarawak, 1997.

cent longhouses, and it is also used as a work area and a drying platform, with rice granaries along its outer margins among some groups. During *gawea* (festivals), altars and ritual poles are erected, and the veranda becomes an important site for ritual celebrations.

Some of the differences between Bidayuh architectural practices and those of the Iban reflect the differing locations in which each place their villages. In the past the various Bidayuh groups built their villages in rugged locations on mountainsides, ridges, and hilltops. Such locations were chosen for security, for Bidayuh villages were liable to attacks both by other Bidayuh ethnic groups on other mountains and by Iban and Malay raid-

ers from the north.[3] In some instances Bidayuh villages could be reached only by climbing. The assent to the village of Peninjau (on the steep side of Serambu Mountain), where James Brooke built his famous cottage (and where Alfred Wallace spent time), required the use of ladders at some points. The location of this village also had the advantage of a magnificent view of the surrounding countryside, including the Sarawak River.[4]

The Iban and other groups also at times built fortified villages on hilltops for defensive purposes, but this was usually a temporary measure for those who normally lived along rivers and depended on stockades and other methods for protection. But for the Bidayuh and related

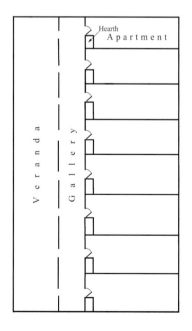

FIG. 4.2 (above).
Two longhouses facing
one another in Bisarat
Village, Serian area,
western Sarawak, 1997.

FIG. 4.3 (right).
Drawing (section
above, plan below) of
a Bidayuh longhouse.

groups in northwestern Borneo, the mountains were a permanent rather than a temporary home. This pattern of adaptation had probably developed over a long period of time. The riverine themes that are so pronounced in the cultures of the Iban, Melanau, Kajang, Kayan, Kenyah, and many other groups are missing from that of the Bidayuh.

The traditional architecture of the Bidayuh reflects this mountainside and hilltop orientation in various ways. Quite apart from influences of social organization, the rugged upland terrain favored by the Bidayuh discouraged the sort of massive building characteristic of some other groups. Bidayuh longhouses and other buildings are usually constructed on foundations of smaller posts. The moving of large, very heavy logs of the sort used by Kayan, Kenyah, and Kajang builders as supporting columns, while difficult enough for the riverine dwellers, would be far harder in the irregular, steep hillsides of Bidayuh country. Nor for similar reasons could longhouses usually be very long, at least if all of the apartments were built on the same level. Occasionally Bidayuh mountainside longhouses are built in a series of terraces. Until recently this could be seen in the remnants of the longhouses at Gayu in Padawan. Even so, the lack of much level ground discouraged the joining together of very many apartments. Unlike those of the Iban, the mountain villages of the Bidayuh, therefore, generally consisted of a series of smaller longhouses, as well as, in some instances, separate family houses. Also, such smaller longhouses and individual houses were not placed in the linear pattern common to the riverine groups but rather oriented to one another at different angles as the terrain allowed.

Men's Houses

The more limited development of Bidayuh longhouses in comparison to those of many other groups is probably also related to the practice of building men's houses. Among most of the other longhouse-dwelling groups nearly all social life and most ritual activity take place in the longhouse, especially in the covered gallery. While among the Bidayuh the longhouse is also a center of social interaction and ritual, some of both is displaced to the men's house—the customary residence of the unmarried male adolescents and men of the village, the guest quarters for visiting men, the place for public meetings, the repository for the village collection of skulls, and the site for the performance of rituals related to the skulls, most important the annual or periodic *gawea mukah* or *panggah*. Commonly known in the Sadong area as "*balai*" or "*balu*," in Padawan as "*panggah*," and in Bau as "*baruk*," men's houses are not isolated from the rest of the village. Although an elevated location relative to the other buildings is important, they are placed in close proximity to the longhouses or individual dwellings and are usually

FIG. 4.4. Small house, rear view, Gumbang, Bau area, western Sarawak, 1997.

FIG. 4.5. Older style house built of traditional materials, Singai, Bau area, western Sarawak.

fig. 4.6. Gayu longhouse, Padawan, western Sarawak, 1996.

connected to them by bamboo platforms and walkways. This can be seen in various existing villages in Padawan, including Sadir, Bunuk, Gumbang, and Anah Rais. Here they are at the center of the village.

The architecture of the men's houses is distinctive. Presumably because of their use for storing and displaying skulls and because they were also used as guest houses in which European visitors commonly stayed, men's houses are usually mentioned or described in accounts of the Bidayuh.[5] Most observers in the nineteenth century described men's houses as round or octagonal with a conical roof, but square and irregular ones were also noted. While different groups of Bidayuh tended to use different designs, the early accounts indicate that the styles varied in the same area and even in the same vil-

lage.[6] The round shape, which is now pervasive in the Bau area, is notable for its distinctiveness as a design in Borneo. Although round or oval shapes occur elsewhere in insular Southeast Asian architecture, they are not characteristic of indigenous Bornean groups, among whom longhouses, granaries, and wooden mausoleums are square or rectangular. At present most of the men's houses in Bidayuh villages in the Sadung and Padawan areas are square, and a few there and elsewhere are octagonal. The round shape characteristic of the Bau area is particularly important for the contemporary Bidayuh as an ethnic symbol and, as will be noted below, has been used as a design motif for various modern buildings.

While some of the design principles used in the construction of the men's house are the same as those of

FIG. 4.7. Round-style men's house (*baruk*) at Opar Village, Bau area, western Sarawak, 1989.

other buildings, certain features are different. At the center there is a large fireplace, the corners of which are formed by four central posts that extend from the ground through the floor and upward to the apex of the roof. These posts, which slope inward as they go up, both provide the vertical framework for the fireplace and carry much of the weight of the roof. In most larger round or octagonal men's houses there is also an outer set of posts that extend from the ground up to the roof at the midpoint between its peak and lower edge. About two meters above the floor, four massive beams (sometimes doubled) extend from one side of the building to the other and cross the four central posts above the fireplace and then intersect with beams supported by the outer set of posts. If the roof is high, there are also crossbeams far-

ther up that are also joined to the central posts and supported by diagonal braces. Finally, a raised platform used for sitting and sleeping extends along the outer wall.

While the term "head house" is less appropriate than "men's house" as traditionally constructed and used, it has some validity in relation to present-day practices. Since unmarried or visiting men no longer sleep or spend much time in these buildings, their uses have been often reduced to the storage and display of skulls and the occasional ritual activities associated with them. In some instances, true head houses have been built—that is, small structures that have room for little else besides the skulls and are used for no other purpose. In Grogo, a Bidayuh Jagoi village in Bau, for example, the skulls were moved out of the *baruk* several years ago into a small shed

FIG. 4.8 (top). Hearth of the men's house at Opar Village, Bau area, western Sarawak, 1989.

FIG. 4.9 (bottom). Skulls kept on display in the men's house at Opar Village, Bau area, western Sarawak, 1989. (Note hornbill carving to the left.)

behind it. Here they are looked after by the few remaining non-Christian male ritual leaders, while the entire village, which is mainly Christian, continues to use the *baruk* as a public meeting hall. They were moved, it was said, so that the children would not be frightened. Some other Bidayuh villages (including Opar and Bunuk) continue to display their skulls in their *baruk* while also using the buildings as village meeting halls, perhaps in part because these villages receive occasional tourists, for whom the skulls are an attraction. Gunung Jagoi Village no longer has a men's house but keeps its collection of skulls in a small shelter, as does Sentah.

THE SHIFT DOWN THE MOUNTAIN

Bidayuh villages tend to be situated more permanently than is generally the case among the other interior swidden cultivators of the region. In particular, the pattern of frequent movements, often involving lengthy migrations, of the Iban, Kenyah, and Kayan is not common among the Bidayuh. Over time communities dependent upon shifting cultivation experience land shortages, especially in land close to the village. Rather than shifting the entire village, however, as was often done by many other groups, the Bidayuh have tended to divide their communities and create daughter villages, which in time have their own daughter villages, a process that is sometimes reflected in village names.[7] Some existing villages claim to be very old, and a few can be traced in European accounts to the middle of the nineteenth century, although this does not necessarily mean they are still in the exact same location.[8] The great majority of existing Bidayuh villages are more newly established, but most of them derive in one way or another from older, generally nearby ancestral settlements.

The main pattern of movement over more than a century has been from higher, more rugged or remote locations to lower, more accessible ones.[9] This movement,

FIG. 4.10. Bunuk Village, showing small longhouse and single houses crowded together, Padawan area, western Sarawak, 1990.

which began in some parts of Sarawak long ago during the Brooke period, often occurred in stages, as part of the earlier village moved to a new, lower location and part remained behind.[10] In overall terms, while a few of the old mountain villages remain, the shift is complete in most regions. The villagers who have established new communities have been mainly left to their own inclinations in arranging their houses and have generally followed the older, mountainside and hillside pattern of placing them close together wherever there is usable space.[11] The common pattern was to initially recreate the older, existing architectural patterns in both form and material. In most cases this meant the construction of longhouses and men's houses in close proximity to one another. Except for their newer, more accessible locations, such villages were often similar to those on the mountain. Sooner or later, however, the inhabitants of many such villages began to move out of longhouses and into separate family dwellings, a process that was eventually also replicated by most of the inhabitants of the remaining mountain villages.

While many of the surviving longhouses and men's houses have been kept in a traditional form (except for the now nearly pervasive use of metal roofing), the single

FIG. 4.11.
Single house built
like a section of
a longhouse,
Gumbang, 1989.

houses that the Bidayuh came to build both in the newer, lower villages and in the older, mountain ones take various forms. Some of them resemble a single apartment section of a longhouse. Such houses, raised on piles, have an open front veranda of split bamboo lath; a small, roofed-in gallery; a main inner room, including hearth and kitchen area; and a raised sleeping platform at the back. Some have the traditional roof-flap window (*komban*).

Modern Houses

Many of the older houses in the Bidayuh villages in the Bau area take the form of a general Malay style. Bidayuh villagers themselves say that they learned to build such houses from Malays or that, in the case of the early ones, Malay carpenters were hired to build them. Such houses

are constructed with light, sawed-wood frames; are raised several feet above the ground; and have a portico or roofed-over front entrance porch rather than an open bamboo front veranda. The more costly versions have walls and floors made from sawed boards and roofs covered with *belian* shingles, and the interior space may include a separate bedroom, as well as a loft area. They also have windows in the walls rather than in the roof—and it is the roof design in particular that distinguishes the Melayu style. Even today the main distinctions that the Bidayuh of the Bau area make regarding house types are based not, for example, on the materials from which a house is made but on the complexity of the roof design. *Basal* houses have simple, two-sided roofs, while *rimas* types have more complicated, hipped roofs or ones that involve intersecting planes, as do Malay houses.

Many Bidayuh are now building single houses that reflect urban influences and have no particular ethnic significance but rather a regional style. While there are some continuities, such modern dwellings are quite different from both the older Bidayuh single houses and the traditional Malay-style ones. The modern dwellings vary regarding both materials and designs. In terms of materials, there are wooden houses and there are brick or concrete block and stucco houses—as well as mixed versions. Houses are generally referred to as being "*kayu*," or wood, if they have sides made from wooden boards. Wooden houses, as well as brick or cement block and stucco ones, may also have cement floors, although some have plank floors. The choice of whether to build a wooden or a brick or block stucco house is a matter of both cost and prestige. An affluent village dweller will build a modern-style stucco house; those less well off will also be influenced by the relative costs of materials, as well as the greater prestige, and, it is believed, the durability of brick and cement block.

Apart from the distinction based on roof form, the main variation in the design of modern houses is between one or two stories and between placing the building directly on the ground or raising it on posts. These two choices are not exactly independent. One-story houses may be built either at ground level or raised, but two-story single houses will almost invariably have the lower floor on the ground. While two-story houses are a modern form, they are, at least as built in villages, a development out of an older design. This can be readily seen in the way that they are built and in houses in different stages of development. In contrast to Western practice, the upper story is built first. This involves raising the upper story two and a half or three meters above the ground on posts, and leaving the area beneath open. This creates a structure very like many longhouses and many traditional Melayu houses, in which the space beneath the building is used for storage, keeping animals, or

work. The more recent innovation involves enclosing this space with walls and adding a concrete floor. Once this is done, it becomes a two-story dwelling, with kitchen and living and bathing areas at ground level and bedrooms on the upper floor.

Modern single-story houses are generally built directly on the ground. This requires that the ground be leveled for the floor, as is true also when the lower part of a two-story house is to be enclosed. In many Bidayuh villages in Sarawak this is now commonly done by a bulldozer, which levels or terraces the entire building site. It also involves covering the floor with concrete or, in the case of the most costly houses, putting in tile over concrete. Modern single-story houses often have covered porches, verandas, and sometimes parking areas for automobiles and motorcycles. The more expensive and prestigious versions tend to have all of these features, as well as complex hipped roofs with intersecting planes and sometimes archways. The styles are set by urban-based elites who have achieved success in government, politics, or business and who build lavish second or retirement houses in or near their natal villages. Simpler versions of such houses are built by middle-income villagers, including schoolteachers and government workers or others with salary incomes. In these cases the houses often take several years or more to complete, with work progressing or halting in relation to the availability of money to buy materials and pay workers.

The simplest versions of the contemporary wooden or cement block house built directly on the ground are smaller, rectangular houses, sometimes with attached kitchens or other rooms made of wood and thatch. Such houses usually have simple, two-sided roofs with gable ends. Since they are usually built by villagers who are dependent to some extent on subsistence farming, they will have drying platforms and storage sheds nearby. The construction of such houses also often goes on over a long period because of the costs involved in acquiring

FIG. 4.12. Simple, small, cement block, built-on-the-ground contemporary house under construction, Singai, Bau area, western Sarawak, 1998.

materials and doing the work in relation to farming or wage labor. They are typically built in front of or beside an existing dwelling, which will continue to be used after the completion of the new house. In the case of an extended or stem family, the new house may be occupied by the younger members while the parents continue to use the older one.

OBTAINING WOOD AND OTHER BUILDING MATERIALS

The relative cost of materials is partly a matter of location and access to wood. All village houses built by the Bidayuh and other groups make use of lumber. Houses built with wooden floors and sides as well as frames will use much more than those that have cement floors and cement block or brick walls. But the latter also have some wooden parts, usually a framework of posts and beams, as well as door and window frames. Wood for construction is sought at the time of a building project or in advance if possible. The accumulation of wood and other materials is a main factor in the pace at which building takes place. Houses can be seen throughout Bidayuh villages, in various states of completion, that have had little or no work done on them for months or years at a time because builders have run out of materials and do not have the money to buy more.

Because of its uses for house building and various

FIG. 4.13. New house (white stucco with blue pillars and trim), Gumbang, Bau area, western Sarawak, 1998.

other purposes, wood is often accumulated even if no building project is imminent. It is a rare house built above the ground that does not have some lumber stored underneath in anticipation of some eventual use. Lumber for construction will not be purchased unless a project is under way or about to be started, but any that can be obtained in other ways will generally be acquired as the opportunity arises. If a villager decides that a tree suitable for lumber needs to be cut down for some reason, he may hire someone to do it and cut it into lumber, or do this himself, and then store the wood for future use. Similarly, wood from buildings that have been torn down is used again if it is in suitable condition. In particular, *belian* posts, beams, and planks will be saved and reused, in

either their existing form or resawed into smaller pieces, much in the same way that a log is cut up.

At present, the entire process of both cutting down trees and making lumber is done with a gasoline-powered chain saw supplemented by the ubiquitous bush knife (*parang*). While all village men engaged in farming make use of chain saws in clearing land for swidden fields, the effort and skill required to cut a log into usable posts, beams, and boards that are straight and of a standard shape and size have made wood cutting a more specialized activity. Men who are skilled at cutting trees and turning them into ready-to-use lumber are often hired to perform this work.

In addition to recycling, village builders obtain wood

from a number of local sources. These vary, of course, depending on local circumstances, especially the location of the village, and include old-growth forest, fallow swidden forest and orchards (some of which resemble old-growth forest), and village lands.

Old-Growth Forest

Many of the trees that are highly valued for construction purposes grow in primary or old-growth forest or at least occur in desirable sizes in such forest. Villagers who live near old-growth forest depend on it as a source of lumber. Access to such forest, however, is limited in the case of most Bidayuh villages. For one thing, the forest may be too distant or too hard to reach, or it may grow on steep mountainsides, where cutting trees or making and moving lumber is difficult. Some Bidayuh villages, especially in the more remote areas, are located near old-growth forest, but in these cases there may be other restrictions. According to state law, residents are permitted to cut trees on interior forest lands for personal use but not for sale. However, this does not include land that has been reserved for other purposes, such as parks, or that has been allocated for logging, which in particular tends to restrict access to old-growth forest.

Villagers are not permitted to cut trees or take wood within the boundaries of logging concessions, even if these are in areas in which they have previously cut wood. In some areas of Sarawak (the upper Baram, for example) timber companies have had to offer villagers various commodities and services to get their agreement to build logging roads across their lands. These may include arrangements to supply timber and other building materials. Such agreements do not appear to have been made in the Bidayuh areas, where relations between villagers and loggers are often hostile. Logging operations, however, are a source of a certain amount of lumber in some places. In addition to those who may cut illegally, villagers who work in timber camps or who have friends or relatives who do may be permitted to salvage lumber from discarded logs. Further, once loggers have left an area, local villagers help themselves to scrap and to logs that had been used to build bridges for logging roads.

Fallow Swidden Areas, Orchards, and Village Lands

Tiboi'e (to use the Singai Bidayuh vernacular term, as will be done throughout the following sections), or land that has been used in recent decades for shifting dry rice cultivation, is also an important source of building materials. *Tiboi'e* that has been left fallow for a few years will yield small poles and in ten or fifteen years will have trees that are large enough to serve as posts in construction. Many kinds of trees desired for building either do not grow on *tiboi'e* land or, if they do, would not become large enough to be of much use before the area is cleared again. Several kinds of trees that are used for construction do, however, grow readily on such land. These include *pora (Cinnamum porrectum)*, a relatively soft and highly aromatic wood that is valued because it repels penetration by insects and is commonly used for siding, and *boyuh (Autocarpus* spp.), which provides bark as well as planks used for various purposes.

Forest orchards *(wong)* and village lands *(kupua)* also provide usable wood. There are various reasons for cutting trees in orchards or on village lands. Almost any kind of larger tree, including some palms, will yield timber or bark that is usable for some building purpose. This includes many of the fruit trees that attain great size. If a new house site has trees growing on it, these will be cut down, and if they are large enough, they will be cut into planks or framing timbers. Fruit trees, including durian, that are no longer bearing or that are growing in places where they might threaten houses will also be cut down and turned into lumber. This will also be done with illipe nut trees growing in orchard land that is to be converted to gardens. A villager needing lumber will therefore cast a critical eye on older fruit and nut trees, wondering if they might not be worth more as building material.

Losing Forests and Buying Wood and Other Materials

Village builders who cannot acquire enough wood from these various local sources have to buy lumber from a sawmill or hardware supplier. In this situation bricks or blocks and cement are usually cheaper than wood. Conversely, villagers who have access to sources of lumber will be somewhat more likely to build wooden houses. This is all the more so if they live in areas where access to construction supplies is more difficult and therefore costly. At one extreme are villages that are not connected to roads but do generally have access to forests. Here wooden houses are common; however, even in such villages builders will generally make some use of concrete for bathing and kitchen areas, although this may mean that heavy bags of cement (as well as metal roofing, windows, and doors) have to be carried by hand for long distances. At the other extreme are villages that have little access to local sources of wood but are connected by roads to nearby suppliers of building materials; in this case the inhabitants will mainly build cement block houses. Many villages are somewhere between these two extremes in terms of access to local sources of lumber, on the one hand, and to commercial suppliers of building materials, on the other. In such villages both wooden and stucco houses are common, although richer builders will choose the latter.

FARMHOUSES, FIELD HUTS, AND TRADITIONAL SINGLE VILLAGE HOUSES

While the Bidayuh are now commonly building modern urban or regional-style single houses, they continue to build farmhouses in traditional styles. Unlike the mod-

FIG. 4.14 (top). Cutting down a tree to make lumber, Singai, Bau area, western Sarawak, 1998.

FIG. 4.15 (bottom). Making lumber from logs salvaged from an abandoned area of a timber concession, Tringgus, Bau area, western Sarawak, 1998.

FIG. 4.16. Farmhouse and drying platform, Singai, Bau area, western Sarawak, 1998.

ern houses, which lack features that make them uniquely Bidayuh, the farmhouses are distinctive and therefore also have some ethnic symbolic value. Farmhouses (*bori omuh*) include the huts and houses built next to swidden or swamp rice fields, as well as those built near main houses and used for storage and for drying rice and other crops. Field houses are used for shelter from heavy rain and for resting or for longer stays during the harvest and when fields are located at longer distances from the village. The smallest and simplest of the *bori omuh* are huts with shed roofs and a front drying platform, all raised a meter or less above the ground. Constructed mainly of bamboo and covered with sago leaf thatch, such structures are sometimes open in the front and can be built in a short time.

Among villagers engaged in farming (as most are) and living in single houses, the practice of constructing separate, nearby farm buildings is common. In the case of villagers living in longhouses, processing and storage activities take place in the longhouse itself or in buildings that are often attached to it. This is also the case with the older styles of single houses, which have drying platforms, sometimes with attached sheds, as well as verandas at the front or side. In the case of newer houses—especially ones built directly on the ground—such facilities are commonly found only on detached buildings, including, sometimes, previous houses that have been kept for this purpose, as well as specially constructed ones.

Beyond their uses for shelter, processing, and storage, farmhouses built in traditional styles serve other social

FIG. 4.17. "Deer's head" farmhouse, Krokong, Bau area, western Sarawak, 1998.

and cultural purposes. Larger farmhouses with cooking facilities may be used to entertain or compensate those who have helped a family with planting or harvesting, as in the *pingiris* labor exchange. Some farmhouses also serve as second or recreational houses. Traditional farmhouses, in general, are desirable from a symbolic perspective. For Bidayuh who live in modern single houses that have little if any particular ethnic character, traditional farmhouses are a way of maintaining or reviving tradition in a rapidly changing world in which little of the old culture is believed to remain. This is particularly the case with the larger and more complicated versions of farmhouses. These include the *bori bak jourat* and the *pongau*, the former built in the southern Bau area, the latter in the north, specifically today in Singai.

The term "*bori bak jourat*" means "deer's head house" and is in reference to its appearance. Such houses have a two-sided roof, side walls that slope outward from the roof to the ground, and three roof-flap windows, one in the front above the door and one on each side. When these windows are raised into an open position the house is thought to resemble a deer's head in its front view. Such houses are constructed with a wood and bamboo framework and covered with sago leaf thatch. They have an internal hearth and a rear raised bench, as well as an open front veranda.

Pongau
In the past *pongau* were built in mountain villages as single dwellings in addition to longhouses, either because

FIG. 4.18 (above).
Pongau and its owner and
builder, Babai Met,
Singai, Bau area,
western Sarawak, 1999.

FIG. 4.19 (right).
Interior of a *pongau*,
Singai, Bau area,
western Sarawak, 1998.

some people preferred to live separately or because the steep and broken terrain permitted only a small longhouse that could not accommodate all families. *Pongau* are covered entirely with thatch and have a unique, bulging shape with a somewhat boatlike interior. The construction of these houses is now being revived in the villages below the mountains (to which all Singai Bidayuh have now moved), both as recreational second dwellings and as farmhouses. In early 1999 there were a half dozen *pongau* in various Singai villages, with several more in the planning.

Pongau are complex structures that are built in different sizes, depending on their purpose. The larger ones, which serve as second houses, are more or less the size of a Bidayuh longhouse apartment, which they resemble in some other respects as well. From front to back there is first an external veranda drying platform, then a narrow covered but open-sided porch with a door. Inside the door is a bathing area on one side of the passageway and a storage area on the other. Beyond these areas is the main room, with a kitchen and hearth at the front, then the living area, and, at the back, the raised sleeping platform with storage beneath. There is also, as in a longhouse apartment, a loft above that is reached by a small, notched-log ladder. *Pongau* that are built to be used as farmhouses also have external drying platforms, either on the front or at the side.

Like the deer's head house, *pongau* have a highly distinctive form. The side walls are quite different than those of most other buildings. The walls are not vertical but instead slope inward from the bottom to the top, so that the floor is substantially wider than the roof. The walls are formed by sloping posts set in the ground about a meter below the floor so that posts, floor, and roof have a blunt "A" shape when viewed from the front. In addition, the side walls are not horizontally straight but are instead bowed outward, so that the floor of the *pongau* is wider in the middle than at the front and rear ends—a feature that, along with the slope of the walls, gives the interior of the building the shape of the cabin of a boat. The side walls of a *pongau* also have the distinctive flap windows, which are hinged at the top and therefore open outward and upward from the bottom. As in the deer's head house, such a flap window is also built into the roof at the front so that when it is raised, it provides access through the door without it being necessary to stoop.

Pongau are constructed with a framework of numerous smaller posts and beams and diagonal braces, rafters, and joists, mainly fastened together by tying. Like the smaller farmhouses and field huts, both side walls and roofs are covered with palm thatch. Some recently built versions combine metal roofs with thatch walls. With their complex design, full-sized *pongau* are not hastily built houses. One constructed in 1998 by a skilled and experienced builder, working nearly every day with an assistant, required more than two months to complete, with palm thatch sheets that were purchased elsewhere.

CHAPTER FIVE TWO PATTERNS OF CHANGE

THE ARCHITECTURAL CHANGES that are taking place among the interior peoples of Borneo are similar in some respects to those occurring among tribal or small-scale societies throughout the world. Such peoples are generally modifying their traditional house forms in the direction of those of influential surrounding or outside groups or toward forms that reflect urban, regional, national, or broader styles. In many places people are of course severely affected by restrictions on access to traditional building materials, as well as by poverty. Many have no houses at all or must do with whatever forms of shelter they can find or create. Whether people do or do not have much choice in the matter, the changes that are occur-

FIG. 5.1. Abandoned Bidayuh longhouse section, Gayu Village, Padawan area, western Sarawak, 1994.

ring can be said to constitute architectural modernization, acculturation, or globalization. In Borneo it has
long been recognized that groups located nearer the
coast, where outside influences are oldest and strongest,
have generally altered their architecture to a greater extent than those in more remote areas of the interior.[1]

Patterns of change among longhouse-dwelling peoples in Borneo, however, have been more complicated
than this. Here change has occurred along two lines. One
of these is the abandonment of longhouses in favor of
separate family dwellings, and the other is the modernization of longhouses. The latter, moreover, is a matter

of many innovations in both materials and design, some
of which have been applied to existing longhouses as
well as to the construction of new ones.

THE ABANDONMENT OF LONGHOUSES

The abandonment of longhouses may be partial, in
which case the village consists of one or more longhouses and a number of individual houses, or it may be
complete. It may be abrupt, as when a longhouse is torn
down and not rebuilt, the households instead building
separate houses, which have perhaps by that time been

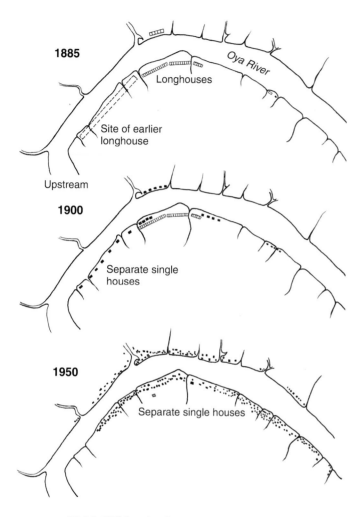

FIG. 5.2. Shift from longhouses to separate houses among the Melanau, Medong Village, Oya River, central Sarawak, 1885, 1900, and 1950.

completed or partially completed. In such instances the abandonment may be voluntary, or it may be the result of government demand or persuasion or a fire that has destroyed the longhouse. The abandonment may also be gradual, as when newly formed families build separate houses rather than establishing an apartment in a longhouse, or when resident families build separate houses where they spend most of their time, perhaps returning to their longhouse apartments only during festivals or for other special occasions. The *adat* of many groups contains rules intended to protect the integrity of the longhouse by prohibiting the abandonment or destruction of a longhouse apartment, but such rules do not seem to have prevented families from having houses elsewhere and spending most of their time in them. Many of the apartments of several of the remaining Bidayuh longhouses in the Bau area are vacant much of the time.

The extent to which longhouses have been kept or abandoned throughout Borneo has varied greatly. The move out of longhouses began early in some areas of Sarawak. Among the Melanau peoples in the coastal zone of central Sarawak, the shift was well under way in the nineteenth century and is now complete. In the 1830s the village of Oya on the lower Oya River consisted of both individual houses and fortress-longhouses raised high (up to thirty feet) above the ground on massive piles.[2] After this the great longhouses began to be dismantled and replaced, either by smaller longhouses, which still enabled nobles to live in a traditional manner, or by individual houses. By 1950 all of the families in Oya Village were living in individual houses spread in a ribbon along the river, and by the mid-1980s (according to my inquiries), longhouses were gone entirely from the entire lower Oya occupied by the Melanau (while retained, however, by the Iban further up the river) and probably from other regions of Melanau country as well. As of 1998 only one Melanau longhouse remained, having a few years before been designated as a special historical building.[3]

In addition to the Melanau, many of the Bidayuh and some of the Iban have also abandoned longhouses. As we have seen in the case of the Bidayuh, longhouses are gone in most of the villages in the Bau region, although several remain in Singai. Other than these and the large Selako longhouse at Pueh in the western corner of Sarawak, most of the existing Bidayuh longhouses are located in Padawan and Serian, especially in the deep interior areas near the Kalimantan border. Among other groups in Sarawak the pattern has varied. In the case of the Iban, the Sebuyau (known after the river whence they came), who migrated to Lundu and Kuching in far western Sarawak, initially built longhouses but eventually gave them up. Other Iban in downriver areas have partially abandoned longhouses, while most of those in the interior have retained them. In the case of the more northerly interior groups of Sarawak, most of the Kayan, Kenyah, and Kajang groups of the Baram and Balui River basins have kept longhouses. Farther still to the north or to the interior, the Lundayeh peoples have remained in longhouses in some instances and abandoned them in others, while the Kelabit appear to have kept them.

The shift from longhouses to individual houses has not entirely been a one-way process. In Sarawak, as well as in earlier periods in Kalimantan, nomadic groups that traditionally lived in single forest dwellings have moved into longhouses as a part of a broader process of settling into larger, more permanent villages and adopting cultivation. Where this has occurred, it has sometimes been with the encouragement and assistance of local longhouse-dwelling groups, who benefit from the increase in forest products the settled hunter-gatherers are able to provide in trade.[4] It has also sometimes occurred as a result of government persuasion and assistance. In any case, it has taken place in areas where longhouses have been retained by other groups and thus presented a model of an appropriate house by a dominant group.

The abandonment and the modernization of long-houses have tended to be alternative processes, not only in the case of specific villages, but also in that of ethnic communities or regions. That is, among groups or in areas where longhouses have been extensively retained, most of them have been modernized. Conversely, where the main tendency has been to abandon longhouses, modernization has been limited, even when new longhouses have been built. Such longhouses tend to preserve characteristics no longer found elsewhere.

This contrast can be seen in Sarawak in the difference between what has occurred among the Bidayuh in the Bau area, who have mainly abandoned longhouses, and among the Iban, Kenyah, Kayan, and Kajang groups of the interior, who have more often retained them. Among the Bidayuh of Bau the few remaining longhouses—including ones built or renovated relatively recently—retain the cooking hearth in the main room, a feature no longer found in the longhouses of the other groups. The contrast can also be seen on a much larger scale between what has generally occurred in Kalimantan, on the one hand, and in Sarawak, on the other. The modernization of those relatively few longhouses that have survived in Kalimantan has been both more recent and more limited than in Sarawak, where longhouses remain pervasive or common in many areas. The differences in what has occurred in Sarawak and Kalimantan can be seen more specifically among the Kenyah and Kayan, who dwell in Sarawak and in Kalimantan. To a large extent the Sarawak Kenyah and Kayan retain longhouses and have been modernizing them extensively for several decades or longer. Most Kenyah and Kayan in Kalimantan live in single houses, although some in the deep interior of East Kalimantan have kept longhouses. The limited and recent changes among those of the Apo Kayan have been noted recently by Timothy Jessup.[5] Here newer, Sarawak-style longhouses began to be built only in the early 1980s.

The same traditional orientation in longhouse design is also evident among the Taman and Maloh of the upper

FIG. 5.3. Bidayuh longhouse kitchen and hearth, still located in the customary place on the front wall of the inner apartment, Anah Rais, 1996.

Kapuas River in the interior of West Kalimantan. These groups customarily build large and massive longhouses raised high above the ground, and some have been renovated or newly built.[6] The renovated houses have some modern features, including covered entranceways and paint, but they have also preserved many older ones, including high foundations of log posts, notched-log entrance ladders, and (in some instances) lattice front walls. The newly constructed versions, including one under construction in 1994 at Eko Tambai on the Kapuas, are placed lower to the ground and have a lighter framework but otherwise also tend to conform to the traditional design.

Reasons for Abandoning Longhouses

Why have some groups abandoned longhouses while others have not? In the past it was sometimes assumed that people built longhouses mainly for defensive pur-

poses, and therefore once the threat of attack had been eliminated through pacification under colonial rule, they would abandon them. The survival of longhouses long after pacification made it apparent that while defense may have been a predominant consideration, it was not the only one, or people continued to find it an attractive or compelling way of life after it was no longer an essential one. At least, the shift to single houses was not an inevitable development.

The abandonment of longhouses, as well as a shift to more modestly constructed ones, has sometimes been attributed to a decline in access to forest resources, especially to mature trees of the right sort for posts and other crucial parts. Stephen Morris suggests that the Melanau began to abandon longhouses in part because the threat of raids by Iban had diminished with the establishment of control by the Brooke regime, and in part because supplies of *belian* timber had been depleted. He notes that traditional Melanau longhouses probably required between two and three hundred mature *belian* trees for posts, crossbeams, rafters, and floorboards. By the late nineteenth century *belian*, which had previously been plentiful in the swamp forests of Melanau country, had been depleted and was available only farther upriver in areas controlled by the Iban.[7]

A similar point has been made regarding the general absence of longhouses among the Ngaju Dayaks of the Mentayan River, on the opposite side of the island in present-day Central Kalimantan. Douglas Miles reports that although longhouses may never have been the only form of houses among the Ngaju of the Mentayan and other rivers, they were occasionally constructed in the past. He found one in the 1960s that had been built on massive ironwood posts and had ironwood floorboards, beams, and shingles. The construction of such a house was not a normal practice but rather the result of the effort and expenditure of several rich and influential men. But in general supplies of *belian* were no longer

FIG. 5.4. Kayan single house, Padua Village, Mendalam River, upper Kapuas area, West Kalimantan, 1994.

available at a near enough point to make the building of such longhouses feasible.[8]

Whatever the importance of a decline in the availability of ironwood in these instances, it has probably not been generally responsible for the abandonment of longhouses. While ironwood is valued enormously everywhere in Borneo for its great strength and endurance, longhouses, including ones using massive construction, are also built with other strong and decay-resistant woods in areas where it is lacking. This is the case in the Apo Kayan plateau, where *belian* is less common than in the lowlands. Here, however, builders circa 1970 reported building more modest longhouses than they had in earlier years owing to difficulties in obtaining

trees for posts and other lumber of the size and quality traditionally used in massive construction.[9] Beyond the availability of ironwood in particular, access to timber with which to build longhouses has probably generally influenced construction practices but not the abandonment of longhouses altogether. The shift to lighter frames of sawn lumber, which is now complete in Sarawak at least, means that the timber and other materials required for longhouses differ little from those of individual houses.

The abandonment of longhouses has also been linked to religious conversion and related influences. The Melanau abandoned longhouses at a time when they were converting to Islam or (to a more limited extent)

FIG. 5.5. Taman longhouse with statues and raised entranceway to the left, Melapi, upper Kapuas River, West Kalimantan, 1994.

Christianity, the former reflecting a long period of Malay influence in the coastal region. Longhouses are not proscribed or discouraged by Islam, but for the Melanau individual houses were a part of a broader shift to a coastal Muslim or Melayu way of life. European missionaries were often against longhouses because they assumed that they were the main basis of the traditional ways of pagan life, including the practice of many ceremonies, the observation of taboos, and the consumption of large quantities of alcohol during festivals. In some instances they also supposed that longhouse life was immoral because premarital sexual activity was often a normal part of courtship and marriage and because the sleeping arrangements of traditional longhouse apartments did not allow for marital activities to be carried out in much privacy from others, including children.

With or without the advice or admonishment of missionaries, Christian converts among the Bidayuh have often abandoned longhouses, in part because of disputes over the observation of traditional ritual practices and taboos, some of which are covered by the *adat*, but to which Christians no longer want to adhere. As a result of the disputes, a village often divides, with the Christians leaving the longhouse and building individual houses, either in the same vicinity or in a new location. In some such instances the remaining non-Christians also convert and move into individual houses. The process of conversion and abandonment has been reported elsewhere,[10] but abandonment appears to have been less common where conversion has occurred *en masse*. In such instances the longhouse community is not faced with the problem of reconciling the opposing ritual

FIG. 5.6. Taman longhouse being built at Eko Tambai Village, upper Kapuas River, West Kalimantan, 1994.

practices and ideologies of people who live in close proximity. In some cases, such as the Mualang, an Ibanic group in West Kalimantan, Christian converts built separate longhouses before moving into single houses.[11] In any case, Christianity is by no means entirely associated with single houses, and large numbers of Christian groups in Sarawak continue to live in longhouses, sometimes alongside *adat* followers, not to mention alongside mixed families, in which the younger members have converted while the older ones have not.

The abandonment of longhouses has sometimes been associated with the migration that has taken place under colonial and postcolonial rule. Along with the numerous other groups located along rivers in central and northern Sarawak and adjacent areas of Kalimantan, the Kayan and Kenyah have moved back and forth in various directions, but in recent decades the main pattern of movement has been from more remote upriver areas, especially ones above extensive rapids, to less remote ones nearer to the coast and the main towns.[12] In both countries the relocation of villages has often been carried out at the initiative of the state, for reasons noted below. In any case, groups that formerly lived in longhouses have in some instances relocated into single dwellings. As with conversion to Christianity, however, while shifts from both hilltop and upriver areas have sometimes involved the abandonment of longhouses, this has not necessarily occurred. In Sarawak at least, the Kenyah, Kayan, and Kajang groups that have relocated downstream have generally reestablished longhouses. Conversely, those groups—including the Melanau, some of the Iban, and many of the Bidayuh—who have moved from longhouses to individual dwellings have often done so at or near the same location rather than because of migration to a new area.

State Intervention and the Abandonment of Longhouses in Sarawak and Kalimantan

The question of why some groups have abandoned longhouses while others have retained them can also be approached by looking at the areas in which each development has been predominant, and here the contrast between Sarawak and Kalimantan is significant. These two national divisions share a common border that runs through much of Borneo on a roughly west-east axis and therefore divides many of the principal groups of the northern part of the island. These include the various Bidayuh and the Ibanic peoples (Iban, Kantu, Mualang) to the west and the Kenyah, Kayan, and other related groups to the east. The groups on both sides of the border have much in common. Most are swidden cultivators of hill rice and other subsistence crops, supplemented by hunting and gathering and, more recently, by pepper, rubber, and other cash crops and by wage labor in rural logging camps and in towns. Most have also been subject to many of the same globalizing tendencies and acculturative influences, including those of mission Christianity.

Yet the architectural differences between the two countries are striking. While longhouses in Sarawak have been abandoned by some groups, they continue to be the main form of housing throughout large areas of the interior. In Kalimantan, on the other hand, longhouses have generally been abandoned.[13] In many or most areas of Kalimantan there are few or no longhouses. Bernard Sellato reports recently, for example, that in Kalteng (Kalimantan Tengah, or Central Kalimantan, in the far south of Borneo) only three longhouses remain among the Ngaju and Ot Danum.[14] It is true that among the Ngaju, longhouses may never have

been very common to begin with. This is not so in the case of other areas, including present-day Kalimantan Barat (Kalbar, or West Kalimantan) and Kalimantan Timor (Kaltim, or East Kalimantan). In these areas longhouses were once pervasive but are now largely gone. The differences between what has occurred in Sarawak and Kalimantan suggest that while the depletion of forest resources, religious conversion, migration, and economic improvement all may play a role in the retention or abandonment of longhouses, the main influence lies elsewhere—specifically in the realm of state intervention.

Throughout Borneo generally state intervention began with colonial rule (including the Brooke regime in Sarawak). Colonial Europeans often found various features of longhouses to be objectionable, as they did also some of the characteristics of native houses elsewhere in Southeast Asia.[15] Longhouses were sometimes regarded as dirty, liable to destruction by fire, and promoting a backward, communal way of life. The extent to which colonial authorities intervened to promote the abandonment of longhouses is another matter. For one thing, longhouses had certain advantages for colonial administrators. They made it easier to keep track of people and their activities, including the number of doors (households) in each village and (in Sarawak, at least) the number of enemy skulls kept, for these were commonly displayed in a central place in the veranda of the longhouse. For another, there was some understanding that the more the traditional societies were threatened or destabilized, the greater the risk of resistance or rebellion.

In Sarawak the Brooke government—which ruled from 1841 to 1941 under three "White Rajahs"—suppressed head-hunting and warfare and sometimes sought to promote peaceful relations among different groups but otherwise did little to promote modernization in most areas of native life and, if anything, favored traditional ways and distrusted development.[16] It is true that especially in the nineteenth century the Brooke government frequently attacked and burned the longhouses of recalcitrant Iban. These were acts of retribution, however, intended as punishment for engaging in head-hunting or other activities deemed illegal, rather than efforts at development aimed at forcing longhouse dwellers into a different form of housing. Although the second raja, Charles Brooke, is said to have regarded longhouses as an impediment to progress, he made no effort to promote their abandonment.[17] During the subsequent rule of Vyner Brooke, the last of the three rajas, the government did attempt to regulate Iban architectural practices by requiring that every longhouse include at least ten doors (that is, household apartments). But this rule, which was intended to help prevent "illegal" migration and to facilitate government administration, would appear to have, if anything, forbidden single houses, as well as the small, scattered longhouses that were deemed to be the problem.[18]

The more orthodox British colonial government that assumed control of Sarawak in 1946 was critical of earlier Brooke policies because while leaving interior peoples alone, they did little to prepare them for life in the twentieth century or eventual self-rule. While making limited efforts at development, this government again, however, did little to alter architectural or village arrangements beyond those already noted. At least in the case of the Iban, the breakup of longhouses into separate family dwellings was opposed in some areas as against the best interests of the people as well as the government.[19]

The Dutch in Kalimantan saw little economic potential in the interior and were drawn into it somewhat later than was the Brooke state to the north. Once they were there, they moved more rapidly than did the Brooke raj in Sarawak and intervened more directly in native life, among other things favoring Malay rulers and expanding their authority over the Dayaks.[20] The main concerns, however, appear to have been similar to those in Sara-

wak: the establishment of minimal administrative authority and the elimination of warfare, head-hunting, slavery, and (where it occurred) human sacrifice. Villages were moved in some areas to create buffers between enemy groups and to protect the inhabitants from head-hunting raids, especially by the Iban from Sarawak.[21] Several scholars who have noted the anti-longhouse policies of the postcolonial republican Indonesian government (discussed below) have remarked that these reflect a continuation of policies begun by the Dutch, but they do not mention any specific examples.[22] The scientific traveler Carl Lumholtz reported early in the twentieth century that longhouses were not being built in southern Borneo and suggested that this might be explained by the fact that the Dutch colonial government did not encourage it.[23]

More recently, Victor King's discussion of change among the Maloh indicates that Dutch efforts to eliminate slavery and to otherwise undermine the power of the aristocracy may have influenced the design of longhouses in the direction of less massive forms and perhaps encouraged a shift to individual houses, a process furthered by conversion to Christianity.[24] By the time of King's fieldwork in 1971, the Maloh on several rivers in the upper Kapuas basin had abandoned longhouses, but this was several decades after the end of colonial rule, and King does not attribute the abandonment directly to Dutch policy or practice. Nor does Herbert Whittier's brief account of the effects of colonial rule in the Apo Kayan in East Kalimantan suggest that longhouse building practices were strongly affected by Dutch interference in other areas of Kenyah social life.[25] At the time of his fieldwork in 1970, the Kenyah told Whittier that they were no longer building the sort of longhouses that they had in the past. However, the main reasons for this—the depletion of old-growth forest and therefore the decline in the availability of the large trees needed for massive construction, as well as large-scale migration to regions

FIG. 5.7. New longhouse built by the government for Balui River communities displaced by the Bakun Hydroelectric Dam, Sungai Asap, Belaga, central Sarawak, 1998.

nearer the coast—had little direct relation to colonial policy.

In the postcolonial period, government involvement in indigenous life, which in some ways built upon the changes and disruptions brought by the earlier colonial regimes, has increased greatly—and here there have been major differences in the two countries. In Sarawak the government, which has ruled the country as a Malaysian state since 1963, has been committed to rapid development and has massively intervened in native society and culture in many ways not even contemplated by earlier regimes. In regard to housing, however, while it has been concerned with improvements in sanitation and in reducing the danger of fires and while it has imposed the resettlement of villages for various reasons, it has often supported longhouses.

To begin with, longhouses are officially viewed as community buildings rather than as an assemblage of private apartments. This means that they are eligible for financial assistance for construction or renovation that is not available for separate dwellings. A longhouse community may be given materials for a new roof or aid in rebuilding after a fire. Such assistance is regarded in the same way as the support provided for the construction of *balai raya* (community halls) or other public buildings, generators, gravity-fed water supply fixtures, village roads, or other facilities, for which all villages may be eligible and for which villagers routinely request assistance. At present such assistance is generally viewed as highly politicized—that is, it is dealt with through the office of the local elected representative and is therefore based on the degree of support from the village in the last election. Several years ago one of the remaining longhouses in the Bidayuh village of Attas in Singai was re-

FIG. 5.8. Penan Lusong longhouse, Long Linau, upper Balui area, Belaga, central Sarawak, 1992.

built with funds supplied by the government, although it remains nearly empty most of the time, for most of the owners also own separate dwellings.

In some instances the Sarawak government constructs longhouses for villagers. This was done when many Iban villages were relocated with the construction of the Batang Ai Hydroelectric Dam and Reservoir in the early 1980s, and it is currently being done in relation to the construction of the large Bakun Hydroelectric Dam on the Balui River in Belaga, a project that involves the resettlement of fifteen mainly large, and mostly Kayan, villages. In both instances the relocated villagers have had to purchase their apartments in the new longhouses that the government has had designed and constructed, and in both instances they have been dissatisfied with resettlement in general and with their new longhouses and their locations in particular. But such government prac-

tices indicate that longhouses are officially regarded as the correct dwelling for villagers who want them.

This can be seen also in the occasional government practice of building or providing materials for longhouses for the Penan and Ukit nomadic hunting and gathering peoples, who had formerly lived in single, temporary dwellings. This practice was also sometimes followed in Kalimantan before the government began to pursue its anti-longhouse policy.[26] In both areas it has involved the assumption that the longhouse is the appropriate form of dwelling in the area and that progress for the hunting and gathering nomads involves emulating the lifeways of the settled peoples and therefore living in longhouses and becoming farmers.

Developments in postcolonial Kalimantan have been very different from those in Sarawak. Here official Indonesian attitudes toward longhouses and other Dayak

FIG. 5.9. *Balai adat* (community hall) at Datah Bilang Village, middle Mahakam River, East Kalimantan, 1994.

architectural arrangements reflect a somewhat ambivalent and contradictory view of traditional indigenous lifeways. On the one hand, there is positive ideological respect for cultural diversity and pride in the architectural achievements of some groups—an attitude that has been reinforced in recent years by tourism. On the other hand, there is the view that the Dayak peoples are backward and inferior to the old civilized societies, especially the Javanese, who have dominated the civilian and military administrations. There is also the view that the entire country must be unified, nationalized, and moved forward and that development and order must be imposed from the center to the periphery.[27]

As a part of its efforts to control, administer, and modernize Dayak societies, the republican Indonesian government eventually began to oppose longhouses. This effort started or gained force in the late 1960s as an initiative of the New Order regime. While the government in some instances recognized the value of the longhouse gallery as a public meeting hall and village cultural center, it sought to meet this need instead through the construction of a separate *rumah desa*, or village hall.[28] Village halls (such as the one at the resettled Kenyah village of Datah Bilang on the middle Mahakam, which was officially opened by President Suharto) could be built in a traditional manner and embellished with traditional carvings and paintings, but they would also fit provincial architectural trends.[29]

The anti-longhouse efforts of the New Order government were based partly on various objections to the buildings themselves that had sometimes been made by earlier colonial authorities (e.g., they were unsanitary and more liable to destruction by fire than separate individual family houses). Longhouses were therefore associated with a primitive and communal way of life that was deemed objectionable both because it held back the individual initiative that was necessary for economic progress and because it had an aura of subversion in a period of intense anti-communism.[30] Such views of longhouses have also been attributed to the ethnic prejudices of government officials from other areas, especially Java, where individual families live in separate houses that are built directly on the ground.[31]

The purge of longhouses was part of a broader policy of forced modernization, an effort to promote or impose development among what were defined as isolated or primitive populations.[32] Generally referred to as "suku terasing," such peoples were encouraged or required to give up animistic beliefs and practices for a monotheistic religion, to bury the dead in the ground rather than placing them in above-ground wooden tombs, to wear more clothing, to be educated and taught family planning, to abandon wasteful swidden cultivation, and, in some instances, to be regrouped into new villages or Respen (an acronym for "Resetelmen Penduduk," or the resettlement of inhabitants) that were less remote and more concentrated.[33]

The anti-longhouse policies of the New Order government were not uniform or, if so, not uniformly applied, for longhouses have survived in parts of the interior. A journalist's account of the anti-longhouse campaign in West Kalimantan as of 1978 noted that in the kabupaten (district) of Sanggau in the central Kapuas, only 8 of 158 villages that had longhouses a few years be-fore still had them.[34] The larger claim made—that only a handful of longhouses remained in the entire province of West Kalimantan—almost certainly underestimates the number that continued to exist in upriver areas. In some instances the abandonment of longhouses was a matter of adamant insistence by local camat (subdistrict officers), backed by police or military force. In others it was more a question of persuasion.[35] In particular, communities that moved to new areas or were regrouped or resettled at government initiative into Respen villages appear to have had little choice but to build single-family dwellings.[36] In some places in West Kalimantan at least, villages were permitted to retain existing longhouses but not to build new ones.[37] In areas in which villagers were in the habit of building massive longhouses and living in them for a long time, the buildings sometimes survived. This is the case, for example, among the Taman, who have kept or restored some of their older longhouses and also built new ones. In general, longhouses seem to have survived, especially in areas remote from centers of administrative power, including the upper Kapuas region in West Kalimantan and the Apo Kayan in East Kalimantan.

Beyond such differences, some groups appear to have been less receptive than others to government efforts to eliminate longhouses. As might be expected, the independent-minded Iban were among those inclined to resist or ignore state efforts to promote the breakup of longhouses, though, again, resistance to government initiatives varied from one region or district to another. According to a recent report by Reed Wadley and Fredrik Kuyah, based on detailed demographic information in the northern central region of West Kalimantan, anti-longhouse efforts in Nanga Kantut District succeeded in getting some villages to give up longhouses, while those in Batang Lupar District failed to do so.[38] As of the late 1990s the great majority of the approximately fourteen thousand Iban in these and other districts were living in longhouses rather than single houses, and in Batang

Lupar, all of them were. Wadley and Kuyah are, however, uncertain about the extent to which the current predominance of longhouses reflects earlier resistence to government longhouse initiatives or a more recent return to longhouses as a result of a subsequent abandonment or reversal of government policies. In either case, the current commitment to longhouses of the Iban in West Kalimantan appears to be comparable to that of their much more numerous upriver counterparts in Sarawak.

The shift in Indonesian government attitudes and policies that was present by the 1990s in Kalimantan was motivated in part by the perception that longhouses could be valuable tourist attractions, a matter to be dealt with in the following chapter. In any case, the newer Indonesian government view is closer to the long-standing, more positive and supportive position of the Sarawak state government. That is, rather than seeking the abandonment of longhouses as a backward and hazardous form of housing, the more recent policy in Kalimantan has been to encourage longhouse dwellers to make improvements—especially the building of separate, semidetached kitchens in order to reduce the likelihood of an entire longhouse being destroyed by the spread of a kitchen fire. Unfortunately, however, the newer government policies in Kalimantan appear to have come too late to reverse the abandonment of longhouses that resulted from the earlier, negative approach throughout many or most regions. In addition, Wadley and Kuyah note some tendency among younger Kalimantan Iban to build separate dwellings near to longhouses instead of establishing household apartments within them—a trend they attribute to a desire both to be free of some of the ritual restrictions of longhouse residence (such as the requirement that kitchen hearths not be without fires for more than three days) and to be modern and therefore follow regional housing styles.[39] Such a tendency is also present in Sarawak, especially among downriver Iban, as well as among some other groups.

THE MODERNIZATION OF LONGHOUSES

The other pattern of architectural change in the interior of Borneo has been the modernization of longhouses. Observers writing about Bornean architectural practices have sometimes noted changes in the size, durability, massiveness, and design of longhouses over time—differences between older versions and those constructed more recently. This has not, however, been a uniform process. Instead, there have again been several trends of change, depending in part on the building traditions of the group concerned.

In the case of groups that customarily build smaller, less massive longhouses, the perceived trend has been toward larger or more substantially constructed ones. Such observations have been made about various Ibanic groups, including the Iban of Sarawak and the Kantu' of the upper Kapuas in West Kalimantan.[40] The explanation is that as these peoples became less mobile and more prosperous with the adoption of the cash crops of rubber and pepper, they began to build larger and more permanent longhouses.

Among groups that traditionally built larger and more massive longhouses, some opposite changes have been noted. Some Kenyah, Kayan, and Kajang builders told observers that their newer longhouses were no match for their older ones, in some instances because timber of the size and type formerly used was no longer available.[41] Also, with the cessation of warfare and headhunting, the need for building fortified longhouses high above the ground disappeared. Changes in social organization have also had an effect in some instances among the builders of once great longhouses. According to Victor King, the elimination of hereditary slavery and the decline of the power and authority of chiefs and other aristocrats over commoners diminished a community's ability to mobilize the labor formerly associated with massive building.[42] The traditional architectural markers of social status and authority characteristic of the hierarchical groups have also declined for the same reason, although they have not yet disappeared. Among the Kenyah of the Apo Kayan (as noted above), the centrally located apartments of the chief and other aristocrats were traditionally larger and higher than those of commoners and slaves or former slaves. While the apartments and galleries of chiefs continued to be larger, in part for utilitarian reasons, their roofs no longer rose above the others, with the result that the vertical dimensions of longhouses were reduced.

Insofar as it is reasonable to generalize from these various observations, there has been some convergence toward a more common longhouse form among the groups that have retained longhouses as the main house type—larger and more solidly constructed than those traditionally built by the Iban and Bidayuh, but less massively built than those formerly put up by the Kayan, Kenyah, and Kajang groups. There has also been a general trend toward larger longhouse apartments and other changes, to be discussed in more detail below.

As with the shift to individual houses, changes in longhouses began in the hilir, or downriver areas. By the 1920s and perhaps earlier, the Iban of the lower Saribas (an early region of outside contact and local innovation) had begun to build larger and more permanent longhouses, with more massive ironwood posts, beams, and wide plank floors.[43] Such buildings were similar in these respects to the traditional longhouses of the Melanau, Kenyah, and Kayan. By around 1940, Saribas longhouses had also incorporated other more distinctly modern innovations, including machine-sawn lumber, new doors, and glass windows: "The wealthy Iban of the Betong District," Edmund Leach wrote at the time, "have converted their former ramshackle bamboo sheds into plank built palaces with panelled walls, glass windows, and modern kitchens."[44]

The modernization of longhouses has been a matter of both materials and design. Modernization also involves new construction techniques, tools, and machinery, especially the chain saw and, more recently (and much more selectively), even earthmoving equipment to level building sites. Modernization involves existing longhouses as well as newly built ones, especially insofar as this involves the substitution of new types of building materials for traditional ones. New roofing or siding, for example, can easily be adapted to an older longhouse, as can also some extensions. More radical forms of modernization, however, usually involve new construction. Indeed, the desire to have a modern longhouse is a common motive for rebuilding.

New Materials

The modernization of longhouse materials involves the substitution of purchased materials manufactured elsewhere for ones that were formerly made or obtained locally. In the past, as noted, longhouses and other buildings were made entirely from wood and other materials gotten from the forests and farms. While builders still rely on local sources—in some areas much more so than in others—longhouses now incorporate many things that have been made elsewhere, a development encouraged in some areas by roads and in others by the advent of large cargo boats that ply the major rivers. The use of purchased materials has also been enhanced by the spread of the cultivation of rubber, pepper, and other cash crops and by employment in downriver areas and in logging operations in the interior. In Sarawak modern building materials are sometimes provided for longhouses by the government and occasionally by logging companies in return for permission to construct logging roads across their lands. The new materials most commonly used include corrugated, galvanized metal sheets, sawed lumber, modern-style doors (at least in the interior of Borneo), glazed windows, and cement.

As perhaps everywhere in the developing world, the

FIG. 5.10. Rumah Engkara, two-story Iban longhouse built of concrete block, finished with stucco, and decorated with false brickwork; Lubok Antu area, western Sarawak, 1999.

modern material that has been most widely used both in refurbishing existing longhouses and in building new ones is galvanized and corrugated metal sheets, generally know in Sarawak as *zin'*. In Sarawak most older longhouses have by now been partly or entirely recovered with metal roofs. Traditional siding in the form of planks, lattice, thatch, bark, or sheets of split bamboo has also been replaced by corrugated metal sheets, although to a lesser extent than roofs. While *zin'* may at one time have been substituted for thatch or shingles because of its prestige as a modern material, it is chosen now for utilitarian reasons, and its drawbacks are well known (it is hot when the sun shines and noisy when it rains). In Kalimantan the shift to galvanized metal roofing has not taken place to a comparable extent. Here ironwood shingles are still being produced in large quantities and are therefore much cheaper, both in absolute terms and relative to other materials, than in Malaysian Borneo. Shingles are still commonly used in Kalimantan both in reroofing older longhouses and (to the extent that this is being done) constructing new ones.

The use of sawed lumber and manufactured windows has also become widespread. While in the past longhouses made relatively little or no use of sawed lumber, most wooden parts of more recently built ones, except for some posts, take the form of sawed boards and framing timbers. The increased use of sawed lumber is associated especially with the spread of the chain saw throughout the interior, for which the primary use is cutting forest for swidden cultivation. While in some instances such lumber is obtained from sawmills or lumberyards, most of it is manufactured by villagers themselves. Skilled lumber makers using hand-held chain saws are able to produce regularly dimensioned boards for siding and flooring, as well as framing timbers. Although sometimes lumber made by chain saw is taken to a lumber mill to be planed smooth, it is commonly used as it is.

The use of sawed framing lumber in the construction of walls simplifies the installation of modern doors and manufactured glazed windows. Large modern doors, which are usually of frame-and-panel construction, appear to have everywhere replaced the smaller, often carved, traditional slab doors. Such doors are used in the entranceways to the inner apartments from the veranda and sometimes to other rooms and to the back areas. Modern doors are usually purchased from specialists who operate cabinet shops in towns or rural areas or from urban suppliers. Manufactured windows, usually in the form of movable glass louvers in steel frames, have also replaced the traditional roof-flap windows used by some groups. In modernized longhouses such windows are built into outside walls. More recently and still less commonly, they have also been incorporated into the front walls that separate the interior apartments from the gallery. Louvered glass windows are widely available from building material suppliers.

In Sarawak cement, paint, and plywood paneling is now also common. Cement is widely used in building activities. Even in remote areas, where heavy sacks of cement (and sometimes sand) have to be transported by river or carried by land over steep trails, it is widely used

FIG. 5.11. Serving rice wine to guests on the cement floor of the gallery of Rumah Engkara, Lubok Antu area, western Sarawak, 1999.

in various ways—for example, in concrete walkways and steps in outside areas as a substitute for bamboo or wood. Cement is also extensively used in modernized longhouses as ground-level flooring for two-story buildings and for bathrooms and kitchens. Kiln-fired bricks or concrete blocks are used in longhouse construction but more selectively. These materials are used especially in areas where suppliers are near, transport by river or road is relatively easy, and adequate supplies of wood are not available. Brick or block may be used to construct kitchen additions or, less often, entire longhouses. While selectively applied, paint and plywood paneling are also now commonly used as finish materials in modern longhouses. Paint is used on either or both interior and exterior walls. Manufactured paneling, while less common than paint, is used to cover interior walls and ceilings.

New Longhouses and New Designs
Some modern innovations can be incorporated into existing longhouses while others can only be used in newly

FIG. 5.12 (above). Modern Berawan two-story longhouse at Long Terawan in which the lower story has concrete floors and the inner gallery has been replaced by a narrow covered walkway; Tutuh River, lower Baram area, northern Sarawak, 1998.

FIG. 5.13 (left). Modern two-story Iban longhouse with road access; Rumah Gensurai, Layar (upper Saribas) River, Betong area, western Sarawak, 1993.

FIG. 5.14 (below). Iban longhouse dwellers sitting in the gallery of the longhouse at Rantau Kembayan Manis, watching a television built into the inner wall; Engkari River, Lubok Antu area, western Sarawak, 1999.

FIG. 5.15. Iban longhouse on the Ai River, otherwise traditionally constructed but with a small kitchen section behind the main longhouse; Lubok Antu area, western Sarawak, 1979.

built longhouses. Older longhouses can be modernized, for example, by replacing worn out palm thatch *attap* or wooden shingles with corrugated, zinc-coated steel sheets or some other type of metal roofing. Traditional siding in the form of lattice, thatch, bark, or sheets of split bamboo can also be easily replaced by corrugated metal sheets or sawn boards—and this has been done extensively, though more commonly for a longer period in Sarawak than in Kalimantan. In addition, modern windows and doors can be added to existing buildings, as can electrical wiring (usually connecting to village generators) and indoor plumbing (usually connected to local gravity-fed water supplies)—all innovations found in many or most longhouses throughout Sarawak at least.

Beyond such changes, older longhouses are often modified through lateral additions. The most important of these is the attached or semi-attached kitchen (*dapur*). All earlier descriptions and diagrams of longhouses throughout Borneo show the main fireplace and cooking area to be in the inner, family apartment, usually next to the front wall. While in Sarawak this arrangement can still be seen in some existing Bidayuh longhouses, for the most part kitchens have been relocated to a separate, much larger back area. Such separate kitchens are often built as attached structures, sometimes with the floor raised to the same level as the main room and sometimes at ground level. They are sometimes covered with a one-sided roof but more commonly a two-sided one, in

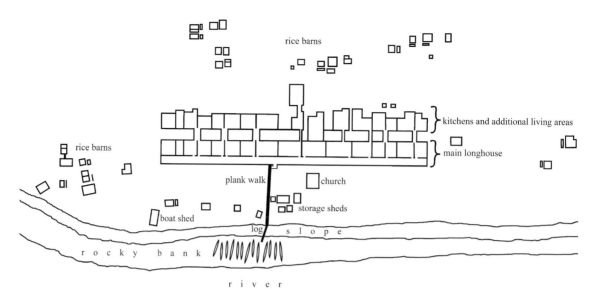

FIG. 5.16. Plan of Long Selatong Lepo Ga', a Kenyah longhouse on the upper Baram River, northern Sarawak, late 1970s; the traditional section was built last and the kitchen extensions first.

which case the profile of the longhouse roof takes the form of an asymmetrical "M." Less often the back side of the main longhouse roof is extended and its pitch decreased to cover the kitchen and eating area, in which case the floor is at ground level. However it is done, the addition of a rear kitchen, which sometimes includes other rooms as well, usually adds a great deal of interior space to a longhouse apartment.

Kitchen extensions are also included in newly built longhouses. In this case they are often built before the main part of a new longhouse is erected. This is done in part as a solution to the problem of where to live while a new longhouse is being built, a process that at present may take several years as materials are gathered and prepared before the final construction. If, as increasingly occurs, a new longhouse is to be built on or very close to the location of an old one, it cannot be begun until the existing building has been torn down. In this case (or if the old longhouse has burned, as also occurs) there are two common practices. One is to build a temporary long-

house while the more permanent one is built nearby. The other is to construct the *dapur* first and use it as a general living place until the main longhouse is finished. Such buildings are begun before the old longhouse is demolished. The extensions are built more or less evenly apart and in the same order as the longhouse apartments will be built, but they can vary in size and shape. Once the new longhouse is finished, the *dapur* remains as such, attached to the main part of the longhouse apartment by a platform, part of which is usually covered over as a walkway and part of which is left open as a drying area. Because such kitchen buildings are commonly used as the main residence for several years or more, they are often large and divided into rooms for sleeping as well as cooking and eating. Further, once the main apartment has been completed, these rooms may continue to be used for some of the same purposes, especially if the family is a large and extended. The back kitchen area usually also contains a bathing area and toilet.

While newer roofing and siding materials, modern

doors and windows, and separate kitchen areas can be incorporated into either existing longhouses or new ones, other innovations can be included only in new or entirely rebuilt ones. The latter include placing the longhouse closer to the ground or (as will be explained below) directly on the ground and adding a second story. In the past longhouses were raised several meters or more above the ground especially for defense, a motive that is no longer relevant. In many instances longhouses are built several meters above ground level, but this is usually so that the lower area can be walled in and a two-story building eventually created. This practice, which is often done in stages, usually requires two innovations that have been common in Sarawak in the last several decades. One of these is grading the site for the longhouse with a bulldozer—usually brought in by river from a nearby logging camp; the other is putting in a cement slab on the ground floor. Two-story longhouses can also be built all at once and with the lower story raised above the ground; in this case the ground need not be leveled, and a wooden floor is used instead of a concrete one. In either case, when a two-story longhouse is created, the lower floor becomes the main living and working area, while the upper one is converted to sleeping rooms. Such two-story longhouse apartments, which also usually have an attached or semidetached kitchen, are often very large, and they can be (and often are) made even larger with front additions that involve extending the gallery area under a shed roof.

Modernization and Improvement

As longhouse dwellers readily point out, the modernization of longhouses should not be simply equated in all respects with their improvement. The older practice of raising longhouses several meters or more above the ground, while perhaps done primarily for defense, also had other benefits, including enhancing the circulation of air. Floors made of split bamboo or loosely joined boards, walls made of bark or split and flattened bamboo, and roofs made of thatch or shingles similarly enhance the circulation of air to a greater extent than do more tightly assembled modern materials. In particular, the corrugated metal roofs that are now common (in Sarawak almost ubiquitous) collect heat and reduce the movement of air in buildings, making them very hot throughout the day.

While the redesign of longhouses has been promoted by governments since colonial rule, in part as a matter of health and safety, the changes appear to have had mixed results. The traditional location of the main fireplace/cooking area in the interior of the apartment, along with other fireplaces in the covered gallery, came to be regarded as a cause of the fires that would often destroy entire longhouses. However, the smoke from the fireplace fires, which were often kept burning or smoldering, also helped preserve the wood or thatch roofs from infestation by insects. Such smoke also keeps mosquitoes away, and some longhouse dwellers now resort to smudging for this reason. The elimination of all or most smoke from the interior of the main part of the longhouse, combined with the lowering of the building above the ground, has thus increased exposure to disease-bearing mosquitoes that fly near the ground. Nor has the danger of fire been eliminated, for many longhouses continue to burn—perhaps because the added safety of detached kitchens has been offset by locally installed electrical wiring attached to village generators. Although government officials and other visitors are sometimes appalled by dirty longhouses, the refuse that may accumulate under and around longhouses can be present to an equal extent in villages composed of single dwellings; conversely, longhouses can be and generally are kept clean, although the shift from traditional organic to non-biodegradable packaging (especially plastic bags) has increased the amount of trash.

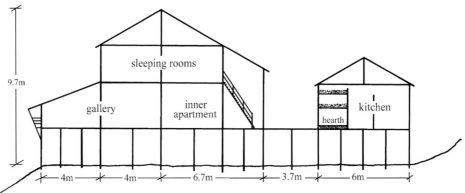

FIG. 5.17 (top). Modern Kenyah longhouse showing the expanded gallery of the chief's quarters, built with a new form of roof design; Long Luyang, Tinjar River, northern Sarawak, 1987.

FIG. 5.18 (bottom). Section drawing of Uma Juman, Long Dupah, Balui River, 1982.

The Modernization of Longhouses on the Balui

The villages on the Balui (the upper Rajang) provide many examples of how far the modernization of longhouses has been carried in some areas. The architecture and lifeways of the Kayan, Kenyah, Kajang, Penan, and other groups of the middle reaches of the Balui have been extensively documented, especially over the last few decades, in anticipation of the large Bakun Dam project. Studies of the transformations of longhouse communities of the Balui were begun in the early 1980s by the Sarawak Museum and other branches of the state government. These include an early survey of longhouse architecture,[45] as well as ethnographic studies of particular communities that included longhouse design and organization.[46] More recently the architecture of fifteen villages that were determined by the government to require relocation because of the planned reservoir to be created by the dam has been further documented by architectural consultants and by the Sarawak Museum (including aerial photographs). Eight of the fifteen villages are Kayan, four are Kenyah, and one is Lahanan (a Kajang group). The remaining two are of former nomadic peoples (one Penan, the other Ukit) who have settled in longhouses. Except for the two nomadic groups, the architectural traditions are similar and involve the use of heavy construction to build large longhouses, in which the apartments of chiefs and sometimes other ranking aristocrats are usually differentiated by size and location.

New-style longhouses began to be built on the Balui around Belaga in the 1960s. By the time that the first survey was carried out in 1982, the modernization of some of the longhouses was already well advanced. Kayan builders in particular had adopted various innovations. These included building two-story structures with large attached or semidetached kitchens and eating areas. These modern longhouses in some instances also had one-story front extensions, formed by adding a continuous shed roof along the entire building. This extension added to the width of the gallery or had a raised floor that was used for sitting. In some instances the entire longhouse was raised on posts so that the lower floor was made of boards in the traditional manner; in other instances, the longhouse was placed directly on the ground and had a concrete floor. Like the Kayan, the Kajang were also by that time building two-story longhouses, but these showed greater variation in the way that the individual apartments were designed. In some instances the design was apparently influenced by the layout of Chinese shop houses in Belaga bazaar. The Kenyah had not modernized their longhouses to the same extent.[47]

In both the Kayan and Kajang longhouses of the Balui in the early 1980s, the apartments of the chiefs continued to be larger than others. Although no higher, these apartments were wider and had galleries that extended farther out in front. This front extension was created in some instances with a wider shed roof. The Kejaman (Kajang) longhouse of Rumah Lasah had enlarged the chief's apartment with a lateral extension with a two-sided roof that joined the main longhouse roof at a right angle.[48] This was a further innovation (now common) that required the use of intersecting roof planes.

The fifteen villages displaced by the Bakun project in the late 1990s represent a cross section of Kayan, Kenyah, Kajang, and other villages of the middle Balui River.[49] The architecture of these villages shows that the modernizing trends noted in some longhouses in the early 1980s have continued to develop and have been extended to others. Although these villages are still sometimes commonly referred to simply as longhouses, most of them are large, complex settlements. The larger ones at least have a government school and clinic, a church, and provision shops, as well as several or more longhouses and sometimes many single dwellings. While Penan Talun, the smallest of the Bakun villages, includes only 104 persons, all of the others have populations of

FIG. 5.19. Uma Juman in 1998: two two-story longhouses built facing one another; since displaced by the Bakun Hydroelectric Dam, 1998.

more than 300. The Kayan villages range from roughly 300 (Uma Balui with 317) to more than 600 (Uma Lesong with 646). The Kenyah villages are by far the largest overall. The smallest of the four of these villages has slightly fewer than 500 inhabitants (Uma Kelap with 477), while the remaining three all have over 1,000 each (Uma Lesong with 1,274, Uma Bakah with 1,056, and Uma Badang with 1,569). The size of the Balui villages has increased substantially in recent years. In the past larger villages would probably have divided, with one or both sections migrating to a new location, but such movement, except where initiated by the state government, has become more difficult.

The size of the Balui villages is related to the number and arrangement of longhouses. The common traditional practice of housing an entire community in a single longhouse built parallel to the main river is followed only in the smallest of the Bakun villages, that of Penan Talun at Long Belangan. All of the others consist of several longhouses, plus individual houses in some instances as well. The main distinction seems to be between villages in which there is one main or large longhouse plus several smaller ones and those in which there are two or more longhouses of equal size, plus others. When there is one main longhouse, it is usually built parallel to the river and extended in a straight line as far as possible. The Kayan longhouse of Uma Nyaving is a notable variation of this practice. This longhouse has two sections joined in an "L" shape, the front one running parallel to the Balui River and the perpendicular side section facing a small tributary stream. In any case, the main, parallel-to-the-river longhouse, which is usu-

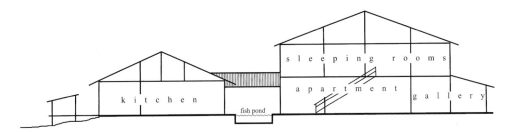

FIG. 5.20. Section drawing of Uma Juman in 1996.

ally the first to have been built, is in most instances supplemented by smaller ones. This can be seen, for example, in the villages of Uma Bawang, Uma Balui, Uma Daro', Uma Ukit, Uma Balui Ukap, Uma Lesong, and Uma Lahanan.

In villages where there are two or more longhouses of equal size, each is sometimes also placed more or less parallel to and facing the river. The Kenyah village of Uma Bakah consists of many small longhouses in several rows, all placed parallel to the river. The Kayan village of Uma Belor includes two main longhouses, both of which face the river. More often, however, many of the longhouses in the larger, multi-longhouse villages are not aligned with the river. In such instances other considerations take precedence. The Kenyah villages, as well as some of the larger Kayan ones, show a preference for grouping longhouses together rather than extending them along and parallel to the river. Here a notable practice—and apparently a recent development in this area—is to place several longhouses so that they face one another across a courtyard. The most spectacular instance of this arrangement occurs in the Kayan village of Uma Juman. This village takes the form of two large, two-story longhouses of equal size set exactly opposite one another and perpendicular to the river. Other instances occur at Uma Ukit, Uma Lesong, and Uma Kulit, although in most of these instances the longhouses are, while placed front to front, arranged in other ways.

The newer arrangements of longhouses reflect several developments. One of these is the increasing size and concentration of village populations. This requires the construction of additional longhouses, the more so in areas where the terrain does not allow for very long buildings. In addition, religious and cultural changes have permitted or encouraged the new arrangements in several ways. Many of the inhabitants of the Balui villages are now Christians and therefore less constrained by traditional ritual restrictions on placing longhouses other than more or less parallel to the river and consequently with definite upstream and downstream ends. Further, the large villages are increasingly differentiated. Some include remnant ethnic populations and different religious groups, for whom separate longhouses are a way of reconciling the advantages of larger settlements (common facilities), including schools and churches, with the tensions and antagonisms associated with increasing diversity.

CHAPTER SIX MODERN USES AND
THE FUTURE OF INDIGENOUS ARCHITECTURE

THE FIRST—AND FOR MANY THE ONLY—view that visitors get of what passes for indigenous Bornean architecture is of various model houses and other buildings that are constructed as part of museums or cultural centers in or near the main urban centers. Visitors may also in some places see government buildings that (as they may or may not realize) have incorporated various indigenous designs into their basic form or into their embellishment. For those who venture somewhat beyond the larger towns there are other opportunities, including tourist longhouses, with all the modern comforts and conveniences, and in some areas, Christian architecture that has drawn upon native elements. While these uses of traditional indigenous architecture may suggest that it remains vital, the extent to which this is so varies greatly from one region to another. In this chapter I offer some final examples of what is occurring.

ARCHITECTURAL APPROPRIATIONS

In Sarawak, indigenous architectural elements have long been incorporated into some hotels and resorts. These range from an occasional statue outside of an otherwise ordinary, international-style medium- or high-rise concrete and glass building to the creation of entire resort complexes on native architectural themes. In Kuching a single concrete representation of a carved grave post sits to the side of the driveway entrance to the high-rise Riverside Hotel, a building that could have been built anywhere in the world and that is, inside and out, otherwise devoid of local influences. The slightly older nearby Hilton is also without local architectural themes but displays old Chinese trade jars, Malay brassware, Iban textiles, head-hunting swords, carvings, and other such artifacts throughout its lobby, lounge, and restaurants. The yet older but also fashionable Holiday Inn, which is located across the road from these hotels on the bank of the Sarawak River, has an interior lobby and lounge area that features extensive indigenous architectural carvings, as well as occasional local artifacts, especially large, polychrome Iban hornbill statues. Farther from Kuching several major hotel corporations have built resorts around longhouses and round men's house themes. Insofar as one can generalize from these and other examples that might be noted, the trend appears to be away from indigenous themes in urban hotel building, except perhaps for the display of local artifacts, but toward it in outlying and upriver resorts.

ARCHITECTURAL THEME PARKS

The largest collections of new buildings intended to represent traditional Bornean houses are in architectural theme parks. These include Taman Mini Indonesia, outside Jakarta, and Sarawak Cultural Village, near Kuching. There are great differences between these two places,

FIG. 6.1 (top). Concrete mortuary post, Riverside Hotel, Kuching, Sarawak, 1998.

FIG. 6.2 (bottom). Hilton Batang Ai Longhouse Resort, with one of the longhouse blocks of guest rooms at the top; Ai River, Lubok Antu area, western Sarawak, 1998.

FIG. 6.3. Kalbar (West Kalimantan) pavilion at Taman Mini, showing a generic West Kalimantan longhouse standing in a pool of water with a copy of the Tugu Katulistiwa, the monument in Pontianak that marks the equatorial boundary; Jakarta, Java.

involving both scale and purpose. Taman Mini was a project of the New Order Indonesian government, undertaken at the initiative of President Suharto's wife, who had been inspired by Disneyland, to which it bears some resemblance. While Sarawak Cultural Village may have been inspired in part by Taman Mini, it has more of the character of an outdoor folk museum.

There are also certain similarities. Both places are supposed to represent the indigenous architecture of the country concerned, and both embody a view of how ethnic architectural diversity is to be organized and displayed. In the case of Taman Mini, the architecture of all of the regions of Indonesia is intended to be in some sense represented, while Sarawak Cultural Village shows that of the main ethnic groups of a much smaller area—

a single state, although Sarawak had an independent existence and identity long enough to regard itself as more than merely a state of Malaysia or a region of Borneo.

Taman Mini

Taman Mini was begun in 1971 and opened in 1975.[1] Its architectural displays are organized on the basis of the twenty-six provinces (*provinsi*) of Indonesia, each of which is represented by a pavilion with a model house. The model house is based on the architecture of the dominant indigenous ethnic group of the province or is otherwise exemplary of it. In the case of Borneo three of the four provinces of Kalimantan are represented by longhouses: for East Kalimantan, a Kenyah longhouse that includes finely painted polychrome wall murals and

FIG. 6.4. Kaltim (East Kalimantan) pavilion at Taman Mini, featuring a Kenyah-style longhouse with a raised roof over the chief's section; Jakarta, Java, 1994.

the raised roof of the chief's central apartment; for Central Kalimantan, a Ngaju longhouse; and for West Kalimantan, a more generic one. Most of the longhouses are idealized creations and would not necessarily be recognizable to the groups whose architecture they are intended to display. However much the longhouses do or do not resemble the structures that they are intended to represent, their display as official architectural representations of all but one of the four provinces of Kalimantan is somewhat ironic. At the same time that Taman Mini was being developed, the real longhouses of Indonesian Borneo were being abandoned and destroyed under government pressure as backward and undesirable forms of housing and village organization.

Sarawak Cultural Village

Sarawak Cultural Village was opened in 1990 as a commercial project located next to two of Sarawak's most opulent beach resort hotels. It was intended to be a living architectural theme park, consisting of authentic indigenous houses, each with costumed natives performing dances, doing crafts, cooking, and showing visitors around. At first, each house was to be staffed by members of the specific groups it represented, but this gave way to a more generalized approach whereby guides from any indigenous ethnic group might serve in any house—an Iban guide in the Bidayuh house or a Bidayuh guide in the Melanau house, for example. Such guides are thought to have enough knowledge of the architecture of any of the houses to handle the inquiries of most

FIG. 6.5. Bidayuh pavilion at Sarawak Cultural Village, showing a round, Bau-area-style men's house (modeled on one in Opar), with a longhouse in the background; near Kuching, Sarawak, 1992.

visitors. The native workers who demonstrate cooking and crafts continue to come mainly from the particular groups represented by each house.

The collection of houses that form Sarawak Cultural Village is not (as it is at Taman Mini) based on the territorial organization of the country. The houses are instead intended to represent the various main ethnic divisions of Sarawak as these are more or less officially recognized and widely known. There is a Malay house (though of a wealthy aristocrat rather than an ordinary villager), a rural Chinese farmer's house (with a dirt floor), a Melanau high fortress house, a Bidayuh longhouse and men's house, an Iban longhouse, and an Orang Ulu longhouse (that is, of the upriver peoples, including the various Kenyah, Kayan, Kajang, Kelabit, and other northern interior groups). There is also a Penan forest shelter.

The longhouses and other buildings representing these various ethnic sectors were designed in consultation with elders of these communities. All are, therefore, based on indigenous designs, but none appear to fully replicate the older materials and forms in use before architectural change had begun to occur. All make some use of sawn lumber as siding, flooring, and framing material, although the main posts are left round in most instances.

The authenticity of some of the longhouses was a matter of interest among members of the various groups who were aware of them at the time Sarawak Cultural Village was developed and opened. An urban Bidayuh leader recounted that the initial Iban longhouse was very modern because the Iban had not wanted to appear to be architecturally backward. But after the Iban were

FIG. 6.6. Orang Ulu (the official and widely used term for the Kenyah, Kayan, Kajang, and other Upriver Peoples of northern Sarawak) pavilion at Sarawak Cultural Village, showing a Kenyah-style longhouse with a larger chief's section with a raised roof; near Kuching, Sarawak, 1992.

criticized by members of other ethnic communities for not having an authentic longhouse on display, a second section was developed along earlier lines. While not representing the oldest form, the result shows the Iban longhouse at two stages of development over the past decades. In contrast, the Bidayuh longhouse and others do not show any of the changes that all longhouses in Sarawak have undergone. The Bidayuh longhouse is based on the terraced design of the old (and now mainly dismantled) ones at Gayu in Padawan but built in larger dimensions than these or other Bidayuh longhouses. The men's house, which is also a part of the Bidayuh exhibit, is based on the round *baruk* at Opar that had been rebuilt several years earlier in a customary style.

The problem of displaying an Orang Ulu longhouse that would represent the traditional styles of the various groups included in this category was resolved (as at Taman Mini) by building a Kenyah-style longhouse—again with the chief's apartment at the center, with a wider front gallery and a roof raised above the remainder of the building. In the case of the Melanau exhibit, the problem was that longhouses had by then ceased to exist in even approximately traditional form. The building that was put up replicates some of the features of the Melanau longhouses known from the nineteenth century, including the massive, high foundation of large ironwood posts.[2] Otherwise the building was not modeled on a Melanau longhouse but rather on the great houses built by some Melanau chiefs for extended families after the abandonment of earlier types of longhouses.

Large nineteenth-century double *klirieng*, outside of the Tun Razak Hall of the Sarawak Museum in Kuching; it is one of the best known and most frequently photographed cultural landmarks of Sarawak; 1992.

MUSEUM DISPLAYS, URBAN LONGHOUSES, AND GOVERNMENT USES OF INDIGENOUS ARCHITECTURE

In addition to architectural theme parks, several museums in Borneo display indigenous houses and other built forms. The Sabah Museum in Kota Kinabalu exhibits five traditional houses built by various Sabah groups. The Brunei Museum, outside of Bandar Seri Begawan, and the Sarawak Museum, in Kuching, both have permanent inside displays of houses or sections of houses. In the Sarawak Museum these include an Iban longhouse *bilik*, constructed with bark walls and other traditional materials and furnished with weavings, customary trade goods (brassware and ceramics), weapons, and a large collection of trophy skulls. There are also smaller displays of architecture and artifacts of the main native ethnic divisions of Sarawak as they are more or less officially noted —Penan, Orang Ulu, Iban, Bidayuh, Melanau, and Malay. The Sarawak Museum does not have open-air exhibits of native houses but does display several magnificent nineteenth-century carved ironwood grave posts and has recently (1998–1999) erected a raised ironwood mausoleum made by Kajang craftsmen from Punan Bah.

Perhaps since longhouses (if mainly in modernized form) remain common in Sarawak and can readily be seen along the Rajang, Baram, and other rivers of central and northern Sarawak, the government has not been inclined to build model versions in urban areas. In Kalimantan, in contrast, existing longhouses are few and far between except in several remote regions. Here, in addition to attempting to preserve some of the few remaining older ones as historical monuments, the government has built models of longhouses in several urban centers, including Pontianak in West Kalimantan, Palangkaraya in Central Kalimantan, and Tenggarong in East Kalimantan. These longhouses are intended to be cultural centers, tourist attractions, and exhibits of indigenous ar-

FIG. 6.8. Rumah Adat; government-built model longhouse, Pontianak, West Kalimantan, 1994.

chitectural traditions.[3] They are also a part of a more general effort to synthesize and reinterpret indigenous architecture, statuary, art, costumes, and dances. Bernard Sellato describes recent efforts:

> Scores of alleged Dayak style road-junction and office-frontyard monuments in bronze, cement, or wood . . . copied from ethnic ritual structures, sometimes reinterpreted in a Soviet Realism way (Kaltim [East Kalimantan]). Interesting modern monuments are more freely inspired by traditional motifs (Pontianak). Many such monuments show little concern for the meaning of the symbols displayed. Sacred Dayak motifs are found stenciled even on garbage bins (Tenggarong). The styles correspond more or less to the culturally dominant groups: Kenyah (Kaltim), Ngaju (Kalteng [Central Kalimantan]), Banjarese (Kalsel [South Kalimantan]), and either a synthetic Dayak or a "Melayak" *kombinasi* style (Kalbar [West Kalimantan]). Though some monuments are strik-

ingly ugly, the Dayak react not against this but rather to their inappropriateness, since most copy traditional funeral or ritual monuments. Recently, Dayak architects have begun designing government office buildings, particularly in Kalteng. The results, hardly more convincing to the rural ethnic peoples, are at least endorsed by the elites.[4]

The purpose of these efforts, as Sellato notes, is to promote tourism, highlight local cultures, and encourage ethnic groups to identify with the province and nation by associating Dayak art and architecture with public buildings. The emphasis here is on creating provincial styles to encourage provincial identities rather than ethnic ones. This may involve either appropriating specific ethnic architectural and other cultural forms (Kenyah longhouses or mural paintings) that are not, however, identified as such or creating synthetic or composite "Melayak" (Melayu-Dayak) ones.

FIG. 6.9. Welcoming arch with Iban shield designs at the entrance to Engkilili Town, Lubok Antu area, western Sarawak, 1999.

In Sarawak, the government—going back to the Brooke period—has also often drawn upon indigenous art and architecture, and for some of the same reasons as in Kalimantan. Roadside monuments and arches with shield designs (perhaps inspired by those seen in Kalimantan) have been erected but appear to be less common. Increasing use, however, is being made of local indigenous architecture in designing local government buildings. In Bau, for example, the town civic center (Dewan Suara) includes a round museum wing modeled on a local Bidayuh men's house, while the civic center in Marudi, on the lower Baram, is designed in the shape of a Kenyah longhouse with its several roof levels. Indigenous artistic designs have also recently been incorporated into places used by visitors and tourists, including the arrival and departure halls at the Kuching Airport, which has hornbill effigy figures and other Iban designs

on the supporting posts, and the downtown River Walk, which has Orang Ulu tendril designs in its spectacular mosaic walkways.

CHURCHES AND INDIGENOUS ARCHITECTURE

Christian churches in some areas have also provided opportunities for the expression of indigenous architectural themes. In earlier periods, Christian missionaries sought not only to convert the indigenous peoples of Borneo to Christianity in terms of belief and ritual practice, but also to profoundly change their attitudes, values, behavior, and lifeways in general, away from the exotic (that is, to the missionaries) customary ones of Borneo and in the direction of the idealized versions of the West. This meant discouraging social and ceremonial drinking and premarital sexual activity; the reliance

FIG. 6.10 (right). Kuching Airport hall with Dayak (mainly Iban) designs on the columns and ceiling; Kuching, Sarawak, 1999.

FIG. 6.11 (below). Dewan Suara (civic center), reminiscent of a Kenyah stratified longhouse with a three-tiered roof; Marudi, lower Baram, northern Sarawak, 1994.

FIG. 6.12. Civic center, designed with a museum wing in the form of a Bidayuh *baruk*, the round style men's house found in the area; Bau, western Sarawak, 1994.

on omens; and the practice of many taboos in relation to birth, illness, death, and agricultural activity, as well as providing Western education and dress—especially in covering the upper body in the case of women and the substitution of pants and shorts for the loin cloth in the case of men. Additionally, conversion was and is often linked with what have come to be regarded as the modern ways of the younger generation, as opposed to the customary ways of the older people.

Because of the widespread association of indigenous architecture (longhouses and in some areas mortuary structures) with traditional religious practices and pagan ways and because of the association of Christianity with Western-style architecture, conversion has generally involved the construction of churches that are poorer and simpler versions of those of the home countries. In the past, village churches in Borneo were—and often still are—generally made of traditional local materials, including split bamboo, but the designs are like those in Western countries—rectangular buildings, usually built directly on the ground, occasionally with a steeple in the front. In more recent decades some Christian authorities have become more tolerant of indigenous, pre-Christian traditions, more willing to accept local practices, and in some instances concerned about the loss of indigenous culture. This changing attitude reflects various developments, including the increasing replacement of European missionaries with local or other Asian clergy and the growing belief among Western-educated indigenous Christians that conversion had required the unnecessary throwing away of local practices and heirlooms that were not counter to Christianity. It also reflects the growing realization that Christianity and Western culture are not the same thing. The Roman

FIG. 6.13. River Walk in the center of Kuching, paved in a stone mosaic of Orang Ulu tendril designs; 1996.

Catholic Church has been especially liberal in accepting and encouraging the preservation or revitalization of local indigenous traditions, including architectural ones. In the case of churches this has mainly involved the incorporation of Bornean decorative motifs into Western-style buildings. In some instances the designs that have been rendered are formalized foliate patterns, especially tendrils, while in others these include explicit indigenous sacred symbols, most notably the dragon.

The use of local design elements in churches and community halls in recent decades has been especially common in Kalimantan, perhaps as a kind of compensation for the massive loss of indigenous architecture. Here, as we have seen, longhouses have been widely abandoned under government pressure, and indigenous Dayak cultural practices in general have been disparaged and discouraged by government officials. The decora-

tion of Christian churches with indigenous relief carving, murals, and statuary has provided an opportunity for the display of symbols of local culture and identity that were previously associated with longhouses and mortuary architecture. Here also the building of new village community halls that have sometimes been lavishly decorated with carving and painting has probably provided a precedent for decorating churches with native art. The embellishment of churches in Kalimantan has occurred especially among groups in which indigenous traditions of architectural carving, painting, and statuary are highly developed, as in the case of the Kenyah, Kayan, and related peoples.

In Sarawak, where longhouses and other indigenous architectural forms have been abandoned or modernized according to local decisions (based on religious conversion and other Western influences rather than

FIG. 6.14. Main entrance doors of Santo Stefanus Catholic Church (dragons painted in polychrome) in the Kenyah village of Datah Bilang, middle Mahakam River, East Kalimantan, 1996.

government pressure), the use of indigenous architectural forms in the construction of Christian churches has generally lagged behind that in Kalimantan.[5] There are, however, some notable exceptions, including the interior of St. Pius Catholic Church at Long San on the Upper Baram.

The New Bidayuh Catholic Complex on Singai Mountain

The new Catholic church and retreat on Singai Mountain is a particularly striking innovation. The design of this church goes beyond the more common pattern of embellishing a basically Western-style building with indigenous decorative designs. It involves the creation of a modern church in the form of a native structure, specifically a round men's house. A dormitory in the form of a longhouse has also been built as a part of the complex. The construction of modern buildings in the form of round *baruk* has, as is also true of longhouses, become common; examples include the museum wing of the civic center in Bau Town, a restaurant in Kuching, and various buildings of several new hotel-resorts at Damai Beach. The construction of a modern Christian church retreat in the form of a longhouse and *baruk* is, however, a new development and one that involves a certain historical irony in that both longhouses and men's houses, with their collections of human skulls, indigenous ritual practices, and social and festive drinking practices, were previously regarded by Christian missionaries as among the main bases of Bidayuh paganism and impediments to conversion and progress.

From the perspective of the Bidayuh, the construction of a new church and longhouse on Singai Mountain represents a synthesis of ethnic and religious concerns and sentiments and perhaps a certain amount of cultural payback or vindication. The church is built on the site of the mission established in the late nineteenth century. It is intended to commemorate the early efforts of the first

FIG. 6.15 (left). Entrance gate to St. Anthony's Church in the Kayan village of Padua; dragon and hornbill ridge crests and finials and statues of doglike *aso'* made of cement and partially painted; Mendalam River, upper Kapuas region, 1994.

FIG. 6.16 (below). Front of St. Anthony's Church, with a painted mural of dragons and a dragon face in the tympanum; 1994.

FIG. 6.17.
Catholic church
under construction
in the form of a
Bidayuh round men's
house, Singai Mountain,
Bau area, western
Sarawak, 1998.

missionary, who lived to see the conversion of only a few souls after many years of effort. The walk up the mountain, along which are located the Stations of the Cross, passes through an old forest-orchard of fruit, nut, and bee trees and giant strangling figs. The walk also replicates one that the villagers made in the past on a regular basis as they returned from their fields below to their villages. The new church is located near the site of the old villages, all of which have now been abandoned for several decades or more. The construction of the church and retreat at this site on the side of the mountain is, therefore, also intended to memorialize the old villages and the traditional way of life, even if these are not places and ways to which many would want to return.

The placing of the new religious complex on Singai Mountain is also intended by the villagers to have a modern political purpose. This is to help retain their ownership rights of the mountain as Native Customary Land.

The mountain is located near to Kuching in an area that is being rapidly developed. The Singai villagers therefore fear that, especially since they no longer occupy the mountain or cultivate gardens there (except for the extensive forest orchards on the lower slopes), it will be appropriated by the government and given to others (perhaps non-Bidayuh) to be developed. The construction of the church, it is hoped, will help to forestall this possibility, although the Singai villagers also speak of reestablishing houses on the mountain as well.

ARCHITECTURE AND TOURISM IN KALIMANTAN

Indigenous architecture is influenced by tourism in varying ways and degrees in different regions. Longhouses in particular are major tourist attractions in both Kalimantan and Sarawak (and to a lesser extent in Sabah, where longhouse architectural traditions are less developed and where tourism is more oriented to nature rather than culture). In Kalimantan tourism has provided an incentive to preserve some of the older longhouses that have survived, to renovate others, and to build new ones along more or less traditional lines as showplaces.

In Kalimantan, where they are few in number in any case, most longhouses do not exist in close proximity to the major urban centers that are the entry points for tourists. Those that survive and are not too distant to attract tourists can be readily identified by the presence of displays of craft items and sometimes snacks and drinks for sale in the gallery. They are listed and often pictured in tourist brochures and well known to the taxi drivers, boat operators, tourist guides, and local proprietors of the shops and inns in the area. Some of the rural longhouses are older buildings that escaped destruction long enough to be recognized as historical relics and regarded as likely objects of tourist interest. They are often otherwise mainly empty. Such longhouses have few counterparts in Sarawak, where longhouses have seldom been preserved without the addition of corrugated metal roofs and other modern materials.

In the few areas of Kalimantan where longhouse living is still a way of life, some of the older buildings have been renovated or rebuilt in a fairly traditional form. The Taman longhouses of Melapi on the upper Kapuas and Semankok on the Mendalam (see figs. 2.10 and 5.5) are good examples. Both, like the newer longhouses also built in the area, are living communities rather than empty relics. Both have covered entranceways and are painted but otherwise preserve many traditional features, including high pile foundations and notched-log entrance ladders with carved figures. These and other longhouses located in the deep interior of West Kalimantan are readily accessible by boat from the district capital of Putissibau and are visited by travelers but not organized as tourist centers.[6]

There are also longhouses in Kalimantan that have been constructed along traditional lines from traditional materials as tourist centers. There are several such longhouses at the Benua' village of Tanjung Isuy—one of the major rural tourist centers of East Kalimantan—on Lake Jempang in the lower Mahakam area. These longhouses are not village dwellings but provide rooms to visitors who wish to stay in them. The villagers in Tanjung Isuy are extensively involved in tourist-related activities, including weaving, carving, and the performance of dances. The longhouses feature carved statues, including a pair of copulating anthropomorphic figures at the top of the entrance log-ladder of one longhouse, perhaps provided more for the amusement of visitors than as traditional guarding deities.[7]

The longhouses that are now gone from most of the villages in Kalimantan have often been replaced by community halls, widely referred to as *balai* (see fig. 5.9). While such buildings predate the widespread abandonment of longhouses during the New Order period, they appear to have been common in Borneo only or mainly among the nonlonghouse dwellers, for longhouses provide places for public and ritual activities within the gallery. The situation is somewhat similar in Sarawak in that modern *balai* tend to be built among groups or in areas where longhouses have mainly disappeared. In both instances, moreover, the funds for the construction of *balai* have often been provided by the government. In Sarawak community halls tend to be simple, utilitarian buildings with corrugated metal roofs and cement floors. In East Kalimantan at least, *balai* are often large, raised wooden structures built along the same lines as longhouse galleries, sometimes with carvings, painted murals, or other decorations.

ARCHITECTURE AND TOURISM IN SARAWAK

In Sarawak, tourism has also become a major economic activity and has focused attention on longhouses and

FIG. 6.18 (above). Eheng, a surviving old longhouse and now a tourist site; Barong Tongkak area, middle Mahakam region, East Kalimantan, 1996.

FIG. 6.19 (right). Souvenir sellers waiting for tourists in the gallery of Eheng longhouse, Barong Tongkak area, middle Mahakam region, East Kalimantan, 1996.

FIG. 6.20. Made-for-tourists longhouse and statuary at Tanjung Isuy, Lake Jempang, lower Mahakam area, East Kalimantan, 1996.

other indigenous buildings as objects of commercial value. Indigenous architecture serves tourism in various ways. Longhouses form part of the passing landscape for travelers in many areas. They are especially common sights and stopping points for the large passenger boats that ply the Rajang, Baram, and other great rivers, and they are well known as popular tourist destinations. Travelers sometimes stop for the night at longhouses.

Organized visits to some longhouses are a major tourist activity. These are often arranged after a visitor arrives in the country, but many involve internationally marketed package tours handled by agents located in Australia, Europe, North America, Japan, Singapore, Taiwan, and elsewhere. Most tours, including those initiated elsewhere, are organized by travel agencies based in Kuching, the local center of the industry and the main entry point for visitors to the country. Except for the part of the tour involving the longhouse itself (and in the case of visits to riverine longhouses, the journey by river to and from them), the visit is in the hands of urban agents—mainly ethnic Chinese—who contract with longhouses and longhouse dwellers for services, including transportation by river. Both the tours organized elsewhere and in Kuching are widely advertised in the travel and tourist media, including websites on the Internet.[8]

While longhouses are very important for the tourist

industry in Sarawak, the direct effect of tourism on long-houses appears to have been more limited. As of 1997 longhouse tourism involved only about thirty long-houses, a very small fraction of the total in the state.[9] Most longhouses have not been organized to receive tourists and have little to do with tourism, except in some instances to serve as scenic points along the river—or increasingly the road. Many are thought to be too modern to be of much interest as tourist destinations, while others that might seem to be sufficiently traditional (or at least rustic) are located too far from cities to be reached in a suitably short time. Organized tourist visits are therefore focused mainly on Bidayuh and, especially, Iban longhouses. These, or rather some of them, have the necessary characteristics to appeal to tourists and are within a day's travel from Kuching.

Bidayuh Longhouses and Tourism

Bidayuh longhouses of tourist interest are in villages located relatively close to Kuching and can be reached entirely by road within an hour or so, although (as explained below) this is not necessarily much of an advantage, especially when the dirt roads are in poor repair. There are three main villages—Bunuk, Gayu, and Anah Rais—all of which consist of several or more long-houses plus some single dwellings. All are located in Padawan District, to the south of Kuching, in the direction of the Indonesian border, and all have been developed to handle tourists arriving by car or van; they have parking areas and entrance signs welcoming visitors and listing entry fees and services. None of these villages, however, is highly commercialized or receives many visitors. All three have had their thatch or wooden shingle roofs mainly replaced by metal ones. Of the three villages, Anah Rais (see fig. 4.1), which is located the farthest from Kuching, has retained its older architecture to the greatest extent. At the other extreme, the once magnificent terraced longhouses at Gayu have been almost en-

tirely dismantled in recent years (see figs. 4.6 and 5.1). In all instances tourists who now visit these villages usually spend a short while walking around, taking photos, and watching villagers pounding rice or performing other chores, and then they leave.

Visits to these villages have been on the wane in recent years, as inhabitants have abandoned longhouses for ordinary single dwellings. Although the villages are located relatively close to Kuching, this is not necessarily much of an advantage, for it means that the economic returns for both tour operators and villagers are relatively small. In recent years at least, nearly all tourist visits to Bidayuh longhouses have consisted of day trips rather than overnight stays, which are part and parcel of Iban long-house tourism. For the tour operator, the sums charged for a morning or afternoon trip to these villages are sufficient to cover the costs of the vehicle and the guide/driver. But the total expenditure is not great in comparison to a two- or three-day "Jungle Adventure" or "River Safari" excursion to an Iban longhouse. Such an excursion includes transportation, a room in the longhouse or separate guest house, welcoming ceremonies, meals, entertainment (costumed dances, blowpipe exhibitions), guided nature walks, and other organized activities.

For many or most of the Bidayuh inhabitants in a tourist-visited longhouse village, therefore, there is relatively little economic reason to be involved with tourism. Bidayuh tourist villages charge very modest entry fees and will, with prior arrangement, provide accommodations, meals, and entertainment (in the form of dancing by villagers in traditional costumes), but these are seldom sought. The result is that little of the limited money that tourists spend to visit Bidayuh longhouses goes to the villagers. Further, Bidayuh villagers have less need for tourist dollars than do Iban villagers living in the more remote locations. If it is relatively easy to bring tourists from Kuching to Bidayuh longhouses, it is also easy for villagers to travel to work on a daily or weekly basis to

FIG. 6.21. Popular postcard on sale in Kuching based on a photo of the Bidayuh village of Bunuk taken several decades ago, before corrugated iron sheets had replaced thatch.

Kuching and to earn wages that are much greater (and more regular) than those to be gained from tourism in the village. Some individuals in Bidayuh villages are tied to the village for various reasons and could benefit from tourism, but not enough to keep the village actively promoting it.

While tourism does not appear to have provided much incentive to preserve existing architecture, several communities have attempted to attract tourists by constructing traditional-looking buildings, but without much success. In the late 1980s Opar built a small longhouse near the center of the village where tourists could spend the night. Several years before the village had, for customary ritual reasons, rebuilt its old men's house in the traditional round shape with a high thatched roof and had held a major festival that gained a lot of local attention. In addition, a dirt road had been completed that connected the village to the main highway near the town of Bau and made the village easily accessible to the outside for the first time. The longhouse was built along traditional lines, with bamboo siding and a palm thatch roof, but since no one lived in it, it did not have the authentic, lived-in look that interests tourists. In addition, the village is located on flat ground and comprised

FIG. 6.22. Small, built-for-tourists longhouse in Sentah Village, with overnight accommodations available; the roof is covered with corrugated metal sheets with a deteriorating overlay of palm thatch; 1998.

mainly of contemporary single houses and is not picturesque, so that except for the impressive *baruk*, there was little for tourists to do or see.

Sentah Village, which is located on a mountaintop off the main highway from Kuching to Serian, took a somewhat different approach in constructing a new men's house and small longhouse for visitors. This village continues to occupy its old mountaintop location, although many of its inhabitants have moved down to several newer communities. The village is reached by a narrow, winding road up the mountain and provides spectacular views of the surrounding country. The village has some basis for attraction, although all of the houses in the main area are contemporary single dwellings, and all that remains of the former men's house is a small, open-sided shelter in which are hung a few human skulls. The reconstructed longhouse and men's house are set apart from and above the main part of the village on a steep

hillside with a fine view and are surrounded by high durian trees. Both buildings are traditional in design, including, for example, roof-flap windows. Both also have palm thatch roofs, but these have been put over metal roofs; the palm thatch roofs (in late 1998) had deteriorated so that large areas of metal had been exposed.

Iban Longhouses and Tourism

Over the past several decades the longhouse tourism industry has been focused much more extensively on Iban than on Bidayuh longhouses.[10] Iban longhouses account for all but a few of those that regularly receive tourists. They have more to offer to tourists than do Bidayuh longhouses—including scenic river travel by longboat and a more distinctly out-in-the-jungle and way-up-the-river rural atmosphere, with fewer signs of modern life. And there is more money to be made by both tour operators and villagers because of the much greater expenditures associated with the longer journey to a faraway village, overnight stays, food, and entertainment. In addition, since Iban tourist villages are much farther from urban areas than Bidayuh ones, villagers have fewer opportunities to pursue urban-based occupations while living in the village or returning to it on weekends. Partly for this reason Iban villagers appear to have been more receptive than the Bidayuh to longhouse tourism—more willing to look after, entertain, and perform for paying guests.

At the same time, the effects of tourism on Iban longhouse architecture have been limited to a few areas. Most or all of the Iban tourist longhouses are situated on the Batang Ai Reservoir (also the location of the Hilton Batang Ai Longhouse Resort) on the Ai River, above the lake; on the Engkari (which flows into the Ai); and on the nearby Lemanak and Skrang Rivers. All of these rivers are relatively small, often fast moving, scenic, and navigable only by longboat, rather than by the large passenger boats, cargo vessels, and log barges that ply the major rivers. The longhouses on these rivers are therefore sufficiently remote that the inhabitants do not have the more abundant economic opportunities or the ready access to modern building materials that are available to Iban communities located on larger rivers or roads or nearer to towns. Conversely, unlike the many Iban longhouses in even more remote locations on smaller or more distant rivers, most of those on the Ai, Engkari, Lemanak, and Skrang can be reached within a day's travel from Kuching (initially several hours by van and then a final hour or so by outboard motor-powered longboat).

Apart from their distinctive not-too-close-but-not-too-far locations, successful Iban tourist longhouses have several architectural features. One is a traditional "jungle look," which is also shown on longhouse postcards sold in Kuching. This means that the longhouse should not appear modern, although it need not necessarily be authentically traditional—something that most tourists (and probably many younger Iban) would not be able to judge. A separate attached or detached kitchen at the back does not, for example, detract from a longhouse's apparent traditional authenticity for tourists, who do not know that longhouses lacked such additions in the past, and, in any case, it is the front of the longhouse that is most important. Nor for much the same reason are modern, wooden-panel doors a problem—no one is likely to know about the smaller, often carved, wooden slab doors that were formerly used to close the passageway through the wall from the gallery to the inner apartment.

Materials that have a natural look are preferable to those that do not—for example, unpainted, sawn wooden boards and timbers, especially those exposed to the sun and rain, which have quickly attained a weathered, rustic appearance. Corrugated metal sheets, on the other hand, are a problem. Commonly used as roofing (and sometimes as siding), these are highly visible and detract from the apparent authenticity of a longhouse. Few if any longhouse roofs in Sarawak (in contrast to most of the remaining ones in Kalimantan) are entirely lacking in metal roofing, and many otherwise traditional-appearing longhouses have all metal ones. Metal roofs are therefore a common source of disappointment to tourists, who have been led to expect that they will be visiting a traditional longhouse.[11] It is for this reason that metal roofs are sometimes covered with a layer of palm thatch.

The liability of metal sheeting, however, also varies with age and condition. Bright, shiny, newly applied sheets are much more objectionable than those that have aged. The least costly and most widely used galvanized corrugated sheets become dull after a few years of exposure; as they lose their zinc coating, they begin to rust and turn a deep and mellow brown before disintegrating. Well-seasoned metal roofing and siding, while not authentically traditional to the discerning tourist eye, at least look rustic, especially in advanced stages of deterioration.

Windows are another point at which the desires and inclinations of longhouse dwellers tend to conflict with the architectural demands of tourism. While traditional flap windows are still incorporated into roofs, in some areas they have been replaced by windows in vertical walls. In most modern or modernized Iban longhouses, louvered glass windows have been built into the wall separating the gallery from the inner apartment. These windows provide light and help with the circulation of air (the latter all the more necessary with the shift to heat-producing metal roofing), but they are readily visible from the gallery, where tourists spend most of their time while at the longhouse. A common solution to the problem of modern metal and glass windows in the gallery wall is to cover them up in some way, although this largely eliminates their usefulness.

Such a strategy of camouflage can also be used in the case of modern-looking plywood paneling, which has also been widely incorporated into older as well as newer

FIG. 6.23. Contemporary postcard of an Iban longhouse with a woman in front feeding pigs and an insert of a boat on the Skrang River. Although the older, wooden-shingle roofing has been almost entirely replaced with corrugated metal sheets, these have extensively rusted, helping to give the longhouse an acceptably ramshackle appearance.

longhouses. Sheets of split bamboo, bark, or bark cloth are used in Iban tourist longhouses to cover up modern windows and paneling and restore a more rustic, "jungle look" to the gallery. Such wall coverings are further enhanced by hanging handicraft items (commonly small weavings, baskets, small wooden figures, blowpipes, and swords) on them. Although the traditionally made versions of such tourist handicrafts are not customarily so displayed, they are thought to enhance the appearance of authenticity of the longhouse gallery. In addition, watching the longhouse dwellers making the handi-

crafts so displayed—the sale of which, moreover, provides a further source of income for the household on whose gallery wall they are shown—is a common tourist activity.

Finally, in addition to the fact that the direct effects of tourism on the indigenous architecture are sometimes more a matter of creating appearances than underlying reality, the economic consequences of successful longhouse tourism have not necessarily served to preserve older, more traditionally built longhouses. Some of the money that villagers earn in successful tourist longhouses is spent on the usual range of contemporary consumer products, including (in addition to chain saws and outboard motors, which are used for transportation and farming) portable electric generators, television sets, and household appliances. These things do not fit with the desired primitive look of the longhouse, but most of them are kept in the inner apartments and therefore more or less out of the sight and hearing of tourist visitors, especially where they are housed in separate guest houses. More obtrusive devices—including power-driven rice mills, television satellite dishes, and large, communal diesel-powered generators—are more problematic and in some cases have led tour operators to move to other longhouses, but such indications of prosperity and modernity can be mitigated by placement and by limiting their use to times that tourists are not present. Moreover, villagers who achieve some degree of economic success through tourism are also inclined to do as villagers who have become relatively prosperous as a result of wage labor at nearby logging operations or by the cash cropping of pepper, coco, or oil palm. This is to build a new longhouse, preferably the best and most modern one on the river. Unless such a new longhouse is built of traditional materials and in a customary way (or made to look like it is—which is not possible in the case of one constructed of cement block and built directly on the ground in a location that has been leveled by a bulldozer), it will be the end of the tourist business. Nonetheless and in spite of the pleas of tour operators and the advice of officials from the Ministry of Tourism, some villages have chosen architectural progress over the economic rewards of tourism. From recent developments on the Engkari River, however, it seems that such choices can also provide neighboring longhouses, which had not formerly been architecturally competitive, with the opportunity to develop tourism, and perhaps therefore with the incentive to maintain or restore the use of customary building materials and forms.

FIG. 6.24. Nanga Ukum longhouse. Although the gallery and exterior (the parts that tourists mainly see) have an authentic, traditional look, the development of the longhouse as a tourist destination has meant that modern innovations be covered up or kept out of sight. The contemporary paneling and glass windows in the wall of the gallery have therefore been covered with bark cloth daubed with paint like camouflage netting (many Iban have served in the military), on top of which have been hung baskets and other handicraft items for sale; 1999.

CONCLUSIONS

Until recently the architecture of the indigenous peoples of the interior had developed in relation to local environmental conditions and nearly limitless forest resources, endemic warfare, a relatively simple but effective technology of hand-forged iron tools, and a highly elaborate ceremonial life focused on head-hunting, fertility festivals, and mortuary practices. Although parts of all of this remain, much of it has either disappeared, become less relevant, or been transformed. While there are notable continuities, Bornean architecture is now intimately associated with the disappearance or commodification of forests in many areas; the use of the chain saw, new modes of construction, and manufactured materials; new—much broader—forms of ethnic identity and political participation; a much greater knowledge of the architecture of other peoples both near and far; conversion to world religions; and the effects of tourism, wage labor, and a cash economy, among other things. Architecture, like life itself, has been globalized.

Longhouses are by far the most important part of Borneo's living indigenous or interior architectural tradition. It remains possible that in the future the use of traditional materials and designs will become the most prestigious and desirable way to build a longhouse. If so, it is possible that once again the magnificent wooden buildings of the past will rise on tall posts along the rivers of Borneo. That prospect would certainly please architects, anthropologists, well-educated urban natives, tourists and tour operators, and perhaps everyone else, including the villagers who would live in them. But even if one were to assume that such buildings would be made of chainsawed or milled lumber rather than hand-cut and hand-hewed timbers and planks and roofed with machine-cut shingles rather than hand-split ones, this is an unlikely prospect for several reasons. One that has already been noted is the declining availability in some, perhaps many, areas of the timber and other materials needed to build traditional sorts of longhouses and the prohibitive costs of purchasing them. Further, in many areas men often work for wages away from the village and are therefore not able or inclined to obtain materials in the customary manner or participate in the traditionally cooperative building practices, which have been further undermined by the decline or abandonment of the ritual requirements that previously sustained such practices.

In limited areas, such as the Engkari River, tourism may encourage the perpetuation or renewal of traditional styles of longhouses as villagers become more aware of their economic value and of the trade-offs involved in architectural modernization. Here the steep slopes of the hills and mountains, while making for spectacular scenery and exciting river travel of the sort appreciated by adventuresome tourists, have little potential for agricultural development beyond swidden cultivation and the small-scale cropping of pepper and other lesser cash crops that can be adapted to the extremely rugged topography. At the same time, the general region of the Engkari and other nearby rivers (where most of the other Iban tourist longhouses are located) is the right distance from Kuching. In such an environment longhouse tourism, swidden cultivation, cash cropping, foraging, hunting, and fishing form an attractive combination to villagers.

Such conditions, however, are not particularly common even in Sarawak—not to mention other areas of Borneo—and at present mainly involve the Iban. Among most other longhouse-dwelling groups in Sarawak the prospect of creating, sustaining, or enhancing tourism by building longhouses in older styles with traditional materials or retaining existing ones is not likely to be taken very seriously. In Kalimantan the situation is perhaps somewhat different. Here there are many fewer longhouses, and here also villagers are considerably poorer and therefore perhaps more inclined to attempt to attract tourists to less likely destinations. Although the distances to be traveled are often great and the transportation difficult, tourism may be a more important motive for saving those longhouses that survived the government assault of the New Order years and for constructing new ones in traditional styles.

Architectural change among the many groups in Sarawak—including most Iban—that has created modern styles of longhouses shows that the pursuit of development and architectural modernity need not involve only the movement into single dwellings. Even in Sarawak, however, where longhouses continue to flourish among many groups, the commitment to them may be less strong or enduring than is suggested by the large numbers to be seen along the rivers and roads of the interior. In some instances longhouse dwellers have built or are living in separate family houses either in the village or away from it in more distant places, including the downriver and coastal urban areas. Those who remain committed to the longhouse but do not want to live in it all of the time can have the benefits of a separate house while retaining an apartment in the longhouse to which they return periodically for social and ceremonial purposes. Although there may be restrictions of ritual and customary law regarding the length of time that apartments can be empty, these no longer seem to be a problem in many communities. If we judge according to what has taken place in some Bidayuh villages, such residence practices work well enough as long as there is a substantial core of families who remain permanently in the longhouse. Once most families begin to live elsewhere most of the time, however, the viability of the longhouse is threatened, at least when the point is reached that it needs to be rebuilt and the question is raised about whether the cost of doing so is worth the limited use that it will have.

The commitment to longhouses therefore varies. In Sarawak the Iban remain most strongly inclined to retain longhouses, with most villages in the upriver areas of the interior lacking single houses. The Melanau, who have all but entirely abandoned longhouses, are at the opposite extreme, followed by the Bidayuh, many of whose villages consist entirely of single dwellings; yet other groups are somewhere in between—that is, they have kept longhouses in most villages but with single houses as well.

While the government of Sarawak supports the maintenance or renovation of longhouses as community projects and builds them itself under some circumstances, it has not sought to preserve older, traditionally built longhouses for their own sake. While officially and politically approved or even lauded as a bastion of native culture, longhouses have only begun to be recognized as significant in terms of Sarawak's evolving concept of historically important architecture. This can be seen in a compendium of historical buildings, monuments, and sites published by the Sarawak Museum in 1995.[12] Here—the official anti-colonial stance of the present-day government notwithstanding—the main emphasis is on the forts and other colonial buildings erected during the Brooke period, followed by mortuary structures; prehistoric or protohistoric megaliths; rock art and archaeological sites; and various Muslim, Christian, and Chinese religious buildings.[13]

Of the remainder of indigenous architecture, prospects are also mixed. Among the Bidayuh, while men's houses have been abandoned as quarters for unmarried men and in most instances as ceremonial centers, the round versions (see figs. 4.7 and 6.5) have been revived as architectural symbols of Bidayuh ethnic identity and pride in modern, multicultural Sarawak.[14] Among the Kenyah and Kayan modern polychrome forms of mural painting have thrived in recent decades and have been put to various new uses.

Architectural carving has declined. In particular, the massive carved mortuary architecture made in Sarawak

FIG. 6.25 (above). Kayan cemetery, Uma Belor, Balui River, 1997.

FIG. 6.26 (right). Punan Bah (Kajang) *salong,* or secondary burial chamber; Tubau, upper Tatau River, Sarawak, 1990.

by the Kenyah, Kayan, Melanau, Berawan, Kajang, and others has mainly ceased to exist as a living architectural tradition. In the far south of Borneo, the creation and use of traditional wooden mortuary architecture has been perpetuated in relation to continuing secondary funeral practices among followers of Kaharingan, but nothing comparable to such a development has occurred in the north. Here, while large raised mausoleums have been made occasionally in recent decades, the klirieng and other massive carved grave posts belong to the past. Made as they were for the political and social elites of stratified societies, the creation of either sort of monumental wooden funerary edifice has been undermined by the emergence of the more egalitarian social orders of the present. In addition, and perhaps more important, the shift to burial among some groups (and, in the case of klirieng, the abandonment of secondary mortuary practices) has also led away from the construction of above-ground mortuary receptacles, although these continue to be found among some groups.[15] Such developments have all, in turn, been further associated with the widespread conversion to Christianity or (to a much lesser extent) Islam.

These developments mean that the survival of massive wooden mortuary structures in the north is mainly a matter of keeping or salvaging those made in the past, especially in the late nineteenth and early twentieth centuries. Here there is a race with time. Built as they are of wood, even if long-lasting belian, the carved and raised mausoleums and funerary posts are subject to decay and collapse and, in the case of those abandoned as villages moved to other locations, to becoming hidden or obliterated by the rapid growth of brush and then forest. The preservation of mortuary structures does not, however, pose the problems present in the case of longhouses. These structures are much smaller and easier to move and restore. The Sarawak Museum has for many years taken an interest in locating, clearing, and protecting old grave monuments, although this has been done much more easily and successfully in the case of grave posts than mausoleums. Some posts have been moved to new locations, including the three that now stand on the grounds of the museum in Kuching. Others, such as the five in the Kajang village of Punan Bah on the Rajang River, stand in their old locations. Many others remain covered in the forest, reminders for those who come upon them of the transience not only of life, but also of most architecture, including the architecture of death, which is intended to last.

NOTES

INTRODUCTION

1. See Waterson's 1998 anthology of Western travelers' accounts. Recent work includes Dawson and Gillow 1994; Fox 1993; Sellato 1989; Waterson 1990; and Winzeler 1998a, 1998b, 1998c.

2. Rudofsky 1964.

3. Oliver, ed. 1997.

4. These include Beccari 1904, Bock 1881, Boyle 1865, Brooke 1866, Furness 1902, Helms 1882, Hornaday 1908, Jongejans 1922, Low 1848, Lumholtz 1920, Molengraaff 1902, St. John 1862, Schwaner 1853–1854, Tillema 1938, and Wallace (1962; originally published 1869), among others.

5. Also Elshout 1926, A. C. Haddon 1901, Mallinckrodt 1924, Nieuwenhuis 1907, Roth 1896.

6. Hose and McDougall 1912, 1:50–55, 203–210.

7. Leach 1950a.

8. Geddes 1957, 48.

9. Geddes 1954 and 1957, respectively.

10. Freeman 1970.

11. G. N. Appell 1976, 1978. For a more recent critique of the emphasis on the autonomy of the household within the longhouse, see Helliwell 1993.

12. Morris 1978, 1991.

13. Rousseau 1980; Freeman 1981.

14. Lévi-Strauss 1963; Waterson 1990. The literature on house societies in Borneo and elsewhere in Southeast Asia should also be noted, including the volumes edited by Carsten and Hugh-Jones 1995, Macdonald 1987, and Sparkes and Howell 2003.

15. The house has sometimes been said to be a representation of the cosmos, with the ground floor sheltering the animals and representing the underworld, the rooms above being the middle world inhabited by humans, and the high roof (where the sacred objects are kept) corresponding to the upperworld. See, for example, Barbier 1982, 47, on the Toba of Sumatra.

16. Schärer 1963.

17. Morris 1991, 77, has made this a part of his explanation of architectural change among the coastal Melanau of present-day central Sarawak, and Miles 1964, 54, has offered it as the reason for the near extinction of longhouses among the Ngaju peoples of southwest Borneo.

18. Jessup 1998.

19. Percentage estimate from Sellato 1994b, 192. Brosius 2001, 130, reports that the Penan in Sarawak number about seven thousand persons, of whom all but about 5 percent (all Eastern Penan) are now settled in permanent villages.

20. Sellato 1994b, 172.

21. Cited in Keppel 1846, 33.

22. Winzeler 1996, 1997, 1998a, 1998b, 1998c.

23. Some of the accounts are included in a volume on architecture and change that I edited for the Borneo Research Council (Winzeler, ed. 1998).

CHAPTER ONE: THE BUILT ENVIRONMENT OF THE INTERIOR

1. See Roth 1896, 1:1–38, for a general summary of these groups for northern Borneo.

2. See Avé, King, and DeWit 1983, 1–33; Lebar, ed. and comp. 1972, 174–199; and Rousseau 1990 for ethnological overviews of the peoples of various areas of Borneo.

3. Rousseau 1990, 103; Schneeberger 1979, 21; Sellato 1994a.

4. In contrast to the practices of many other peoples, including some of those in Southeast Asia (and, as we shall see, in contrast to modern practices in Borneo), Bornean builders made no use of mud or bricks in constructing longhouses or other buildings, with the minor exception of the clay commonly used in hearths.

5. Stewart 1984.

6. Christensen 2001.

7. Soerianegara and Lemmens, eds. 1994, 22; see also Anderson 1980.

8. Avé and King 1986, 15.

9. This is a practice that an officer of the Timber Research Center in Kuching suggested has the effect of reducing the starch that attracts pests.

10. Described, for example, among the Ma'ayan by Hudson 1972, 97–100.

11. Hudson 1972, 23–24.

12. Lumholtz 1920, 2:299.

13. Ibid., 298.

14. Ibid., 307.

15. Tsing 1996, 195–198.

16. From several accounts, the situation has not changed much in the more recent period. In her ethnographic account of the Meratus people, Tsing 1993, 63–66, notes dispersed houses and *balai* but does not describe the latter as residential places (though she does not say that they were never used in this way). On the other hand, a recent entry in the *Encyclopedia of Vernacular Architecture* describes the Meratus ("Orang Bukit") village of Malaris: "The complete village consists of a single edifice, which is inhabited by 34 families comprising 167 people. . . . The house is situated on the top of a hill and is surrounded by forest. Within an hour's walk there are several rice barns in the paddy-fields" (Oliver, ed. 1997, 1137–1138). The authors of this entry go on to provide an account, though in greater detail and with photographs and drawings, of the same *balai* described by Lumholtz. However, insofar as it is intended to represent Meratus housing and village patterns in general (and no single

houses are noted), it is not in accord with the accounts of either Lumholtz or Tsing.

17. Guerriero 1992; 1997, 1139; 1998, 70.

18. That is, in Sarawak at least, excluding the Selako.

19. Rousseau 1990.

20. See Sellato 1994a, 158–160, on mortuary practices of the nomadic peoples.

21. Metcalf and Huntington 1991, 103, citing Gomes 1911 and Jensen 1974.

22. Metcalf and Huntington 1991, 104, citing Gomes 1911 and Perham 1896; see also Sather 1993, 94–103.

23. Uchibori 1984, 20.

24. They are or were also practiced by some other groups, including at least one Kenyah village in present-day East Kalimantan, as well as by the Ngorik (Schneeberger 1979, 41), the Kayan of the Apo Kayan (Rousseau 1998, 317, citing Nieuwenhuis 1907, 2:118). On secondary treatment in northern Borneo, see T. Harrisson 1962; Metcalf and Huntington 1991, 85–97; Lebar 1972, 172, 175; Metcalf 1975; Nicolaisen 1984; and Rousseau 1990, 28.

25. However, Nicolaisen 1984, 4, reports that among the Punan Bah Kajang the purpose of placing *klirieng* (grave posts) near longhouses was to be able to guard the remains that they contained.

26. Buck 1933, 165; Jamuh 1949. In East Kalimantan and Sarawak uncarved grave posts are also common. These are also notched at the top to receive either a coffin or a jar of remains. Those that are made to hold a jar, like a *klirieng*, are capped with a large, flat stone, while those that are made for a coffin are often covered with a wooden roof.

27. As is the very large *klirieng* on the grounds of the Sarawak Museum in Kuching, where it was eventually placed after having been moved from the Kejaman (Kajang) village of Lasah on the Balui River just above Belaga Town.

28. In actuality, the relationship of grave posts and mausoleums to secondary mortuary practices is somewhat complicated. In the recent past at least, both of these structures have been used both by groups that have secondary mortuary practices and by adjacent ones that (while having well-developed death rituals) do not—that is, in Sarawak by the Kayan of the Balui or upper Rajang. Because of this occurrence and because the grave post itself is made to be a repository for remains

stored in a jar rather than a coffin, it has sometimes been assumed that it originated with the Kajang groups and was later adopted by Kayan aristocrats of Kajang descent. On the other hand, groups such as the Berawan and the Punan Bah Kajang erect *salong* as well as *klirieng* (Metcalf 1976). One explanation for the latter practice in the case of the Punan Bah is that *salong* were adopted after a ban on secondary burial made it impossible to build *klirieng* (Langub 1991, 69).

29. In Sarawak at least, *salong* appear to represent the opposite pattern of diffusion from that of the *klirieng*—that is, they were probably brought by the Kayan and/or Kenyah and adopted from them by the Kajang and other practitioners of secondary mortuary treatment.

30. Metcalf and Huntington 1991, 150.

31. Ibid., 151; see also Metcalf's 1976 report on Berawan mausoleums.

32. Rousseau 1998, 316–317.

33. Langub 1991, 69; Nicolaisen 1984, 5. Neither of these authors states when the ban on secondary mortuary practices was put into effect, but it was probably during the early decades of the twentieth century.

34. Metcalf 1976, 134.

35. On secondary treatments in southern Borneo, see T. Harrisson 1962; Hudson 1972, 125–126; Metcalf and Huntington 1991, 97–100; Lebar 1972, 188, 192; and Schiller 1997.

36. Schiller 1997, 60–61.

37. Schiller 2001a, 75–76.

38. Gill 1968, 143–146.

CHAPTER TWO: THE LONGHOUSE

1. Keppel 1846, 32–33.

2. Blust 1987, 89–95.

3. Leach 1950a, 64.

4. Southwell 1959, 49; T. Harrisson 1959, 321.

5. Freeman 1970, 9–10; see also pp. 61–62.

6. Freeman 1970, 75–78. According to Freeman's account of the Baleh River Iban, in 1947 one-fourth of all Iban longhouses had fewer than ten apartment sections (p. 61).

7. Pringle 1970, 279.

8. Rousseau 1998, 53.

9. Avé and King 1986, 55–56.

10. Hose and McDougall 1912, 1:210.

11. The other Ibanic groups include the Kantu' (Dove 1985) and the Mualang, Seberuang, Desa, and Ketungau peoples (Avé, King, and DeWit 1983, 24–28), all located in the tributaries of the middle Kapuas in West Kalimantan.

12. King 1985a, 82; Arts 1992.

13. Jessup 1998 notes movements in regard to the Kenyah and Kayan in the Apo Kayan highlands of East Kalimantan during three periods, beginning early in the nineteenth century. These groups moved very frequently in the period 1825–1874 (the Kenyah groups moved on average once every seven years, the Kayan ones every five), somewhat less so in the period 1875–1924 (the Kenyah once every ten years and the Kayan once every eight). Movement slowed greatly in the last period, 1925–1984 (the Kenyah moved once every thirty years, the Kayan once every twenty). The changes that are reflected in these figures are, again, related to pacification and the establishment of increasing central administrative control, first by colonial and then by postcolonial political authorities over the area. Developments in Sarawak among the Kenyah and Kayan of the Balui and Baram areas appear to be similar.

14. Gill 1968, 240.

15. Morris 1991, 42.

16. Rousseau 1990, 106–107; Miles 1964; Schneeberger 1979, 25–26; see also Janowski 1995 on modern longhouses among the Kelabit.

17. Sutlive 1978, 55; see also Schneider 1975, 208, on the Selako Bidayuh.

18. Sather 1993, 83.

19. Reproduced in Roth 1896, 2:15.

20. Morris 1978, 47.

21. Freeman 1970, 9.

22. Rousseau 1978, 82–83.

23. Geddes 1954, 34. Men's houses are built and maintained collectively by the men of the village, indicating that communal action is not totally lacking among the Bidayuh.

24. G. N. Appell 1976, 78–79.

25. Freeman 1981, 25–42.

26. See, for example, King 1993, 39, 41–57.

27. For example, according to Whittier, the Lepo' Tau Kenyah of the Apo Kayan "may be said to be composed of three classes: *paran* (aristocrats); *panyin* (commoners) and *panyin la-*

min (slaves, war captives or the descendants of either). Each of these classes in turn has its internal ranking, which is most clear in the *paran* class. The *paran* class is collectively referred to as *lelunan ketau; panyin* and *panyin lamin* may be lumped together and called *anak buah* (children/followers). *Panyin lamin* may be separated from society at large with the appellation of *ula'* (slave)" (1973, 69).

28. Alexander 1992; Armstrong 1992; Sather 1996.

29. Roth 1896, 2:209.

30. See Crain 1970a and 1970b on the Lun Dayeh, Janowski 2003 on the Kelabit, and Hudson 1972, 92–93, on the Ngaju.

31. Beyond the influence of other groups, the differential effects of colonial rule, or various modern developments, the matter of why some groups have highly stratified social orders, others moderately hierarchical ones, and yet others more egalitarian ones cannot be easily accounted for. The geographical distribution of more and less hierarchical societies mentioned above does not have the evident sort of environmental or ecological basis that anthropologists have sometimes noted or hypothesized in efforts to explain the development of social stratification (or chiefdoms or states). The more hierarchically ordered societies of Borneo do not, for example, inhabit richer or more diverse environmental zones (or inland versus coastal, highland versus lowland, or circumscribed versus open terrain) than do the less or nonhierarchical ones. Nor do they exploit the environment with different forms of production (wet rice versus dry rice, more reliance on swidden cultivation and less on hunting and gathering), utilize different technologies or different crop regimes (rice versus sago), or have more trade.

Nor is it known whether more or less hierarchical forms of social organization are older or which, if either, might have prevailed if indigenous or more localized developments had not been overtaken by Western colonial rule in the interior of Borneo. While in terms of the longer sweep of human history it can generally be concluded that hierarchical societies developed later than nonhierarchical ones, there is no basis for inferring this in the case of the longhouse-dwelling societies of Borneo. If it is correct to infer (as Bellwood 1996, 20–21, has suggested) that hierarchy was already a characteristic of the proto-Austronesian peoples who settled in Borneo (where all indigenous languages, including those of hunter-gatherers, are Austronesian) and absorbed or replaced pre-Austronesian ones, then the nonhierarchical forms appear to be a later development—that

is, a matter of devolution. However, neither more nor less stratified societies appear to have had a competitive advantage in terms of success in warfare or political domination, at least in central and northern Borneo. While the hierarchical Kenyah and Kayan have both been powerful and expansive groups, the nonhierarchical Iban have been more successful than either over the course of the last 150 years or so (for which historical information exists) in terms of spreading into and gaining control over new areas. But, on the other hand, the Iban appear to have had no peers among other nonhierarchical societies in this regard.

Finally, the culture of hierarchy has diffused in some instances, but this has not always occurred, even in situations of close proximity between hierarchical and nonhierarchical groups. The Iban appear in some instances to have acquired some artistic designs from the Kenyah or Kayan, along with the notion that such designs are restricted according to rank, and the Iban of the Saribas River appear to have developed hereditary hierarchy as a result of Malay influence, but the Bidayuh in somewhat similar geographical (if not political) circumstances have not. Among the Melanau of coastal and subcoastal central Sarawak, hierarchy may have been further encouraged as a result of strong Malay influence, but the Melanau were almost certainly stratified before they moved to the coast and came into substantial contact with Malays, for they are closely related to the also hierarchical Kajang groups of the interior. The political circumstances of these various relationships (Iban-Kayan, Iban-Malay, Bidayuh-Malay, Melanau-Malay) differ in each case.

32. Avé and King 1986, 55.

33. Hose and McDougall 1912, 1:210.

34. Jessup 1998.

35. Hose and McDougall 1912, 1:208, on the Kayan. See also Nieuwenhuis 1907, 2:95, as well as Rousseau 1990, 175.

36. See Schneeberger 1979, 19, on the Tinggalan of East Kalimantan.

37. King 1985a, 90.

38. Morris 1991, 42.

39. Ibid., 77.

40. King 1985a, 90.

41. Whittier 1973, 167–168.

42. *Adat Bidayuh* 1994, i.

43. Freeman 1970, 122.

44. See King 1985a, 83, on the Maloh.

45. Schneeberger 1979, 19.

46. Schärer 1963, 66; Schiller 1997, 47–48.

47. Freeman 1970, 63.

48. Ibid., 119–120.

49. Ibid., 79. In a more recent discussion, Clifford Sather, who writes specifically of the Paku River (a tributary of the Saribas), stresses that the Iban ideally place their longhouses so as to face both the river and the rising sun, which requires a longitudinal alignment along a north-south axis. He states that the sun should rise in front of the longhouse and set behind it and that it should not rise and set over the ends of a longhouse, but he does not say anything about a diagonal alignment. In symbolic terms the sun is associated with the open veranda (tanju'), which is always on the front of an Iban longhouse. Here sun-based drying activities take place, along with rituals held in the daytime (but not feasting), in contrast with nighttime rituals, which take place mainly in the interior gallery (ruai) of the longhouse (Sather 1993, 79). This at least is the ideal arrangement on the Paku River, though how many Iban longhouses there are actually fully or closely aligned in this way is not reported. Sather 1993, 109, states that thirty-two of thirty-three longhouses on the Paku are aligned with the river but does not say how many of these are also built on the west side of the river, where it also flows along a north-south axis, so as to face the rising sun. He also provides a drawing of longhouse alignment relative to the river and the axis of the travel of the sun. Of the three hypothetical longhouses shown, two are located on the west bank of the river and face it. The remaining longhouse is placed on the opposite or east bank of the river. This longhouse is presumably in an anomalous position in that while it is also aligned parallel to the river, it faces the sun, not the river. This suggests that the importance of facing the sun is greater than that of facing the river, although Sather does not otherwise say that this is the case or discuss what happens when a choice has to be made between facing the rising sun and facing the river. He does say, however, that the east-west orientation of a longhouse is much more variable than the upriver-downriver orientation (owing to the difficulty of finding suitable, level sites for building) and that departures from the ideal arrangement are sanctioned by bird divination (Sather 1993, 110).

50. In Sarawak the flow of many rivers is roughly from south to north, although the axis of any one stretch of any river can be in any direction. Therefore, while "ulu" can be north, south, east, or west, it is in general terms to the south in Sarawak, while "illir" is to the north. With the exception of Sabah, which forms a peninsula, the same general principle applies to other areas of Borneo as well—that is, "ulu" is generally westward in East Kalimantan, northward in Central and South Kalimantan, and eastward in West Kalimantan. In all of these instances it is toward the center of the island. "Ulu" is also, and perhaps rather obviously, the general direction of the highest ranges of mountains (although there are exceptions to this) so that to travel upriver is usually to go not only into the interior, but also up in elevation—sometimes fairly abruptly, sometimes, as with the Kapuas River of West Kalimantan (the longest river in Indonesia) and the Barito of Central Kalimantan, very gradually.

51. In the case of the Baram River, for example, the earlier processes of conversion occurred in the headwaters, among the most remote longhouses, and then moved downriver, reaching the Berawan of the Tinjar and Tutuh (major tributaries of the lower Baram) only later (Metcalf 2002, 112). Such instances appear to be interesting anomalies, explicable in terms of the vicissitudes of the history of mission efforts and political patterns in the interior.

52. King 1985a, 93.

53. Schärer 1963, 73.

54. According to Sather 1993, 77, the Iban apply the upstream-downstream principle to the alignment of lumber in building longhouses. Once a tree is cut for lumber, its base is kept track of. Timbers (at least presumably those that form parts that run lengthwise or parallel to the river) must have their base and tip ends always placed in the same direction (usually pointing from upstream to downstream). Further, where such timbers overlap in slots or mortises in posts, the base end of a timber must be on top of the tip end of the adjoining one.

55. Sandin 1970, 30; Sather 1993, 71.

56. Rousseau 1998, 51, citing Nieuwenhuis 1907, 1:107.

57. Rousseau 1998, 51–52, citing Nieuwenhuis 1907, 2:174–175.

58. Rousseau 1998, 8, citing Bernard Sellato.

59. Hose and McDougall 1912, 1:204; Rousseau 1998, 52.

60. Rousseau 1998, 52, on the Kayan; Sather 1993, 76–77, on the Iban.

61. Rousseau 1998, 52.

CHAPTER THREE: THE ARCHITECTURAL SYMBOLISM OF LIFE AND DEATH

1. Sellato 2001.

2. In low-relief carving on bamboo, the negative areas of the design that have been removed are colored with red or black pigment further to enhance the remaining surface. Alternatively, white lime is often rubbed into the carved depressions of designs carved in dark wood, with the result of greatly emphasizing the contrast between the relief and the remaining areas. Similarly, in the *ikat*, or tie-and-dye technique used in weaving by the Iban and some other groups, images are created by protecting the area to be the figure from the penetration of the dye. In representational beadwork, images are created directly or positively, but the negative technique is often imitated, as, for example, when figures are created in white or other light colored beads surrounded by a background of black ones.

3. Gill 1968, 187–188.

4. Sellato 1989.

5. Gill 1968, 186.

6. Sellato 1989, 103.

7. King 1980.

8. Conley 1973, 97–99; Hose and McDougall 1912, 2:40–41; Metcalf 1982, 237–238; Rousseau 1998, 96–97.

9. Gill 1968, 63–64, 242, illustration 9.

10. King 1985b; Sellato 1989, 36.

11. King 1985b, 129.

12. Schärer 1963.

13. Sellato 1989, 44.

14. Gill 1968, 109; E. B. Haddon 1905, 115; King 1985b, 132–134; Leach 1950b, 134.

15. Heine-Geldern 1966, 196–198.

16. Sellato 1989, 44; Rousseau 1998, 47.

17. Whatever its origins, one common resolution of the dog-or-dragon issue is the use of the term "dog-dragon," either for all instances referred to as "*aso'* " or for those in which the figure resembles a dog or has a combination of dog and reptilian features. The only problem here is that the term "dog-dragon" has no apparent counterpart in Bornean languages, which have only terms for dragons or dragonlike serpents or water spirits and for dogs, and not for combinations. Finally, it is also relevant to point out here another basic characteristic of Bornean design, which is the practice of having one thing turn into another, as when tendrils from dragons become hornbill birds or two dragons in profile are put together to form a demon face as seen from the front.

18. Metcalf 1976, 133.

19. Rousseau 1998, 94.

20. Metcalf 1976, 133.

21. On the general importance and uses of jars in Borneo, see Roth 1896, 2:284–287, and especially B. Harrisson 1986, as well as Sellato 1989, 45; see also Kaboy and Moore 1967 on the use of ceramics among the Melanau.

22. Sellato 1989, 45.

23. B. Harrisson 1986, 19.

24. B. Harrisson 1986, 25–27; King 1985b, 137; see also Kaboy and Moore 1967 on the Melanau.

25. B. Harrisson 1986, 25.

26. Ibid., 27.

27. Ibid., 24.

28. Ibid., 27.

29. Holt 1967, 17–18.

30. See T. Harrisson 1951 on the human uses of the casque, head, and feathers of the rhinoceros hornbill and other hornbills in Borneo.

31. Gill 1968, 110, 143; Sellato 1989, 45–46. Just why, among these groups, the hornbill should be used to represent another bird god rather than being one itself is uncertain. It may be somewhat analogous to referring to or transforming the dragon into a dog, but in an opposite way—that is, perhaps if the dragon is too dangerous to be invoked by name, then the hornbill is not sufficiently ferocious to be regarded as a chief god for warrior societies.

32. Sellato 1989, 45; see also King 1985b, 131, on the hornbill in Maloh culture and Rousseau 1998, 63–65, on the Kayan.

33. Wessing 1986.

34. Sellato 1989, 47.

35. Ibid.

36. For example, the Moon of Pedjeng drum in Bali shown in Holt 1967, 27.

37. Sellato 1989, 46.

38. Rousseau 1998, 93, 257.

39. Schärer 1963, 24, facing 26, 67, 68, 69, 71, and 72.

40. Sellato 1989, 46.

41. Ganjing 1988, 168–183.

42. Gill 1968, 99.

43. Ibid., 99–100.

44. Sellato 2001, 139; Whittier 1973, 169.

45. Ibid., 138.

46. Metcalf 1976, 133.

47. King 1985b, 129.

48. Metcalf 1976, 133.

49. Ganjing writes that "According to Iban belief, those who do not belong to the upper class or those who are in poverty, are not allowed to decorate their rooms with designs of the dragon, human being, tiger, or giant forms. Any violation of this prohibition can bring ruin to the offenders" (1988, xiii).

50. In this regard, however, it is interesting to note that Armstrong, who conducted two years of fieldwork among the Badang Kenyah of Sarawak, observes in an article aimed at disputing the significance that has been attributed to hierarchy that "it is . . . striking that very few people use status symbols to which they are not entitled" (1992, 203).

51. See Mashman 1989 for an account of developments in Sarawak among the Kenyah and Kayan as of the late 1980s.

52. That is, those shown in photos taken before World War II in East Kalimantan (e.g., Tillema 1989, 95), as well as later in the Belaga area of Sarawak (Leach 1950b, 134).

53. Mashman 1989.

CHAPTER FOUR: THE DEVELOPMENT OF BIDAYUH ARCHITECTURE

1. Roth 1896, 2:2–9.

2. Guerriero 1997, 1998, 70; Rousseau 1990, 109–110.

3. It has also been suggested that the Bidayuh occupation of hilltops and mountainsides was a relatively recent development in the precolonial period. Malcolm MacDonald, a high-ranking colonial administrator, has asserted in a popular book on the Dayaks of Sarawak that the Bidayuh preference for high ground was a response to raids by the more numerous and powerful groups, including the Iban and Brunei Malays (MacDonald 1985, 51). However, the Bidayuh adjustment to mountain life is highly skilled and does not suggest a temporary shift. Further, the linguistic diversity of the Bidayuh (in contrast, for example, to the general homogeneity of the Iban), in terms of which the occupants (or former occupants) of one mountain tend to be differentiated from those of the next, is well developed. Finally, many Bidayuh villagers continued to occupy rugged and remote higher locations, long after the Brooke government ended Malay and Iban raiding in the First Division of the 1840s. At present, most Bidayuh communities that formerly occupied less accessible hilltops or mountainsides have shifted to lower, more open valleys or slopes, and in some instances to riversides and roads, although some remain in their old locations, while others have only recently moved down. Tringgus, one of the last of the nineteenth-century villages in Bau (see Grant 1884, 37, for a description in 1858), moved from its previous site only in the early 1980s. While security from raids or coercion by non-Bidayuh may be part of the explanation of Bidayuh settlement patterns, other factors—including the local head-hunting practices of the Bidayuh themselves—are also relevant.

4. St. John 1862, 1:154.

5. For example, Low 1848; St. John 1862; Wallace 1962, summarized in Roth 1896, 2:157.

6. Roth 1896, 2:157.

7. Grijpstra 1976, 63.

8. Jagoi Gunung, which (according to C.T.C. Grant, a Brooke government official who toured the region) was established following the defeat and destruction of Bratak, is one such example (Grant 1884, 99); Gumbang, which at the time of Grant's visit in 1858 had shortly before been moved a few hundred yards to resolve a border dispute with the Dutch in Sambas, is another (Grant 1884, 62).

9. Across the Indonesian border in Sambas, the mixture of older, highland villages and newer, lowland ones suggests a similar development.

10. In Bau the large village of Gumbang remains near its old location, as does the small village of Jagoi Gunung, but each of these ancestral settlements has lower daughter villages. On the other hand, the old villages on Serambu and Singai Mountains, which were often referred to in the nineteenth-century accounts, have all moved down. In upper Padawan and elsewhere some of the older villages remain in or near their older locations.

11. In the Bidayuh areas of West Kalimantan, where heavier government or military authority has been brought to bear, houses in relocated or regrouped Bidayuh villages are apt to be well spaced and set out in a rectangular grid, sometimes in neat rows. In upper Sambas, for example, this influence can be seen in the contrast between the old, high, mountainside community of Tamong, where houses are closely clustered in relation

to the irregularities of the setting and connected by winding bamboo walkways, and the new and lower community of Lemat, where the houses are set apart in two orderly lines.

CHAPTER FIVE: TWO PATTERNS OF CHANGE

1. Leach 1950a, 64–67.
2. Morris 1991, 44.
3. *Historical Buildings, Monuments and Sites in Sarawak* 1995, 50.
4. Sellato 1994b, 163–168.
5. Jessup 1998, 27.
6. Described by King 1985a, 82, for the Maloh.
7. Morris 1991, 76–77.
8. Miles 1964, 54.
9. Whittier 1973, 52.
10. Pearson-Rounds and Crain 1998, 61, concerning the Lundayeh–Lun Bawang.
11. Drake 1998, 120. See also Whittier 1973, 57, on the Kenyah of the Apo Kayan in East Kalimantan.
12. Laway 1998 on the Kayan of East Kalimantan.
13. Laway 1998; Mudiyono 1994.
14. Sellato 1998, 202.
15. Waterson 1990, 31–34.
16. Pringle 1970, 320–349.
17. Ibid., 280.
18. Ibid., 279–280.
19. Leach 1950a, 63.
20. Rousseau 1990, 33–37.
21. King 1985a, 63.
22. Laway 1998; Dove 1982, 19.
23. Lumholtz 1920, 2:317.
24. King 1985a, 195–198. See also Fried 2001, 82–83, on anti-longhouse efforts and their effects among the Bentian of East Kalimantan.
25. Whittier 1973, 38.
26. Sellato 1994b, 172; see also Langub 1974.
27. See Hooker and Dick 1993, 4.
28. Laway 1998, 48–50.
29. See Sellato 1998, 199–200, and Sellato n.d.
30. Dove 1982, 18; Frans and Kanyan 1994, 205.
31. King 1993, 287; Muller 1992, 49.
32. See Appell-Warren 1985, 10–15; Avé and King 1986, 98; and Tsing 1993, 155–156, for discussions of these notions; for a

general anthropological critique of development attitudes and policies in Indonesia, see Dove 1988.
33. Appell-Warren 1985, 14.
34. Jenkins 1978, 23.
35. Drake 1998, 134–135, regarding the Mualang of West Kalimantan.
36. See, for example, G. N. Appell 1985 and Appell-Warren 1985 on the Bulusu' of northeastern East Kalimantan.
37. King 1985a, 195–196.
38. Wadley and Kuyah 2001, 722–723.
39. Ibid., 723.
40. Dove 1982, 39–40; Leach 1950a, 26; Pringle 1970, 205–206.
41. Whittier 1973, 52.
42. King 1985a, 102.
43. Ibid., 103–104, 195–196.
44. Leach 1950b, 63.
45. Kelbling 1983.
46. For example, Alexander 1993.
47. Kelbling 1983, 140–144. Since no specific examples are described or illustrated, it is difficult to know how much the longhouses had been changed by that time.
48. Kelbling 1983, 146–147.
49. *Design Brief, Bakun Resettlement Project, Part B, Existing Longhouses* 1996.

CHAPTER SIX: MODERN USES AND THE FUTURE OF INDIGENOUS ARCHITECTURE

1. On Taman Mini, see Pemberton 1994, 152, and Sellato n.d., 11–12.
2. Morris 1991, 42, 77.
3. While those in Palangkaraya and Tenggarong are supposed to be based on existing longhouses, the one in Pontianak is a composite and bears little resemblance to any existing West Kalimantan longhouse but, instead, replicates the one in the Kalbar pavilion in Taman Mini. See Sellato 1998 and n.d.
4. Sellato n.d., 11.
5. This is so even in areas occupied by the same groups (the Kenyah and Kayan) that have created indigenous carvings, paintings, and statuary in churches in Kalimantan.
6. As of 1994 at least.
7. See Schiller 2001b for a description of a Kenyah tourist

longhouse in the village of Pampang, near the provincial capital and tourist gateway of Samarinda in East Kalimantan.

8. Look for "Sarawak," "longhouse," and "Borneo" on the Internet, although searches for the last will also yield ads for East Kalimantan tours.

9. Masing 1997, 10.

10. On tourism among the Iban, see Kedit and Sabang 1992, Kruse 1998, and Zeppel 1992.

11. Kruse writes the following: "In the field I was presented with one scenario time and time again. It involved tourists standing by the river bank, having just stepped from their longboat, and gazing at the sight of a four-hundred foot long wooden longhouse built on stilts, only to say, 'This is not a "real" longhouse, it has a tin roof.' . . . For the Iban in the longhouse it was a common joke but also a cause of some bitterness" (1998, 144–145).

12. *Historical Buildings, Monuments and Sites in Sarawak* 1995.

13. Only two entries for longhouses are included. One of these (page 50) is to the last existing Melanau longhouse (at Kampung Sok in Matu, declared a historical building), and the other (page 66) is to the site of an Iban longhouse in Saratok that in an early morning of 1833 was attacked and burned by a rival group of Iban from Banting and Lingga, with a loss of life of 133 occupants—the historical significance being, in part, that it was the longhouse of Temenggong Tandok, an Iban chief appointed by the sultan of Brunei to oversee the Krian Tengah region, which was then (more or less) under Brunei control.

According to James Masing (an Iban, an anthropologist, and minister of tourism in the state government of Sarawak), the problem with designating longhouses as historic sites subject to rules or efforts at preservation is that there are so many of them. In addition, the ownership of longhouses is based on *adat* and is in the hands of the owners of the individual apartments, who therefore have the right to modify or retain their apartments as they (within limits) choose.

14. The round men's house in Opar Village has been designated a historical building.

15. These include the Kayan in Sarawak (see Rousseau 1998, 301) and the Taman in West Kalimantan.

BIBLIOGRAPHY

Adat Bidayuh 1994
  1994 Kuching, Sarawak: Majalis Adat Istiadat.
Alexander, Jennifer
  1992 "Must Ascribed Status Entail Inequality? Reproduction of Rank in Lahanan Society." *Oceania* 62:207–226.
  1993 "The Lahanan Longhouse." In Fox., ed., *Inside Austronesian Houses*, pp. 31–43.
Anderson, J. A. R.
  1980 *A Check List of the Trees of Sarawak.* Kuching: Dewan Bahasa dan Pustaka Cawangan Sarawak, For Forest Department, Sarawak.
Appell, G. N.
  1976 "The Rungus: Social Structure in a Cognatic Society and Its Ritual Symbolization." In *The Societies of Borneo: Explorations in Cognatic Social Structure*, ed. G. N. Appell, pp. 146–151. Washington, D.C.: Special Publication of the American Anthropological Association, No. 6.
  1978 "The Rungus Dusun." In King, ed., *Essays on Borneo Societies*, pp. 143–171.
  1985 "Resettlement of the Bulusu' in Indonesian Borneo." *Borneo Research Bulletin* 17(1):21–31.
Appell-Warren, L. P.
  1985 "Resettlement of the Bulusu' and Punan in Indonesian Borneo: Policy and History." *Borneo Research Bulletin* 17(1):10–20.

Armstrong, Rita
  1992 "The Cultural Construction of Hierarchy among the Kenyah Badeng." *Oceania* 62:194–206.
Arts, Henry
  1992 "Ulu' Banua, a Longhouse of the Taman-Daya." *Borneo Research Bulletin* 24:68–78.
Avé, Jan B., and Victor T. King
  1986 *Borneo: The People of the Weeping Forest, Tradition and Change.* Leiden: National Museum of Ethnology.
Avé, Jan B., Victor T. King, and Joke G. W. De Wit
  1983 *West Kalimantan: A Bibliography.* Leiden: Koninklijk Instituut Voor Taal-, Land En Volkenkunde.
Barbier, J. P.
  1982 "The Batak of Sumatra." In *Art of the Archaic Indonesians*, ed. W. Stöhr et al., pp. 46–54. Geneva: Musée d'Art et d'Histoire.
Beccari, Odorado
  1904 *Wanderings in the Great Forests of Borneo.* London: Archibald Constable.
Bellwood, Peter
  1996 "Hierarchy, Founder Ideology and Austronesian Expansion." In *Origins, Ancestry and Alliance: Explorations in Austronesian Ethnology*, ed. James A. Fox and Clifford Sather, pp. 18–40. Canberra: Department of Anthropology, Australian National University.
Blust, Robert
  1987 "Lexical Reconstruction and Semantic Reconstruction: The Case of Austronesian 'House' Words." *Diachronica* 4(1–2):79–106.

Bock, Carl

  1881 *The Head-Hunters of Borneo: A Narrative of Travel up the Mahakkam and down the Barito.* London: Sampson, Low, Marston, Searle and Rivington.

Boyle, Fred

  1865 *Adventures among the Dyaks of Borneo.* London: Hurst and Blackett.

Brooke, Charles

  1866 *Ten Years in Sarawak.* London: Tinsley Brothers.

Brosius, J. Peter

  2001 "Local Knowledge, Global Claims: On the Significance of Indigenous Ecologies in Sarawak, East Malaysia." In Grim, ed., *Indigenous Traditions and Ecology,* pp. 125–157.

Buck, W. S. B.

  1933 "Notes on the Oya Milanos." *Sarawak Museum Journal* 4(2):157–174.

Carsten, Janet, and Stephen Hugh-Jones, eds.

  1995 *About the House: Levi-Strauss and Beyond.* Cambridge: Cambridge University Press.

Chin, S. C.

  1985 *Agriculture and Resource Utilization in a Lowland Rainforest Kenyah Community.* Special Monograph No. 4. *Sarawak Museum Journal* 35 (56).

Christensen, Hanna

  2001 "Botany." In *Encyclopaedia of Iban Studies,* gen. ed. Vinson Sutlive and Joanne Sutlive, vol. 1, pp. 239–262.

Conley, W. W.

  1973 "The Kalimantan Kenyah: A Study of Tribal Conversion in Terms of Dynamic Cultural Themes." Ph.D. dissertation, Fuller Theological Seminary. Published in 1976 as *The Kalimantan Kenyah: A Study of Tribal Conversion in Terms of Dynamic Cultural Themes.* Nutley, N.Y.: Presbyterian and Reformed Publishing.

Crain, Jay

  1970a "The Domestic Family and Long-House among the Mengalong Lun Dayeh." *Sarawak Museum Journal* 18:186–192.

  1970b "The Mengalong Lun Dayeh Long-House." *Sarawak Museum Journal* 18:169–185.

Dawson, Barry, and John Gillow

  1994 *The Traditional Architecture of Indonesia.* London: Thames and Hudson.

Design Brief, Bakun Resettlement Project

  1996 *Part B, Existing Longhouses.* Kuching: State Planning Unit, Government of Sarawak.

d'Estrey, Meyners

  1891 *A travers Borneo.* Paris: Hachette.

Dove, Michael R.

  1982 "The Myth of the 'Communal' Longhouse: The Kantu' of West Kalimantan." In *Too Rapid Development: Perceptions and Perspectives for Southeast Asia,* ed. Collin MacAndrews and Chia Lin Sien, pp. 14–78. Athens, Ohio: Ohio University Press.

  1985 *Swidden Agriculture in Indonesia: The Subsistence Agriculture of the Kalimantan Kantu'.* Berlin: Mouton.

  1988 "Introduction: Traditional Culture and Development in Contemporary Indonesia." In *The Real and Imagined Role of Culture in Development,* ed. Michael R. Dove, pp. 1–37. Honolulu: University of Hawai'i Press.

Drake, Richard Allen

  1998 "The Politics of Longhouse Architecture among the Mualang of Belintang Hulu." In Winzeler, ed., *Indigenous Architecture in Borneo,* pp. 119–137.

Elshout, J. M.

  1926 *De Kenja-Dajaks uit Apo Kajangebied: Bijdragen tot de kennis van Centraal-Borneo.* The Hague: Martinus Nijhoff.

Florus, Paulus, Stepanus Djuweng, John Bamba, and Nico Andasputra, eds.

  1994 *Kebudayaan dayak: Actualisasi dan transformasi.* Jakarta: PT Grasindo.

Fox, James G., ed.

  1993 *Inside Austronesian Houses: Perspectives on Domestic Designs for Living.* Canberra: Department of Anthropology, Australian National University.

Frans, S. Jacobus E., and L. Concordius Kanyan

  1994 "Rumah panjang sebagai kebudayaan dayak." In Florus, Djuweng, Bamba, and Andasputra, eds., *Kebudayaan Dayak,* pp. 199–210.

Freeman, Derek

  1970 *Report on the Iban.* London: Athlone Press. London School of Economics Monographs on Social Anthropology, No. 41. (Originally published in 1955.)

  1981 *Some Reflection on the Nature of Iban Society.* Canberra: Research School of Pacific Studies, Australian National University. Occasional Paper of the Department of Anthropology.

Fried, Stephanie

2001 "Shoot the Horse to Get the Rider: Religion and Forest Politics in Bentian Borneo." In Grim, ed., *Indigenous Traditions and Ecology*, pp. 71–99.

Furness, W. H.

1902 *The Home-Life of Borneo Headhunters: Its Festivals and Folklore*. Philadelphia: Lippincott.

Ganjing, Augustine Anggat

1988 *Basic Iban Design: An Introduction*. Kuala Lumpur: Dewan Bahasa dan Pustaka.

Geddes, W. R.

1954 *The Land Dayaks of Sarawak: A Report on a Social Economic Survey of the Land Dayaks of Sarawak Presented to the Colonial Social Science Research Council*. London: H. M. Stationery Office. Colonial Research Studies, No. 14.

1957 *Nine Dayak Nights*. Melbourne: Oxford University Press.

Gill, S.

1968 "Selected Aspects of Sarawak Arts." Ph.D. dissertation, Columbia University.

Gomes, E. H.

1911 *Seventeen Years among the Sea Dyaks of Borneo*. Philadelphia: Lippincott.

Grant, C. T. C.

1884 "A Tour of the Dayaks of Sarawak: Borneo in 1858." London.

Grijpstra, B. G.

1976 *Common Efforts in the Development of Rural Sarawak, Malaysia*. Amsterdam: Van Gorcum.

Grim, John A., ed.

2001 *Indigenous Traditions and Ecology: The Interbeing of Cosmology and Community*. Cambridge, Mass.: Center for the Study of World Religions, Harvard Divinity School. Distributed by Harvard University Press.

Guerriero, Antonio. J.

1992 "La structure villageoise Modang Wehèa." In *Architectures et cultures*, Cahiers de la recherche architecturale, no. 27–28: 71–88.

1997 "Modang." In Oliver, ed., *Encyclopedia of Vernacular Architecture of the World*, vol. 2, pp. 1139–1140.

1998 "The Modang Men's House in Regard to Social and Cultural Values." In Winzeler, ed., *Indigenous Architecture in Borneo*, pp. 69–87.

Haddon, Alfred C.

1901 *Head-Hunters: Black, White and Brown*. London: Methuen.

Haddon, Ernest B.

1905 "The Dog-Motive in Bornean Art." *Journal of the Royal Anthropological Institute* 35:113–125.

Harrisson, Barbara

1986 *Pusaka: Heirloom Jars of Borneo*. Singapore: Oxford University Press.

Harrisson, Tom

1951 "Humans and Hornbills in Borneo." *Sarawak Museum Journal* 3:400–413.

1959 *World Within: A Borneo Story*. London: Cresset Press.

1962 "Borneo Death." *Bidragen tot de Taal-, Land- en Volkenkunde van Nederlandsch Indie* 118:1–41.

————, ed.

1959 *The Peoples of Sarawak*. Kuching: Sarawak Museum.

Heine-Geldern, Robert

1966 "Some Tribal Art Styles of Southeast Asia: An Experiment in Art History." In *The Many Faces of Primitive Art*, ed. Douglass Fraser, pp. 161–221. Englewood Cliffs, N.J.: Prentice-Hall.

Helliwell, Christine

1993 "Good Walls Make Bad Neighbors: The Dayak Longhouse as a Community of Voices." In Fox, ed., *Inside Austronesian Houses*, pp. 44–62.

Helms, Ludvig

1882 *Pioneering in the Far East, and Journeys to California in 1849 and to the White Sea in 1878*. London: W. H. Allen.

Historical Buildings, Monuments and Sites in Sarawak.

1995 Kuching: Sarawak Museum.

Holt, Claire

1967 *Art in Indonesia: Continuities and Change*. Ithaca, N.Y.: Cornell University Press.

Hooker, Virginia M., and Howard Dick

1993 "Introduction." In *Culture and Society in New Order Indonesia*, ed. Virginia M. Hooker and Howard Dick, pp. 1–23. Kuala Lumpur: Oxford University Press.

Hornaday, William T.

1908 *Two Years in the Jungle: The Experiences of a Hunter and Naturalist in India, Ceylon, the Malay Peninsula and Borneo*. New York: Charles Scribner's Sons. Originally published in 1885.

Hose, Charles, and William McDougall

1912　*The Pagan Tribes of Borneo*. 2 vols. London, Frank Cass.

Hudson, A. B.

1972　*Padju Epat: The Ma'anyan of Indonesian Borneo*. New York: Holt, Rinehart, and Winston.

Jamuh, G.

1949　"Jerunei." *Sarawak Museum Journal* 5:62–68.

Janowski, Monica

1995　"The Hearth-Group, the Conjugal Couple and Symbolism of the Rice Meal among the Kelabit of Sarawak." In *About the House: Levi-Strauss and Beyond*, ed. Janet Carsten and Stephen Hugh-Jones, pp. 84–104. Cambridge: Cambridge University Press.

2003　"Who's in Charge Around Here? Struggle for Leadership in a Changing World among the Kelabit of Sarawak." In Sparks and Howell, eds., *The House in Southeast Asia*, pp. 95–113.

Jenkins, David

1978　"The Dayaks: Goodby to All That." *Far Eastern Economic Review*, June 30, pp. 22–26.

Jensen, Erik

1974　*The Iban and Their Religion*. Oxford: Clarendon Press.

Jessup, Timothy C.

1998　"House Building, Mobility and Architectural Variation in Central Borneo." In Winzeler, ed., *Indigenous Architecture in Borneo*, pp. 16–41.

Jongejans, J.

1922　*Uit Dajakland: Kijkjes in het leven van den koppensneller en zijne omgeving*. Amsterdam: Meulenhoff.

Kaboy, Tuton, and Eine Moore

1967　"Ceramics and Their Uses among the Coastal Melanaus (a Field Survey)." *Sarawak Museum Journal* 15:10–29.

Kedit, Peter, and Clement Sabang

1992　"Tourism Report: A Restudy of Skrang Longhouse Tourism." In King, ed., *Tourism in Borneo*, pp. 45–58.

Kelbling, Sebastian

1983　"Longhouses at Balui River." *Sarawak Museum Journal* 32:133–158.

Keppel, Henry

1846　*The Expedition to Borneo of HMS Dido for the Suppression of Piracy, with Extracts from the Diary of the Journal of James Brooke, Esq., of Sarawak*. New York: Harper and Brothers.

King, Victor T.

1978　"The Maloh." In King, ed., *Essays on Borneo Societies*, pp. 193–214.

1980　"Structural Analysis and Cognatic Societies: Some Borneo Examples." *Sociologus* 30:1–28.

1985a　*The Maloh of West Kalimantan: An Ethnographic Study of Social Inequality and Social Change among an Indonesian Borneo People*. Dordrecht, Holland: Forris Publications. Verhandelingen van het Koninklijk Instituut voor Taal-, Land- en Volkenkunde, 108.

1985b　"Symbols of Social Differentiation: A Comparative Investigation of Signs, the Signified and Symbolic Meanings in Borneo." *Antropos* 80:125–152.

1993　*The Peoples of Borneo*. Oxford: Blackwell.

———, ed.

1978　*Essays on Borneo Societies*. Oxford: Oxford University Press. Hull Monographs on South-East Asia, No. 7.

1992　*Tourism in Borneo: Papers from the Second Biennial International Conference, Kota Kinabalu, Sabah, Malaysia, July 1992*. Borneo Research Council Proceedings, Series No. 4.

Kruse, William

1998　"Tourism, Cultural Change and the Architecture of Iban Longhouses in Sarawak." In Winzeler, ed., *Indigenous Architecture in Borneo*, pp. 138–169.

Langub, Jayl

1974　"Adaptation to a Settled Life by the Punan of the Belaga Sub-District." *Sarawak Museum Journal* 22:295–301.

1991　"Orang Ulu Carving." In *Sarawak Cultural Legacy: A Living Tradition*, ed. Lucas Chin and Valerie Mashman, pp. 61–74. Kuching: Society Atelier Sarawak.

Laway, Balan

1998　"The Traditional House of the Uma' Leken Kayan of East Kalimantan." In Winzeler, ed., *Indigenous Architecture in Borneo*, pp. 42–51.

Leach, E. R.

1950a　*Social Science Research in Sarawak: A Report of the Possibilities of a Social Economic Survey of Sarawak Presented to the Colonial Social Science Research Council*. London: H. M. Stationery Office for the Colonial Office.

1950b　"A Kejaman Tomb Post from the Belaga Area of Sarawak." *Man* 218:133–136.

Lebar, Frank M., ed. and comp.

    1972   *Ethnic Groups of Insular Southeast Asia.* Vol. 1: *Indonesia, Andaman Islands and Madagascar.* New Haven, Conn.: Human Relations Area Files Press.

Lemmens, R. H. M. J., I. Soerianegara, and W. C. Wong, eds.

    1995   *Plant Resources of South-East Asia, No. 5 (2): Timber Trees: Minor Commercial Timbers.* Leiden: Backhuys.

Lévi-Strauss, Claude

    1963   *Structural Anthropology.* New York: Basic Books.

Low, Hugh

    1848   *Sarawak. Its Inhabitants and Productions: Being Notes Taken during a Residence in That Country with H. H. the Rajah Brooke.* London: Bently.

Lumholtz, C. S.

    1920   *Through Central Borneo: An Account of Two Years' Travel in the Land of the Headhunters between the Years 1913 and 1917.* 2 vols. New York: Scribner.

Macdonald, G., ed.

    1987   *De la hutte au palais: Sociétés "à maisons" en Asie du Sud-Est insulaire.* Paris: Editions du CNRS.

MacDonald, Malcolm

    1985   *Borneo People.* Singapore: Oxford University Press. (Originally published in 1956.)

Mallinckrodt, J. M.

    1924   "Ethnografische Medeelingen over de Dajak in de Afdeling Koalakapoeas." *Bidragen tot de Taal-, Land- en Volkenkunde van Nederlandsch Indie* 80:555–567.

Mashman, Valerie

    1989   "Ethnic Arts and Society." *Sarawak Museum Journal* 61. Special Issue No. 4, Part 3:215–229.

Masing, James

    1997   "Tourism and the Protection of Indigenous Cultures." Paper presented at PATA Conference, Beijing, April 22.

Metcalf, Peter

    1975   "The Distribution of the Treatment of the Dead in Central Northern Borneo." *Borneo Research Bulletin* 7:54–59.

    1976   "Berawan Mausoleums." *Sarawak Museum Journal* 24:121–136.

    1982   *A Borneo Journey into Death.* Philadelphia: University of Pennsylvania Press.

    2002   *They Lie, We Lie: Getting on with Anthropology.* London: Routledge.

Metcalf, Peter, and Richard Huntington

    1991   *Celebrations of Death: The Anthropology of Mortuary Ritual,* 2d ed. Cambridge: Cambridge University Press.

Miles, D.

    1964   "The Ngadju Longhouse." *Oceania* 35:45–57.

Molengraaff, G. A. F.

    1902   *Borneo-Expedition: Geological Explorations in Central Borneo (1893–94).* Leiden: Brill; London: Kegan Paul, Trench, Trubner.

Morris, Stephen

    1978   "The Coastal Melanau." In King, ed., *Essays on Borneo Societies,* pp. 37–58.

    1991   *The Oya Melanau.* Kuching: Malaysian Historical Society.

Mudiyono

    1994   "Perubahan structure pedesaan masyarakat Dayak: Dari rumah panjang ke rumah tunggal." In Florus, Djuweng, Bamba, and Andasputra, eds., *Kebudayaan dayak,* pp. 211–221.

Muller, Kal

    1992   *Indonesian Borneo: Kalimantan.* Hong Kong: Periplus Editions.

Nicolaisen, Ida

    1984   "Heritage, Identity and Cultural Policy—The Case of Sarawakian Burial Posts." *Sarawak Gazette,* vol. 110, no. 1384 (July 1984): 3–6.

Nieuwenhuis, A. W.

    1907   *Quer durch Borneo: Ergebnisse seiner Reisen in den Jahren 1896–97 und 1898–1900.* Leiden: Brill.

Oliver, Paul, ed.

    1997   *Encyclopedia of the Vernacular Architecture of the World,* vol. 2. Cambridge: Cambridge University Press.

Pearson-Rounds, Vicki, and Jay B. Crain

    1998   "From 'Bang Tetel' to 'Bawang': Patterns of Transformation and Coherence in Lundayeh-Lun Bawang Architecture." In Winzeler, ed., *Indigenous Architecture in Borneo,* pp. 52–68.

Pemberton, John

    1994   *On the Subject of Java.* Ithaca, N.Y.: Cornell University Press.

Perham, J.

    1896   "Petera or Sea Dyak Gods." In Roth, *The Natives of Sarawak and British North Borneo,* 1: 168–213.

Pringle, R.
1970   *Rajahs and Rebels: The Ibans of Sarawak under Brooke Rule,*
        1841–1941. London: Macmillan.

Roth, Henry Ling
1896   *The Natives of Sarawak and British North Borneo.* 2 vols.
        London: Truslove and Hanson.

Rousseau, Jérôme
1978   "The Kayan." In King, ed., *Essays on Borneo Societies,* pp.
        78–91.
1980   "Iban Inequality." *Bijdragen tot de Taal-, Land- en Volken-*
        kunde 136:52–63.
1990   *Central Borneo: Ethnic Identity and Social Life in a Stratified*
        Society. Oxford: Clarendon Press.
1998   *Kayan Religion: Ritual Life and Religious Reform in Central*
        Borneo. Leiden: KITLV Press.

Rudofsky, Bernard
1964   *Architecture without Architects: An Introduction to Non-Pedi-*
        greed Architecture. New York: Museum of Modern Art.

St. John, Spenser
1862   *Life in the Forests of the Far East.* 2 vols. London: Smith,
        Elder.

Sandin, Benedict
1970   "The Old Fashion Iban Longhouse." *Sarawak Gazette,*
        February 28, 1970, pp. 29–32.

Sather, Clifford
1993   "Posts, Hearths and Thresholds: The Iban Longhouse
        as a Ritual Structure." In Fox., ed., *Inside Austronesian*
        Houses, pp. 64–115.
1996   " 'All Threads Are White': Iban Egalitarianism Recon-
        sidered." In *Origins, Ancestry and Alliance: Explorations in*
        Austronesian Ethnography, ed. James G. Fox and Clifford
        Sather, 70–110. Canberra: Department of Anthropol-
        ogy, Australian National University.

Schärer, H.
1963   *Ngaju Religion: The Conception of God among a South Bor-*
        neo People. Translated by R. Needham. The Hague:
        Nijhoff.

Schiller, Anne
1997   *Small Sacrifices: Religious Change and Cultural Identity*
        among the Ngaju of Indonesia. New York: Oxford Univer-
        sity Press.
2001a   "Mortuary Monuments and Social Change among the
        Ngaju." In *Social Memory, Identity and Death: Anthropo-*
        logical Perspectives on Mortuary Rituals, ed. Meredith

Chesson, pp. 69–78. Washington, D.C.: Archaeologi-
        cal Papers of the American Anthropological Associa-
        tion, No. 10.
2001b   "Pampang Culture Village and International Tourism
        in East Kalimantan, Indonesian Borneo." *Human Or-*
        ganization 60 (4):414–422.

Schneeberger, W. F.
1979   *Contributions to the Ethnology of Central Northeast Borneo*
        (Parts of Kalimantan, Sarawak and Sabah). Berne: Insti-
        tute of Ethnology, University of Berne.

Schneider, William M.
1975   "Aspects of Architecture, Sociology, and Symbolism
        of the Selako House." *Sarawak Museum Journal* 23:207–
        219.

Schwaner, C. A. L. M.
1853–1854   *Borneo: Beschrijving van het Stroomgeblied van den*
        Barito. 2 vols. Amsterdam: P. N. Van Kampen.

Sellato, Bernard
1989   *Hornbill and Dragon: Kalimantan, Sarawak, Sabah, Bru-*
        nei. Jakarta: Elf Aquitaine Indonesie.
1994a   "Social Organization, Settlement Patterns and Ethno-
        linguistic Boundaries in East Kalimantan." Paper pre-
        sented at Third Biennial Conference of the Borneo
        Research Council, Pontianak, July 10–14.
1994b   *Nomads of the Rainforest: The Economics, Politics and Ideol-*
        ogy of Settling Down. Honolulu: University of Hawai'i
        Press.
1998   "Modern Architecture and Provincial Identity in Ka-
        limantan." In Winzeler, ed., *Indigenous Architecture in*
        Borneo, pp. 198–234.
2001   "High Status and Low Relief: Carved Doors and Pan-
        els of Borneo." *Arts and Cultures* 23(2):137–155.
n.d.   "Spatial Organization and Provincial Cultural Iden-
        tity: Historical Factors and Current Trends in Kali-
        mantan." In *Beyond the State: Essays on Spatial Structura-*
        tion in Insular Southeast Asia, ed. M. Charles. Paris:
        LASEMA-CNRS.

Soerianegara, I., and R. H. M. J. Lemmens, eds.
1994   *Plant Resources of South-East Asia, No. 5 (1): Timber Trees:*
        Major Commercial Timbers. Bogor: PROSEA Founda-
        tion.

Southwell, H.
1959   "Kayans and Kenyahs." In Harrisson ed., *The Peoples of*
        Sarawak, pp. 39–56.

Sparks, Stephen, and Signe Howell, eds.

2003　*The House in Southeast Asia: A Changing Social, Economic and Political Domain.* London: Routledge Curzon.

Stewart, Hillary

1984　*Cedar: Tree of Life to the Northwest Coast Indians.* Seattle: University of Washington Press.

Sutlive, Vinson H., Jr.

1978　*The Iban of Sarawak: Chronicle of a Vanishing World.* Prospect Heights, Ill.: Waveland Press.

Tillema, H. F.

1938　*Apo Kayan: Ein Filmreis naar an door Centraal-Borneo.* Amsterdam: Van Munster.

1989　*A Journey among the Peoples of Central Borneo in Word and Picture.* Edited by V. T. King. Singapore: Oxford University Press.

Tsing, Anna Lowenhaupt

1993　*In the Realm of the Diamond Queen.* Princeton, N.J.: Princeton University Press.

1996　"Telling Violence in the Meratus Mountains." In *Head-hunting and the Social Imagination in Southeast Asia,* ed. Janet Hoskins, pp. 184–215. Stanford, Calif.: Stanford University Press.

Uchibori, Motomitsu

1984　"The Enshrinement of the Dead among the Iban." *Sarawak Museum Journal* 28:15–32.

Wadley, Reed, and Fredrik Kuyah

2001　"Iban Communities in West Kalimantan." In *Encyclopaedia of Iban Studies,* gen. ed. Vinson Sutlive and Joanne Sutlive, vol. 2, pp. 716–734.

Wallace, Alfred R.

1962　*The Malay Archipelago: The Land of the Orang-utan and the Bird of Paradise, a Narrative of Travel, with Studies of Man and Nature.* New York: Dover Publications. Originally published 1869.

Waterson, Roxana

1990　*The Living House: An Anthropology of Architecture in South-East Asia.* Singapore: Oxford University Press.

———, ed.

1998　*The Architecture of Southeast Asia through Travelers' Eyes.* Singapore: Oxford University Press.

Wessing, Robert

1986　*The Soul of Ambiguity: The Tiger in Southeast Asia.* De Kalb: Center for Southeast Asian Studies, Monograph Series on Southeast Asia, Northern Illinois University. Special Report No. 24.

Whittier, Herbert Lincoln

1973　"Social Organization and Symbols of Social Differentiation: An Ethnographic Study of the Kenyah Dayak of East Kalimantan (Borneo)." Ph.D. dissertation, Michigan State University.

Winzeler, Robert L.

1996　"Bidayuh Architecture: Tradition, Change, Revival." *Sarawak Museum Journal* 50:11–24.

1997　"Modern Bidayuh Ethnicity and the Politics of Culture in Sarawak." In *Indigenous Peoples and the State: Politics, Land and Ethnicity in the Malayan Peninsula and Borneo,* ed. Robert L. Winzeler, pp. 201–227. New Haven, Conn.: Yale University Southeast Asian Studies. Monograph No. 46.

1998a　"Introduction." In Winzeler, ed., *Indigenous Architecture in Borneo,* pp. 1–15.

1998b　"Men's Houses and the Representation of Culture among the Bidayuh." In Winzeler, ed., *Indigenous Architecture in Borneo,* pp. 170–197.

1998c　"Two Patterns of Architectural Change in Borneo." In Winzeler, ed., *Indigenous Architecture in Borneo,* pp. 88–118.

———, ed.

1998　*Indigenous Architecture in Borneo: Traditional Patterns and New Developments.* Borneo Research Council Proceedings, Series No. 5.

Wood, J. G.

1870–1872　*The Uncivilized Races of Man in All Countries; Being a Comprehensive Account of Their Manners and Customs, and Their Physical, Social, Mental, Moral and Religious Characteristics.* 2 vols. Hartford, Conn.: J. B. Barr and Hyde.

Zeppel, Heather

1992　"Getting to Know the Iban: The Tourist Experience of Visiting an Iban Longhouse in Sarawak." In King, ed., *Tourism in Borneo,* pp. 59–66.

LIST OF SOURCES AND CREDITS

Photographs and illustrations are by the author except as noted below.

0.1. Reports of the Rheinische Missionsgeselshaft, October 1874.

0.2. Schwaner 1853–1854, 2: facing p. 22.

0.3. St. John 1862, 2: facing p. 123.

0.4. Wood 1870–1872, 499.

0.5. Boyle 1865, frontispiece.

0.6. Molengraaff 1902, 77–78.

0.7. Nieuwenhuis 1907, 2: illustration 30, following p. 164.

0.9. Drawn by Robert L. Winzeler (RLW), based in part on King 1994, 39, and Sellato 1989, 7.

1.1. Drawn from a photo in *Historical Buildings, Monuments and Sites of Sarawak* 1995, 74, by Timothy Pyles (TP).

1.7. Hornaday 1908, facing p. 484.

1.10. Drawn from a photo in Sellato 1998, 221, by TP.

1.11. Drawn from a photo in Guerriero 1998, 77, by TP.

1.15. Photo by Lim Yu Seng (LYS), used with the permission of the Sarawak Museum.

1.18. Wallace 1962, 60.

1.20. Photo, Sarawak Museum archives, used with permission of the Sarawak Museum.

1.23. Drawn from a photo by RLW by TP.

1.24. Drawn from a photo in Schneeberger 1979, 129, by TP.

1.26. Photo by LYS, used with the permission of the Sarawak Museum.

1.27. Photo by LYS, used with the permission of the Sarawak Museum.

1.29. Drawn from a photo in Molengraaff 1902, facing p. 284, by Barbara Erickson (BE).

1.31. Photo by LYS, used with the permission of the Sarawak Museum.

2.1. Hornaday 1908, facing p. 357.

2.4. Photo by Allen Drake (AD).

2.5. Photo by LYS, used with the permission of the Sarawak Museum.

2.6. Photo by LYS, used with the permission of the Sarawak Museum.

2.7. Photo by LYS.

2.8. Photo, Sarawak Museum archives, used with permission of the Sarawak Museum.

2.9. Photo, Sarawak Museum archives, used with permission of the Sarawak Museum.

2.14. Drawing based on Schneeberger (1979, 26—Murut and Kelabit) and Miles (1964, 47—Ngaju) by RLW.

2.15. Photo by Bernard Sellato (BS).

2.16. Photo by George Appell.

2.17. Drawn after Whittier 1973, 54, by BE and RLW.

2.19. Photo by BS.

3.1. Drawn from a photo by Allen Drake by BE.

3.2. Drawn from a photo in Molengraaff 1902, facing p. 392, by BE.

3.3. Drawn from a photo by RLW by BE.

3.4. Drawn from a photo by RLW by BE.

3.5. Drawn from a photo in Hose and McDougall (1912, 1: plate 123, facing p. 228) by BE.

3.7. Nieuwenhuis 1907, 2: illustration 27, following p. 162.

3.11. Drawn from a photo in Hose and McDougall (1912, 1: plate 124, facing p. 230) by BE.

3.12. Drawn from a photo in Sellato 1989, 103, by BE.

3.13. Photo by LYS, used with the permission of the Sarawak Museum.

3.14. Photo by LYS, used with the permission of the Sarawak Museum.

3.19. Drawn from a photo in Schärer (1963, illustration 17, following p. 229) by BE.

3.20. Drawn from a photo by LYS by BE.

3.21. Photo by LYS, used with the permission of the Sarawak Museum.

3.22. Drawn from a photo by RLW by BE.

3.23. Drawn from a photo in Sellato 1989, 105, by RLW.

3.24. Drawn from a photo in Sellato 1989, 104, by RLW.

3.25. Photo by LYS, used with the permission of the Sarawak Museum.

3.26. Photo by LYS, used with the permission of the Sarawak Museum.

3.27. Photo by Jennifer Alexander.

3.28. Photo by Aloyssius Lau.

5.2. Drawing after Morris 1991, 101–103, by BE.

5.7. Photo by LYS, used with the permission of the Sarawak Museum.

5.8. Photo by LYS, used with the permission of the Sarawak Museum.

5.13. Photo by LYS, used with the permission of the Sarawak Museum.

5.15. Photo by LYS, used with the permission of the Sarawak Museum.

5.16. Drawn after Chin 1985, 35, by RLW.

5.17. Photo by LYS, used with the permission of the Sarawak Museum.

5.18. Drawn after Edmund Kurui (Kelbling 1983, 143) by RLW.

5.19. Photo by LYS, used with the permission of the Sarawak Museum.

5.20. Drawn after *Design Brief, Bakun Resettlement Project* (Part B, *Exiting Longhouses*, B.8, Umah Juman) by RLW.

6.11. Photo by LYS, used with the permission of the Sarawak Museum.

6.21. Photo scan of postcard by RLW.

6.23. Photo scan of postcard by RLW.

6.25. Photo by LYS, used with the permission of the Sarawak Museum.

6.26. Photo by LYS, used with the permission of the Sarawak Museum.

INDEX

Page numbers in **boldface** *refer to illustrations.*